To Barry

Thank you for all your
help and friendship
With wishes for health
and happiness

Fall 5769 - 2009

CHASIDIC PERSPECTIVES

A FESTIVAL ANTHOLOGY

CHASIDIC PERSPECTIVES

A FESTIVAL ANTHOLOGY

Discourses by the
LUBAVITCHER REBBE
Rabbi Menachem M. Schneerson
זצוקללה"ה נבג"מ זי"ע

Adapted by
Rabbi Alter B. Metzger

Published By
KEHOT PUBLICATION SOCIETY
770 Eastern Parkway • Brooklyn New York 11213

CHASIDIC PERSPECTIVES
A FESTIVAL ANTHOLOGY

Published and Copyright © 2002
by
Kehot Publication Society
770 Eastern Parkway / Brooklyn, New York 11213
(718) 774-4000 / FAX (718) 774-2718
Order Department:
291 Kingston Avenue / Brooklyn, New York 11213
(718) 778-0226 / FAX (718) 778-4148
www.kehotonline.com
ISBN 0-8266-0467-6

Printed in the United States of America

Table of Contents

INTRODUCTION

The Lubavitcher Rebbe, Rabbi Menachem M. Schneerson, of blessed memory, has provided spiritual and practical guidance for Jews as well as for mankind in general. With broad vision he has delineated a path toward self-actualization for all who have come in contact with him and for society as a whole. Revered by his disciples and adherents for his exemplification of spiritual qualities and by others for his concern with ethical and humane values, he has had a profound influence on our era.

A multifaceted personality, he synthesizes various roles—Talmudist, *halachist* (codifier), Biblical exegete, and Rebbe of the Chabad Chasidic tradition—in the vast array of his Torah discourses. In these discourses the Rebbe explicates the various aspects of the relationship among G-d, Torah, and Israel. Readers or listeners are provided a panorama of all levels of Torah study: *peshat* (literal) *remez* (allusion), *drush* (ethical/homiletical), and *sod* (mystical). All are viewed through the prism of Chabad Chasidic thought and blended into a cohesive whole.

This work contains a limited selection of *sichot* (discourses), all dealing with the Jewish holidays. Nevertheless, these discourses, forty-seven in all, provide an overview of the primary concepts of Chabad *Chasidut*, which focus on 1) the G-d-Jew, Jew-G-d relationship; 2) the Jew as a member of a collective community; 3) the individual Jew in relation to himself. The key to these relationships is the unity between G-d and the rest of creation, with an underlying unity among G-d, the Torah and the Jewish people. The Rebbe's thought profoundly elucidates this unity, yet his stress does not lie upon intellectual effort alone. Recurrently he emphasizes the

I

practical implications for Jews and their service to G-d. Indeed, the quest for self-knowledge, for communion with the divine, and for unity among the Jewish people, ultimately inheres in the task of revealing Divinity in the everyday world.

Evocative both intellectually and emotionally, these discourses form a body of teachings which bear in-depth study. Indeed, the sight of devotees of Chabad thought animatedly discussing these sichot in a fragmentary, allusive manner is reminiscent of Talmudic scholars engaging in erudite discussion by brief phrases and mere citations of folio pages. These discourses have inspired and directed the efforts of his emissaries and followers, enabling them to exert a profound influence on the international Jewish community.

Some of the discourses in this book concern the following questions and concepts:

In one of the Rebbe's best-known talks, Hannah's plea for a child is analyzed: Why must Jews ask for mundane, physical needs on Rosh Hashanah, the time of the solemn coronation of G-d as King of the Universe? The answer: Requests for physical needs in prayer derive from a Jew's inner essence and transcend selfish concerns. A Jew prays for physical needs to fulfill G-d's will, the realization of spirituality within the world.

On the second day of Rosh Hashanah, the *Akeidah* (the binding of Isaac on the altar as a sacrifice) is read. Abraham's willingness to offer his son conveys the astonishing capability of the Jewish people to display self-sacrifice for Judaism. Although Abraham had already proven himself through nine previous tests, a puzzling Talmudic statement indicates that the significance of those tests depended on his success in the last one. What, then, was this test's crucial quality? The answer: There is a difference between self-sacrifice based on intellectual reason for the furtherance of an ideal and self-sacrifice based on total trust and submission to G-d, which is contrary to intellect. According to Chasidic thought, Abraham's final test opened the "spiritual channel" of self-sacrifice for all further generations of the Jewish people. It is this heroic quality which has enabled the Jews to overcome the "ordeals and challenges of exile," and through which they will ultimately reach the Messianic Redemption.

The selflessness of the Jew is also expounded in a *sicha* on Yom Kippur. Before entering the Holy of Holies, the high priest, must don white linen garments. The question arises: Why wasn't this greatest of all services performed in the sumptuous garments of gold usually worn by the high priest? The Rebbe answers that the garments of linen exemplify the elemental relationship of the Jew's essence with G-dliness, and the entrance of the high priest into the Holy of Holies is reenacted by all Jews through their prayers on Yom Kippur.

The centrality of Torah to Jewish life permeates the Rebbe's thought. A famous Midrash on Sukkot states that among the "four kinds," the *lulav* (date-palm branch) represents the Torah scholars, whereas the *hadasim* (myrtle twigs) represent Jews who mainly perform good deeds. The *etrog* (citron) represents Jews who excel in both scholarship and good deeds, while the *aravot* (willow branches) represent Jews who neither learn nor do good deeds. Why then, the Rebbe asks, does the blessing over the "four kinds" refer only to the *lulav*, when the *etrog* evidently represents excellence in both modes of spiritual service? The answer lies in the unity among Jews achieved though Torah knowledge and observance.

In a *sicha* for Simchat Torah, the holiday following Sukkot, the Rebbe asks why the festival associated with Torah is not observed instead on Shavuot, the holiday commemorating the giving of the Torah. His answer differentiates between two modes of G-dly service, one of *tzaddikim* (righteous individuals) and the other of *baalei teshuvah* (returnees to Judaism). Thus, this *sicha* stresses the primacy of repentance in the Jew's relationship to G-d.

A *sicha* for the "Chasidic holiday" of the 19th of Kislev, celebrating the release from prison of Rabbi Schneur Zalman of Liadi, founder of the Chabad movement, begins with reflections on the nature of time, and places the emergence of Chasidic thought in the 17th and 18th centuries squarely within the context of the continuous development of Torah and the emergence of mystical thought throughout general history.

A *sicha* for Chanukah compares the laws governing the lighting of the Chanukah menorah to the laws for lighting the menorah in the Temple. In the time of King Solomon's temple, the menorah was lit inside, during the day, with the number of candles remaining constant (seven). Chanukah candles, in contrast, were lit at night, in a position to illuminate outward, and on each progressive, the number of candles increased, until eight were lit on the last night. This increase in light has obvious symbolic implications. The differences delineate the character of the holiday itself. At the time of exile, Jewish people must constantly generate and increase light to overcome the forces of darkness.

In the Purim narrative, Mordecai and Esther react in a puzzling manner to Ahasueros's decree against the Jewish people, caused by Haman. Mordecai seemingly should have tried to use his political influence among his esteemed colleagues, particularly those who sat at "the gate of the king." Why, then, did he choose instead to don sackcloth and ashes? And why did Esther fast three days, then go to the king? Certainly, her weakened condition would have marred the beauty which had caused her to find favor with him in the first place. This *sicha* delineates their proper response for Jews in times of adversity, times of "concealment of the Divine countenance," which depend first and foremost on *teshuvah* (repentance)—and the renewal of the spiritual connection between G-d and the Jewish people.

So too, the Rebbe draws on the past to discuss the future, a future bright with hope and promise. A *sicha* for Passover explores the four courses of action proposed when the Jews were pursued by the Egyptians prior to the splitting of the Red Sea: leaping into the sea, returning to Egypt, praying to G-d, and waging war against the Egyptians. Each of the "plans" represents an approach to spiritual service; each contains valid elements. Ultimately, however, G-d declares the primary goal: "*Daber el B'nei Yisrael* (Speak to the Jewish people)"—"*veyisa'u* (that they should go forward)." They must "go forward" for the G-dliness at the splitting of the Red Sea and its manifestation at Sinai, which in actuality is a prelude to the even loftier manifestation of G-dliness in the Messianic era.

Concerning Shavuot, the Midrash relates that the Jews went to sleep the night before receiving the Torah at Sinai and that G-d was displeased. How was it possible for the Jews not to stay awake prior to such an auspicious event? This is especially puzzling, given the Jews' counting of forty-nine days following the Exodus from Egypt in anticipation of receiving the Torah. According to the Rebbe, sleep entails the separation of the soul from the body and its elevation, which the Jews thought would be the most fitting mode of preparation.

However, the receiving of the Torah was a historically transformative event and the commencement of a new era. Previously, the spiritual realm and the physical realm remained completely separate from each other. Jews by their individual actions could affect the spiritual world but not the physical. After Sinai, however, Jews could now irradiate their entire environment through the performance of *mitzvot* with physical objects. Thus, the proper mode of preparation for the giving of the Torah was not achieved through departure from the physical realm. In its highest form, this merging of the physical and the spiritual will be revealed in the Messianic era, when sublime G-dliness will be revealed in the mundane.

A *sicha* for the 12th of Tammuz, the date of the sixth Lubavitcher Rebbe's release from Soviet prison, asks why the Rebbe refused to travel on Shabbat in the course of his release, although Jewish law would not only allow but demand the breach of Shabbat to save his life. The answer lies in the Rebbe's steadfast desire to remain committed to Jewish observance, under the most perilous circumstances.

The Rebbe's focus on the inherent good even within the bad is never more apparent than in a *sicha* on the Three Weeks, the period beginning with the 17th of Tammuz, when the walls of the Temples were breached by enemy forces, and ending with the 9th of Av (Tisha B'Av), when both the First and second Temples were destroyed. These Three Weeks are considered a period of sadness for the Jews, and the entire day of Tisha B'Av is observed by fasting and mourning. Yet, the Rebbe comments, a month seemingly associated with negative events is also known as *"Menachem Av,"* appending the word "comforter" to the name of the month. His answer explores the difference between consolation and mercy, and relates ultimately to the "mercies" and "consolation" of the Messianic redemption.

As the cycle of the year approaches closure, a *sicha* for the 18th of Elul, the birthday of the Baal Shem Tov, the founder of the Chasidic movement and Rabbi Schneur Zalman of Liadi, focuses on the significance of birthdays. The Rebbe's predecessor, Rabbi Yosef Yitzchak Schneersohn, revealed a special set of customs for observing birthdays, and the Rebbe addresses the question of why birthdays should be given special emphasis. The answer is that the birthday is the prototype for man's spiritual service—each day a person must be "reborn" in the continual quest for self-betterment and greater attachment to G-dliness. Moreover, in Chasidic thought, the succession of pregnancy followed by birth also represents exile followed by redemption, the culmination of the spiritual service of the Jewish people collectively.

As the preceding examples have shown, the train of thought in the Rebbe's *sichot* frequently reminds the reader that Judaism posits an optimistic view of history and human existence. In contrast to Maimonides' emphasis of G-d as omnipotent, Chasidism focuses on G-d's omnipresence and His constant vivifying and sustaining of all of creation. Thus, Divine Providence is impelled by G-d's concern for the well-being of all creation.

In the *Tanya*, his classic primary work of *Chasidut*, Rabbi Schneur Zalman of Liadi speaks of this omnipresence as being a source of great joy and inspiration, motivating an individual in the service of G-d. Even alienated Jews possess the spiritual level of *Yechida shebenefesh*, the divine spark which inevitably will be the impetus for return and commitment to the Torah heritage.

In the Messianic redemption, the ultimate manifestation of the divine spark within every Jew, and indeed within all of creation, will occur. Evil will be banished and Humanity's capacity for good will reach its highest expression.

Despite the anguish of the past and the agony of the Holocaust in our recent era, Jews affirm the culmination of the Messianic redemption. Chasidism emphasizes the revelation of G-dliness at that time; and the resultant era of universal peace, tranquility, and harmony is a frequent theme in the Rebbe's teachings. Yet, a Jew cannot be passive in this historical process, as the Rebbe frequently stresses in connection with the verse "As the days of your departure from Egypt I will show [you] wonders." The Rebbe does not simply regard this prophecy as a simple assurance of a future event, but rather as an assertion: If Jews display the tenacious spiritual heroism of their ancestors in Egypt, they will merit the wonders of the Messianic era. Thus, they are not merely passive observers, but catalysts in this historical process of universal redemption.

I would gratefully like to acknowledge the following people and institutions:

Rabbi Yosef B. Friedman of the Kehot Publication Society. Dr. Binyomin Kaplan, whose sustained and dedicated efforts in the editing of this work are deeply appreciated. Rabbi Avraham D. Vaisfiche, for significant help with footnotes and research for the text. Rabbi Shmuel Marcus, for his persistent efforts to bring this project to completion. Rabbi Shalom DovBer Levin, head librarian of the Agudas Chasidei Chabad-Lubavitch Library and Archive Center; Rabbi Ari Chitrik for his initial impetus for this project; Chaya Sarah Cantor, and Rabbi Yosef Yitzchak Jacobson, for their editorial suggestions.

Rabbi Yehuda Krinsky of Lubavitch World Headquarters, a friend for more than four and a half decades.

The Levi Yitzchak Library of the Lubavitch Youth Organization; the Yeshivah University Uptown Campus Library; the Stern College Library, for making available their research sources.

My earliest teachers in Chabad *Chasidut*: Rabbi Dovid Raskin and Rabbi Beryl Junik; Rabbi Mordechai Altein, an early mentor in the study of Chabad; and his wife Rebbetzin Rochel Altein, editor of the English section of *Di Yiddishe Heim*, the Chabad Women's Journal, where much of this material first appeared.

Dr. Lawrence Shiffman of New York University, and Dr. Schneur Zalman Leiman of Yeshivah University and City University of New York; Dr. David Kranzler and Dr. Charles Bahn, members of the faculty of the City University of New York, for their perceptive insights and comments.

Rabbi Dr. Norman Lamm, president of Yeshivah University, for his general interest in Chasidism and his particular focus on its existential ramifications. Karen Bacon, Dean of Stern College for Women, and Rabbi Dr. Ephraim Karnafogel, Chairman of Rebecca Ivry Department of Jewish Studies of Stern College, for their general encouragement of scholarly endeavors. My thanks also to Professor Sheina Sara Handelsman of Bar Ilan University and Rabbi Yaakov Jacobs, for their gifted expertise in editing segments of this work.

My wife Yehudit, for her constant support and suggestions. Our parents of blessed memory—Chaim Yitzchak Moshe and Charna Metzger; and Rabbi Abraham Mordechai Hershberg and Rebbetzin Mintcha Hershberg; whose dedication to the ideals of Judaism sensitized me to the significance of the concepts in this work.

Rabbi Alter B. Metzger

Chof-Beis Shevat, 5762

LUBAVITCHER REBBE
Rabbi Menachem M. Schneerson
זצוקללה״ה נבג״מ זי״ע

NOTE ON TRANSLATION:
The translator has endeavored to retain, as far as possible, the flavor, rhythm and sequence of the original Hebrew or Yiddish *sichot* as they appear in *Lekkutei Sichot*. The translator also provided the reader with brief introductions to each *sicha*.

ROSH HASHANAH

THE CRY OF THE *SHOFAR*
TWO CHASIDIC PARABLES

The sounding of the *shofar* is the central observance and focal point
of the holiday of Rosh Hashanah, as indicated by the statement in
the Talmud that the spiritual themes of coronating G-d as King and
bringing the remembrance of the Jewish people before G-d are
actualized by blowing the *shofar*. The following excerpt from a *sicha*
presents two elaborate Chasidic parables for the deeper meaning of
the blowing of the *shofar* and then relates them to the major themes
of Rosh Hashanah observance.

BY WHAT MEANS?

The Talmudic sage Rabbah declared:[1] "G-d says to the
Jewish people: On Rosh Hashanah, recite before me (verses of
Kingship, (verses of) remembrance, and (let there be heard)
the sound of the *shofar*. Kingship, that you proclaim Me as King
over you; remembrance, that memory of you will come before
Me; by what means?—through the sounding of the *shofar*."

What is the meaning of the Talmud's statement that *shofar* is
the means for proclaiming G-d as King and evoking the
remembrance of the Jewish people? We find two parables
regarding the blowing of *shofar* in Chasidic works. One parable
is related in the name of Rabbi Israel Baal Shem Tov.[2]

---

1. *Rosh Hashanah* 32b.
2. See *Hemshech VeKacha* 5637, ch. 38. This parable is also printed in the Supplements
   to *Keter Shem Tov* (Kehot edition), ch. 108.

THE BAAL SHEM TOV'S PARABLE

There was once a king who had an only son, who was very learned and the "apple" of his father's eye. The king decided that it would be beneficial for the prince to travel to far-off lands and acquire wisdom and knowledge of human behavior. The king provided his son with a large escort, a group of noblemen and eminent government officials, and a retinue of servants to serve them. The king also bestowed great wealth upon his son, so that he could journey in ease and luxury to the many lands and remote islands. He hoped that the prince would thus attain a great increase in wisdom and experience.

During the extended journey, the son, accustomed to great luxury, squandered the money in pursuit of personal pleasure; his lifestyle became an ever-increasing quest for sensuality and self-gratification. This finally resulted in the sale of all that he possessed.

Finally, the prince ended up alone in a remote, distant land, where the greatness of his father was unknown. In dire distress, he decided to travel home. But so much time had elapsed that he had forgotten his native language. On returning to his own country, he tried to communicate in sign language that he was the king's son, but the people did not comprehend. He finally reached the castle courtyard, and once again tried sign language with the people there, but to no avail. In desperation he decided to cry out in a loud voice, hoping that his father would recognize him. The king suddenly discerned that this was his son's voice, crying with great pain and anguish. This awakened his fatherly love and compassion, and he embraced and kissed his son.

This allegory expresses the relationship between G-d and the Jewish people, for all Jews are described as the sons of G-d. The souls of Israel are dispatched to earth to acquire wisdom, in a manner similar to the lengthy journey of the prince. In spiritual terms this means that through Torah and *mitzvot*, the soul can rise to ever higher levels. However, the body's physical desires and the search for sensual pleasure bring the soul to a place very remote, where it is alienated from its Father, and it loses all recollection of its native tongue—Torah. Only upon returning to the King and through a simple, but heartrending cry, is the soul reunited with G-d, the Father of the Jewish people. This is the significance of the Rosh Hashanah *shofar* blast, the outcry which rises from the depths of the Jewish heart. It is actually a profound expression of repentance, of remorse for the past and sincere commitment for the future, to obey the Father—G-d's will. This outcry evokes a compassionate, G-dly response; He manifests His love for His only son with forgiveness for his past deeds.

RABBI LEVI YITZCHAK OF BERDITCHEV'S PARABLE

The second parable is described in *Kedushat Levi*,[3] a Torah compendium of the Chasidic teachings of Rabbi Levi Yitzchak of Berditchev:

A king once traveled to a great forest. He penetrated so deeply into the forest until he was lost, and could not find the correct, direct path home. In the depths of the forest he met simple peasants, and asked them to lead him out of the forest, but they were unable to help him, for they had never heard of the king's great highway, which led directly to the royal palace.

The king then found a wise and understanding man, and requested his aid. The sage discerned immediately that this was the king, and was deeply moved by their encounter. In his wisdom, he immediately led the king to the correct, direct path, guided him to his royal palace and aided him until the king was finally restored to his true honor and seated on his majestic throne. The rescuer, of course, found great favor with the king.

Time passed, and this wise man acted improperly in ways that angered the king. The king ordered him to be regarded as one who had violated the royal law and brought to trial. The man knew that he would be dealt with very severely. In great anxiety, he fell before the king and implored that he be granted

---

3. *Drush LeRosh Hashanah*, "*Bechatzotzerot*."

one plea: before the trial and the judgment would be passed on him, he wished to be garbed in the very same clothing he had worn when the king first encountered him in the forest. The king, too, was to don the original clothing he was wearing then.

The king acceded to this request. When the forest encounter was re-enacted by their dressing in the original garments, the king vividly remembered the life-saving kindness of his rescuer. Great mercy was aroused within him as he recollected how he had been restored to the royal throne. With compassion and mercy, the king magnanimously forgave his rescuer and restored him to his place of high honor.

This narrative, too, is descriptive of the relationship between G-d and Israel. At the time of the great Sinai revelation, G-d went from nation to nation and offered them the Torah, but they declined it. We, the Jewish people, accepted the Torah with gladness and joy, affirming that "we will do and we will hear,"[4] accepting the Torah even prior to hearing its specific teachings. We declared our loyalty to G-d, "accepting the yoke of the Heavenly kingdom," proclaimed G-d's majesty as king over us, and affirmed that we would fulfill His commands and be loyal to His holy Torah.

Now we have sinned and rebelled against Him. A primary Chasidic concept states that the *mitzvot* are the spiritual "garments" of the soul.[5] When the *shofar* is blown, it is comparable to being garbed in the "garments" of *mitzvot*. Remembrance of the Jews' original acceptance of the Torah evokes G-d's forgiveness for all our sins, and He inscribes us immediately for a good life, etc.

These two parables can be compared to the themes of the blessings we say for *Malchiot* (kingship) and *Zichronot* (remembrances) at the time the *shofar* is blown during the Rosh Hashanah prayer services. The first parable emphasizes the actions of

---

4. Exodus 24:7.

5. *Tanya,* ch. 4

the king's son: his return and simple, heartfelt outcry, allegorically expressing our acceptance of "the yoke of (G-d's) Kingship." The second parable emphasizes the remembrance of the outstanding quality of the Jewish people made manifest at the time of the giving of the Torah, which in later times evokes that "your remembrance should come before Me (G-d) for benevolence."

We can thus understand the aforementioned Talmud: "How can kingship and remembrance be evoked?" and the answer: "by means of the *shofar*," for the sound of the *shofar* is a replication of our outcry as we repent and accept G-d's sovereignty anew in the service of "proclaim Me to be King over you." It also elicits the remembrances related to the mitzvah "garments" of the Jewish people which "come before Me for benevolence."

(*Likkutei Sichot*, vol. 34, pp. 183-185)

Rosh Hashanah

The Prayer of Hannah—
A Woman Teaches Us
How to Pray

Tefilah, praying to G-d, is on the one hand a simple process, and on the other hand an amalgam of praise of G-d; supplication; thanksgiving, with a strong element of introspection and contemplation. The Talmud[1] derives many of the laws governing *tefilah* from the experience of Hannah, who turned to G-d when she found herself childless. Nevertheless, Eli the high priest mistook her for a "drunken woman" upon observing her heartfelt prayer. In this *sicha*, the Rebbe explores the deeper meaning of Eli's accusation and Hannah's reply.

A Prayer for a Child

The *Haftorah* (the section from the Prophets) which is read on the first day of Rosh Hashanah concerns Hannah. She had been childless[2] until, by prayer, she stirred divine mercy and gave birth to a son of great stature, the prophet Samuel.

The portion of the Torah read on each Shabbat and *Yom Tov* has an intrinsic connection with the time it is read.[3] The Hannah narrative is intrinsically connected to the day of Rosh Hashanah: Hannah conceived on that day.[4] But beyond that fact, there is a more timeless connection which can serve as a guide to each Jew in the experience of Rosh Hashanah. Since her prayer at Shiloh brought her a son, from her prayer

---

1. *Berachot* 31a.
2. I Samuel 1:2.
3. See *Shelah, Torah Shebiktav*, beg. *Parshat Vayeishev*.
4. Psalms 107:5.

15

experience we can glean guidance for our own efforts to evoke divine mercy through prayer.

We must, therefore, first deal with the puzzling response of Eli the high priest, who sees her lips moving silently. Concluding that she is intoxicated, he scolds her for coming to the sanctuary in such a state. Hannah humbly responds that she is childless and that she has come to appeal to G-d to bless her with a child. [5]

ELI'S ERROR

The question arises: how can Eli be so wrong about Hannah; how can he be oblivious to the intensity of her prayer? and, assuming he is, why is it necessary to record this event and to thus disparage Eli? Moreover, why does Eli, believing her to be intoxicated, not scold her until after she finishes?

THE DECORUM OF PRAYER

These questions force us to conclude that Eli does not suspect that Hannah is intoxicated in the conventional sense. The unusual length of her prayers is not in keeping with the norms of prayer, which call for simple and brief petitions. Eli believes that her petition to G-d is inappropriately self-assertive, standing as she is before G-d and in the "House of G-d." Hannah apologetically explains that she is pouring out her heart in spontaneous prayer and that she is not "intoxicated in prayer," not being overly assertive. She explains that hers is a sincere personal supplication, an "outpouring of soul."

This dialogue between Hannah and Eli provides us with a proper mode of prayer, and offers us insight into the prayers which comprise the Rosh Hashanah liturgical service.

THE PARADOX OF ROSH HASHANAH

Rosh Hashanah, on the one hand, is the time when Man's material and spiritual needs are examined. Regarding this day it

---

5. I Samuel 1:13-15.

is written in Psalms, "For it is a *chok* for Israel, a judgment for the G-d of Jacob."[6] The word "*chok*" (a decree not to be questioned or rationalized) can also be understood in the verse in the sense of "Feed me with the bread of *chuki* (my allotment)."[7] This refers to the divinely ordained allotment of "bread"—of all Man's material needs for the coming year, which is determined on Rosh Hashanah. And the latter part of the verse, "judgment for the G-d of Jacob," is the divine allotment of spirituality for each person.[8] It is for this reason that we petition the Almighty on Rosh Hashanah for material sustenance—for life, for children, for economic gain, and also for *hashlama*, for personal growth in the realm of spirit.

Paradoxically: Rosh Hashanah is the time of, as it were, "crowning" the Almighty as our King,[9] a motif which recurs throughout the liturgy. It is a time when Man is in a state of total self-nullification, to the point that he is totally oblivious to his personal desires and submits himself without reservation to the divine will. And it is this self-nullification which elicits acceptance of the coronation from the divine King.

These two aspects of what is asked of us on Rosh Hashanah appear to be contradictory—mutually exclusive. The paradox is sharpened by the statement in the Kabbalistic work *Tikunei Zohar*[10] that those who pray on Rosh Hashanah for "food, sustenance, forgiveness and life" are like hounds that cry "Give!" because they think only of themselves and show no concern with the Divine Presence. Yet these very supplications for material needs have been incorporated into the liturgy by our Sages because Rosh Hashanah is a propitious time for such petitions to be fulfilled. Hence, our *kavanah*, the devotional

---

6. Psalms 81:5.

7. Proverbs 30:8; *Likkutei Torah, Rosh Hashanah* 54d, 55d , etc.

8. *Sefer Hama'amarim 5710*, p. 15.

9. See *Likkutei Sichot*, vol. 4, p. 1145 and ff., p. 1354 and ff., etc.

10. *Tikkun* 6 (22a). See *Or Torah* of the Maggid of Mezeritch, beg. *Parshat Vayigash*; ibid., *Al Agadot Chazal*—"*Ein Omdim*" (108c)

intention of our prayers, should include our own needs. It is, however, no contradiction to be at the same time permeated with the humbling sense of self-nullification.

ROSH HASHANAH PRAYER AND PRAYER DURING THE YEAR

This seeming contradiction becomes apparent not only in the Rosh Hashanah liturgy, but in the daily *Amidah*, the prayer said three times each day, recited as "one who stands before the king"[11] in such self-abnegation that making the slightest untoward gesture would be deemed an act of sacrilege.[12] Yet, in the twelve intermediate benedictions, the Sages have ordained supplications for our most mundane needs.

This question can be resolved, however, by distinguishing between the prayers of the High Holy Days and those of the entire year. During the course of the year, subsequent to the coronation Rosh Hashanah, G-d the King is, metaphorically speaking, conducting the everyday affairs of His state.

However, Rosh Hashanah marks the onset of G-d's sovereignty, when the Jews must crown G-d as King by submitting to His authority. At that time He is exalted and transcendent, above guiding the world, as it were, and greater and profounder self-nullification is required, to the degree that nothing can be apprehended aside from the Omnipresence and Omnipotence of G-d as King. And therefore this problem is specifically linked to Rosh Hashanah: how can Man be in such a state of total humility and yet pray to the King for his personal needs?

CROWNING THE KING

The explanation of the above problem is that the prayer of a Jew for his needs on Rosh Hashanah is not due to his quest for personal gain, nor great material possessions, or even lofty spiritual qualities. His striving is totally derived from his

---

11. See *Shabbat* 10a.

12. See *Chagigah* 5b.

endeavor to fulfill the spiritual service of "Coronate Me as King over you."[13]

The prayerful plea of "Reign upon the world in Thy Glory,"[14] that G-d's majesty should be manifestly perceived in all worlds, is actualized by means of a Jew's concerning himself specifically with worldly matters and transforming them into an abode for His Divine Presence.

The material world at large contains "sparks of sanctity." Each individual Jew is charged with refining and uplifting those sparks uniquely designated to him,[15] these being his specific "share" and responsibility in his spiritual endeavor. Therefore, the Jew prays for G-d's material blessing, for only in this way can he accomplish G-d's "Reign upon the whole world" in relation to the specific spiritual mission assigned to him.

Thus, a Jew's self-awareness does not compromise the purity of his Rosh Hashanah prayers, for he pleads with the sole intention of fulfilling G-d's Will.

Moreover, this supplication is carried out through self-nullification at the time of the King's coronation, since the spiritual goal of uplifting the sparks of sanctity is linked to the very essence of the Jewish soul. Just as the divine will that "G-d desired to have an abode in the lower realms"[16] is rooted in G-d's absolute Selfhood,[17] so too is this quest is simultaneously rooted within the essence of the souls of the Jewish people, and it is they who implement this spiritual task.

INDIVIDUAL NEEDS

The question can still be posed: the prayers of the Rosh Hashanah liturgy were fixed by our Sages for all Jews, regardless of their level and status; and among them are surely some whose pleas for both material and spiritual acquisitions

---

13. *Rosh Hashanah* 16a, 34b.

14. Liturgy, Rosh Hashanah.

15. See *Keter Shem Tov*, sec. 218.

16. See *Tanchuma, Naso* 16; *Tanya*, ch. 36.

17. See *Sefer Hama'amarim 5666*, p. 446.

are not solely motivated by a desire to fulfill G-d's will, but to some degree from anxiety over their own dire straits. They pray with the basic hope that G-d will fulfill their mortal needs from His "full and generous hand." Indeed, the commandment to pray is, in essence, that one ask for one's personal needs, as is obvious in the blessings of the silent prayer, each being an explicit request for fulfillment of a specific need. This is, in fact, the unique and surpassing effect of prayer,[18] that through prayer the sick person is cured, and the needed rain actually does fall.

HUNGER FOR HOLINESS

This enigma can be resolved by bearing in mind the Baal Shem Tov's interpretation[19] of the verse, "Hungry and thirsty, their soul prayerfully yearns within them":[20] that the hunger and thirst of the body for food or drink is rooted in the fact that "the soul prayerfully yearns." The soul desires to refine the spark of sanctity within food and drink which is specifically granted to that person and which "he must set aright." In other words, although a Jew experiences physiological hunger, the true "hunger" is the longing of the soul for the sparks of sanctity in the food which are uniquely related to him.

Although prayers on Rosh Hashanah that G-d grant material and spiritual needs, may appear to result from selfish personal desire for "children, life and food needs," nevertheless, within even a simple Jew, the inner force behind the "outpouring of soul" is the "hunger" and yearning of the spirit to fulfill G-d's will for "the creation of an abode for Him in mundane world." Moreover, the very fact that we perceive the strongest awakening while praying for our needs in "U'nesaneh tokef"—asking "Who will have a placid life, etc." from the depth of the heart with an intensity of feeling exceeding that when praying "and reign upon the entire world in Thy Glory"— indicates that this indeed is the essential content of our prayer.

---

18. See *Tanya, Kuntreis Acharon*, Essay 4.

19. *Keter Shem Tov*, sec. 194, and see *Likkutei Sichot*, vol. 1, p. 177.

20. Psalms 107:5.

This, therefore, is the reason that the most intense feelings are experienced specifically during the prayers for one's personal needs: the inner motivation of these prayers is the soul's basic drive to fulfill the divine purpose of creation, transforming the world into an abode for the Almighty.

To return to our original question, we may conclude that the *haftorah* of Hannah, describing her heartfelt prayer and Eli's challenge, "How long will you be drunken," was designated for the day of Rosh Hashanah in order to underscore this spiritual concept.

Eli's argument was that while one stands "before G-d... before the Holy of Holies,"[21] there should be no outer distractions; the sole concern should be the profound awareness of actually being "before G-d." It is then wholly inappropriate to ask for material matters and personal needs, even so heartfelt a plea as "Give Your maidservant a child."[22] In addition, Hannah prayed "at length," in a state of spiritual "intoxication," impelled by desires which, in Eli's view, were essentially self-centered. Eli believed that Hannah's desire to have a child was so powerful that she was not adequately mindful of where she stood— "before G-d."

To these words of Eli, Hannah replied, "And I poured out my soul before G-d." Her prayer for a child was not an expression of "intoxication" and selfish obsession. On the contrary, it was an outpouring of the innermost aspect of her soul, specifically related to her "standing before G-d." As the Psalms state, "For You (G-d) does my heart say 'Seek My face,' Your face, O G-d do I seek."[23] Interpreted according to *Chasidut*, the word "*panai*" (my face) is understood to be related to "*penimiyut*"— inwardness.[24] Hannah was crying out from the innermost depths of her being, and her desire did not stem from will for

21. Ralbag, I Samuel 1:11
22. Ibid.
23. Psalms 27:8.
24. *Likkutei Torah*, Deuteronomy 44b, c.

self-gain; her entire existence was characterized by the yearning to be "bound and united with You."

It is thus clear why concurrent with her plea Hannah vowed that if "You will give Your maidservant a child," then "I will give him over to G-d for all the days of his life."[21] His entire life would not be for personal endeavor, but would be dedicated to the service of G-d. Her prayer for a child did not emerge from a selfish desire, but from yearning to serve G-d, a drive which she experienced within the innermost realm of her soul.

This, then, is the spiritual implication for every Jew from the Rosh Hashanah prayer: That only the essence of a Jew is dedicated to G-d is not sufficient. This essence must emerge and become manifest. Thus, when a Jew prays on Rosh Hashanah, beseeching G-d for his material or even spiritual needs, the "high priest Eli" within his soul contends: "How long will you be drunken?" At this time of G-d's coronation, it is utterly inappropriate to think of worldly matters and personal needs.

Notwithstanding this, a Jew must yet ask for these needs, for indeed it is this very challenge which evokes the reply from the "Hannah" within each Jew. Even someone who, on the conscious level, is only aware of his personal needs has within him the essential yearning for "I poured out my soul before G-d." This is the true desire of the essence of the soul which is "bound and united with You," joined in oneness with G-d in His essential Selfhood.

Just as Hannah's response totally resolved Eli's challenge and caused him to offer his own blessing and assurance that "the G-d of Israel will grant the plea that you have pleaded of Him,"[25] similarly, G-d will fulfill every Jew's request for a good and sweet year, even in the most literal sense, for "children, life

---

25. I Samuel 1:17.

and economic sustenance," and all of them in a generous and abundant manner.

(*Likkutei Sichot*, vol. 19, pp. 291-297)

ROSH HASHANAH

BLESSINGS, PRAYER, AND THE SONG OF HANNAH

> In the previous *sicha*, the Rebbe explores the issue of prayer for personal needs on Rosh Hashanah. In the present *sicha*, also dealing with the many lessons to be learned from the prayer of Hannah, the Rebbe explores the ability of prayer to break through the boundaries of normal existence and bring about that which is truly new.

THE UNIQUENESS OF HANNAH'S PRAYER

The Talmud states: "Rav Hamnuna said: Many profoundly significant laws can be derived from, the verses describing how Hannah prayed for a child:[1] *'She spoke in her heart'*—from this we derive that the one who prays must concentrate his heart with *kavanah*, devotional intent; *'Only her lips moved'*—this teaches us that he who prays must move his lips; *'her voice could not be heard'*—from here we learn that it is prohibited to raise one's voice in prayer."[2]

Everything in the Torah is stated with exact precision. The Pentateuch abounds with references to the concept and proper manner of prayer in the Pentateuch in those sections which relate to the prayers of Abraham, Isaac, Jacob, and Moses. Why does the Talmud cite "significant laws" based on the Book of Samuel, which is one of the books of the Prophets, rather than citing those derived from the Pentateuch itself? We cannot say that the case of Hannah is unique because of her profound plea

---

1. I Samuel 1:1.
2. *Berachot* 31a; I Samuel 1:13.

25

for a child, for the Torah itself relates the story of Isaac's intense prayer because his wife Rebecca had no children. [3]

Indeed, the Talmud declares that our patriarchs established the three traditional daily prayers: Abraham—*Shacharit*—the morning prayer, Isaac—*Minchah*—the afternoon prayer, and Jacob—*Arvit*—the evening prayer. Nevertheless, the prayer of Hannah in particular serves as the model for "significant laws." What is the special uniqueness of her prayer?

There are two categories of prayer: the prayer which an individual "recites and prays every day"[4] for his, everyday, constant needs, and the prayer expressed at "special times" for a specific need, as at a time of danger or catastrophe.

Some of our Sages regard the mitzvah to pray as deriving directly from the Torah, while others regard it as a Rabbinic obligation. Even the latter agree that at times of adversity prayer *is* a Biblical obligation.[5] Thus, the law states "a person should pray...at a time of danger," or when faced with a pressing personal need.

THE NATURE OF BLESSING

There is a difference between the concept of *tefilah* (prayer) and *berachah* (blessing). The root of the Hebrew word *berachah* is related to the word *breichah*, a pool or stream of running water. The nature of water is to run downward, from above to below. *Berachah* is also related to *hamavrich*—one who bends a grapevine down on to the earth to grow another vine. Thus, the word *berachah* connotes drawing forth from the spiritual source above to provide humanity with some form of benefit.[6]

A blessing can be effective only when the desired outcome already exists above, although it is still separate from the individual who requires it. The bestowal of a *berachah* hopefully causes the descent of that bounty from its spiritual source to the

---

3. Genesis 25:20.

4. Maimonides, *Hilchot Tefilah* 1:2.

5. *Derech Mitzvotecha*, p. 229.

6. See *Likkutei Torah, Devarim* 19a.

physical world below. Thus, the Torah states about Jacob's blessing of his sons, "Each one according to *his* blessings did he bless them."[7] Jacob elicited and brought down from above the unique and appropriate blessing for each one of the brothers.

This provides us with insight into Jacob's blessings for his grandsons, Menasseh and Ephraim. Jacob reversed his hands, "His right hand...on the head of Ephraim, the younger child... and his left hand on the head of Menasseh."[8] Joseph requested that the right hand be placed on the head of Menasseh, the first born, but Jacob replied that Ephraim would be "a ruler. of nations," surpassing his brother.[9] Seemingly, if Jacob is *giving* the blessing, he should indeed have blessed Menasseh with the major blessing. In accordance, however, with the definition of a blessing—that the effluence is not created anew, but is essentially "drawn down;" a *divine* bestowal from its spiritual source— Jacob could not effect a change in the *berachah* but only bring it down to the world below.

It is otherwise in the case of prayer. Our plea of *Yehi ratzon* (May it be Your will) requests that G-d should, so to speak, have a new "will," thus granting us something totally new in response to our specific need.

This can, perhaps, explain the opinion that prayer is Biblically ordained only at times of danger and adversity. Prayer is a plea to G-d, *Yehi ratzon*, for something totally new, not the provision of our daily, regular needs. Thus, true prayer transforms, brings about new conditions: significant change, rescue, or cure in cases of danger and adversity.

It is thus apparent that the depth and intensity of prayer is related to the degree of change and transformation necessary for the prayer to be granted. The traditional heartfelt prayers for rain during a drought, or for G-d to cure a seriously ill person are examples of such pleas. This differs nonetheless, from the

---

7. Genesis 49:28.

8. Genesis 48:14.

9. Genesis 48:19.

prayer of a childless woman, which requires a radical change in the pattern of nature, childlessness being itself the creation of G-d. This expresses the power and loftiness of prayer with even greater force.

PRAYING FOR A *TZADDIK*

The prayer of Hannah is indeed in a category of its own, different also from the prayers of our patriarchs. We are told: "She made a vow and said 'G-d of Hosts, if You will perceive the pain of Your maidservant and You will give Your maidservant offspring that are men.'"[10] Rashi interprets the latter phrase, "offspring that are men" as connoting individuals who are *tzaddikim*—outstandingly pious. Hannah did not pray merely for children, but for *tzaddikim*—for a child of *great piety*. She did not ask for one who had the *potential* to be a *tzaddik*, but for an individual who would be an actual *tzaddik*, in all his deeds. In her concluding vow, Hannah declares "I will give him to G-d all the days of his life," that in practice he will be utterly devoted to G-d for his whole life.

Since she ultimately gave birth to the prophet Samuel, who, in fact, possessed the qualities for which she had prayed, and who was indeed dedicated to the service of G-d, it is likely that this occurred because G-d completely fulfilled her request.

This stands in sharp contrast to the natural order of things established by G-d, including Man's free will. It is written that the angel who oversees conception declares about the new human being: "he or she will be strong or weak, rich or poor, handsome or ugly, etc. However, no statement is made regarding whether the child will be a *tzaddik*, (a virtuous person,) or a *rasha*, (a wicked person)."[11] This is because "everything is in the hands of Heaven except for the fear of Heaven."[12] "G-d has given Man free choice, and if he desires to turn to the path of virtue and be a *tzaddik*, it is totally up to

---

10. I Samuel 1:11.
11. *Niddah* 15b.
12. *Niddah* 16b.

him...This is a primary principle and a pillar of Torah and its commands."[13]

We see that the prayer of Hannah superseded the patterns of nature, which are in accord with the constraints and boundaries that G-d established in His Torah as a fundamental principle and "pillar."

This also has *halachic* consequences. The *Mishnah* declares that the Prophet Samuel was a *Nazir*, one who is required to abstain from wine and from cutting his hair. In describing Samson, who was also a *Nazir*, the Bible, declares: "And no razor shall come upon his head."[14] Hannah used the very same words in her prayers for a child.[15] The Talmud declares that this conveys to us that just as Samson was a *Nazir*, so too, Samuel was a *Nazir*.[16] Indeed, Maimonides declares this as law: "Samuel of Ramot was a life-long *Nazir*."[17]

There is a well-known *halachic* question: How could Hannah's vow create the obligation for Samuel to be a *Nazir*? The problems are twofold: Samuel did not exist at that time, and had he been alive, the vow of a parent cannot impose the status of *Nazir* upon a child.[18]

The answer is that Samuel became a *Nazir* when he willingly accepted this status as an adult.[19] By not objecting, and by acquiescing to his mother's vow, he, in effect, elicited the spiritual sanctity of the *Nazir* retroactively.

This underscores the loftiness of Hannah's prayer and vow. She was aware that her vow could not make Samuel into a *Nazir* on its own if he objected to it upon maturity. Nevertheless, she was profoundly confident in the fulfillment

---

13. Maimonides, *Hilchot Teshuvah* 5:1-3.
14. Judges 13:5.
15. I Samuel 1:11.
16. *Nazir* 66a.
17. Maimonides, *Hilchot Nezirut* 3:16.
18. *Nazir* 25b.
19. *Likkutei Sichot*, Vol. 18, p. 66 and ff.

of her prayer, anticipating that he would commit himself to that level of G-dly service for his entire lifetime.

There are two dimensions to prayer, the devotional thought—*kavanah*—and its actual verbalization. The primary aspect of prayer is obviously the concentrated, devotional thought; this unique quality of prayer is what differentiates it from other *mitzvot* which require speech. In such other *mitzvot*, *kavanah* is an extrinsic condition, but in prayer the *kavanah* is inherent to the actual verbal fulfillment of the mitzvah.

This may be why there is no similar emphasis on *kavanah* regarding a *berachah*. Since the purpose of a *berachah* is to elicit a divine bestowal from its spiritual source to be revealed in our physical, material world, the primary emphasis of the *berachah* is the aspect of speech which reveals the inner thought. In prayer, however, which creates real change in the physical world "so that the sick person should be cured, that rain should descend from Heaven causing birth and growth,"[20] we elicit, as it were, "a new will" of G-d. Essentially, this is the result of the devotional *kavanah* of the person praying, "to remove from his heart all distracting thoughts and to perceive himself as standing before G-d's presence."[21] The verse describes Hannah's prayer: "And her soul was embittered and she prayed to G-d, weeping internally."[22] When an individual nullifies all personal thoughts and desires, and humbles himself as a servant before his Master, this evokes a reciprocal divine response, "As water reflects face to face."[23] Devoted thought of the heart— *kavanah*—is the first of the principles we learn from Hannah and it is the basis, the inner content, of the other profound principles.

---

20. *Tanya, Kuntreis Acharon*, Essay 4.
21. Maimonides, *Hilchot Tefilah* 4:16
22. I Samuel 1:10.
23. Proverbs 27:19.

EVOKING THE WILL TO BE KING

The account of Hannah's prayer is read as the *Haftorah* on Rosh Hashanah. One reason for that is because her prayer was said on that day. There is also a thematic link between Rosh Hashanah and her prayer. On the first day of the New Year we evoke "a new will from G-d for all creation" by accepting G-d as our King and spiritually dedicating ourselves to Him as King of the Universe.

In human terms, a person truly worthy to be king is superior to the extent that he is "taller than all the people from his shoulder and upward."[24] The acceptance of kingship is a descent from this superior person's lofty level in order to become involved with the mundane affairs of the kingdom. His subjects must make every effort to arouse within the king the will to reign. This is accomplished through the self-nullification of the populace; its submission to the king is manifested through the act of coronation.

How much more so does this apply to G-d, Who is exalted beyond the attribute of kingship, completely above all created existence. The service of the Jewish people on Rosh Hashanah manifests their acceptance of the yoke of the Heavenly kingdom and evokes within G-d, so to speak, the will to be King.

With the blowing of the *shofar* we make G-d our King, as the Talmud states, "Say before Me *Malchiyot* (verses regarding G-d's kingship) that you accept Me as king, *Zichronot* (verses of remembrance of G-d and His deeds) so that your remembrance should come before me for benevolence. How?—with a *shofar*."[25]

The sound of the *shofar* is an elemental sound, which comes from the essence of the heart. In service to G-d, it is the elemental cry of a Jew which comes from the innermost realm

---

24. I Samuel 10:23.
25. *Rosh Hashanah* 16a.

of the heart, as it is written, "Their heart cried out to G-d."[26] In this way G-d's innermost *will* for kingship, *His* acceptance of the coronation as king of the Jewish people and thereby King of the universe is achieved, until the profound revelation of his kingship "And G-d shall be King of the entire world; on that day G-d will be One and His Name One."[27]

(Likkutei Sichot, vol. 29, pp. 182-188)

26. Lamentations 2:18.
27. Zechariah 14:9.

Rosh Hashanah

The Uniqueness
of the *Akeidah*

On the second day of Rosh Hashanah the *Akeidah*—the binding of Isaac upon the altar—is read. This account conveys the unique capability of the Jewish people for self-sacrifice for Judaism. Though Abraham had undergone nine previous tests, his self-sacrifice in those instances could be explained as based upon reason and intellect for the furtherance of an ideal. In the *Akeidah*, however, he acted in a manner of total faith and submission to G-d. Indeed, for acquiescing in a manner contrary to intellect, Chasidic thought tells us that Abraham opened the spiritual channel of self-sacrifice for all future generations of the Jewish people. It is with this heroic quality that Jews will be able to overcome the ordeals and challenges of exile until the time of the Messianic redemption.

The Culmination of the Ten Trials

The *Akeidah* was the primary and loftiest trial experienced by our Patriarch Abraham. It was the most difficult of the ten trials with which our forefather was tested.[1] When G-d spoke to Abraham about the *Akeidah,* He said, "*Kach nah et bincha*" (*Please take your son*)."[2] The Talmud states that since the word *nah* is an expression of request, G-d was actually stating "I have tested you with nine trials, and you have passed them all successfully. I now ask you, *please* stand firm and succeed in this trial, lest the world say that your earlier triumphs were of no true significance."[3] Why would Abraham's failure to pass the test of the *Akeidah* nullify the meaning and significance of all his

---

1. *Avot* 5:3.

2. Genesis 22:2.

3. *Sanhedrin* 99b.

33

earlier ordeals? Would it not merely indicate that his capacity for self-sacrifice fell short of the specific trial of the *Akeidah*, without reflecting on the value of all the earlier tests? Why should they be retroactively subject to challenge and doubt? Yet G-d's emphasis indicates that the *Akeidah* was of a higher dimension, totally incomparable to the earlier trials.

THE *AKEIDAH* IN HISTORICAL PERSPECTIVE

The *Akeidah* must be viewed from a general perspective because of its profound significance in Jewish history. Abarbanel states:[4] "It is the entire *keren* (literal translation "capital"—here in the sense of spiritual might) and merit of Israel before their Father in Heaven; indeed, this is the reason we recite the *Akeidah* narrative in our daily prayer."

It has frequently been asked: Why do we constantly invoke the memory of the *Akeidah* and Abraham's willingness to sacrifice Isaac more than the martyrdom of all the pious and holy individuals throughout our history who willingly sacrificed themselves for the sanctification of G-d's name?[5] Did his sacrifice exceed that of, for example, Rabbi Akiva and his fellow rabbis, and the sacred martyrs in every generation? Moreover, G-d spoke to Abraham directly, which was not the case for the innumerable holy martyrs who gave their lives for the sanctification of G-d's name without G-d's speaking to them.[6]

We cannot answer that it is a far more difficult ordeal to sacrifice one's child, as in the *Akeidah*, than to give up one's own life, for we find in a later generation the moving incident of Hannah and her seven sons. As she herself cried out, "You, O Abraham, sacrificed one son, and I sacrificed seven children."[7] Indeed, throughout Jewish history many individuals

---

4. Genesis, ibid.
5. See *Ikarim, Ma'amar* 3, ch. 36.
6. *Tanya, Igeret Hakodesh,* ch. 21.
7. *Gittin* 57b; *Yalkut Shimoni* on Psalms, *Remez* 873.

not only willingly gave up their own lives, but also endured the anguish of sacrificing their children.

REQUESTS AND COMMANDS

The philosophical work *Ikarim*, explains that the uniqueness of the *Akeidah* is that it possessed no element of necessity or coercion. Nor was it obligatory for Abraham to accede to G-d's word.[8] This is indicated by our Sages in their comment[9] on the verse *G-d shall see:*[10] Abraham said before G-d: "Master of the world, it is revealed and manifest before You that when You said to me, 'Take, I ask of you, your only son Isaac and offer him up as a whole-offering,' I could have said, "Have You not already declared to me 'through Isaac shall be called your seed' (i.e. descendants). I did not say this, but suppressed my feelings of mercy and did not question (the hidden motives of) Your ways." This text suggests that Abraham was not obligated to obey this command, for he could cite a valid rationale for not doing so if he wished (and indeed the *Ran* in his *Derashot*[11] (Sermons) states that G-d's use of the word *nah* (please) implies that it was a matter of choice and not duty). Unlike Abraham, Jewish martyrs willingly sacrificed their lives for the sanctification of G-d's name in later generations in compliance with G-d's *command* "And I shall be sanctified amidst the children of Israel."[12]

This answer, however, can be challenged. Firstly, the argument that Abraham could have sought exemption from G-d's words is somewhat problematic. After all, when *G-d Himself* requests something (even if there is the remote possibility of demurring), it is self-evidently obligatory.

Even among the aforementioned martyrs of later generations, there were some whose martyrdom was not due to

---

8. *Ikarim*, ibid.
9. *Bereishit Rabbah* 56:6.
10. Genesis 22:14.
11. No. 6 (p. 105 and ff.).
12. Leviticus 22:32.

Torah obligations or commands. On the contrary, these individuals needed to find *halachic* justification for their acts, as reflected in the well-known *halachic* controversy concerning whether it is *permissible* to give up one's life when the legal ruling is "He should (better) transgress and not be slain."[13]

OPENING THE CHANNEL

There is a well-known Chasidic resolution to this problem.[14] The unique accomplishment of Abraham was the fact that he was the *first* person who successfully overcame the test of self-sacrifice.

The beginning of any endeavor entails difficulties; in the words of our Sages, "All beginnings are difficult."[15] Only after Abraham opened the channel of self-sacrifice was the capacity for such heroism made possible for future generations. It was therefore a lesser ordeal for his descendents because Abraham instilled this capability within them.

The problem with this rationale is that Abraham had already elicited this quality, even *before* the ordeal of the *Akeidah,* when he underwent the test of Ur Kasdim.[16] He stood with resolute courage then to eradicate all forms of idolatry and to promulgate an awareness of G-d in the world, to the point that "The king desired to kill him (for his promulgation of monotheism) and a miracle occurred."[17]

Moreover, in Ur Kasdim there seems to be an element surpassing the ordeal of the *Akeidah,* for in that instance G-d did not address Abraham directly, while at the time of the *Akeidah* he did. If the *Akeidah* was indeed not the first instance of self-sacrifice, then we are once again confronted by our initial problem: What is the uniqueness of the *Akeidah?*

---

13. *See Tur* and *Shulchan Aruch, Yoreh Deah* beg. Ch. 157, and commentaries there.

14. *Sefer Hama'amarim 5678, 5688, Ashreinu; Likkutei Sichot,* vol. 10, p. 46.

15. *Mechilta* and Rashi, Exodus 19:5.

16. See *Pirkei DeRebbi Eliezer,* ch. 26.

17. Maimonides, *Hilchot Avodah Zarah* 1:3.

THE NATURE OF SELF-SACRIFICE

An analysis of the nature of *mesirat nefesh* (self-sacrifice) will clarify the problem. The explanation that Abraham opened the channel of self-sacrifice in the world implies that without his courageous act, it would have been utterly impossible for this quality to exist here on this earth.

Self-sacrifice, on the one hand, entails total self-nullification. Creation, on the other hand, implies that the Creator has created a specific, limited entity. It is obvious that this created being cannot transcend the conditions of its creation.[18] As the Rabbis say: "A prisoner cannot free himself from prison"[19] —he is subject to the limits of his existential situation. The endowment of power from a loftier source is necessary to enable the ascent to the level of self-sacrifice.

One could object that the capacity for self-sacrifice exists even among the nations of the world. Moreover, there is an opinion that a *ben Noach* (non-Jew), even among those who lived before Abraham, is also commanded to endure self-sacrifice under certain circumstances.[20] There are many examples in history where non-Jews gave their lives for the sake of perceived, though often erroneous, ideals.

This can perhaps be explained by the fact that an individual's willingness to give his life for G-d does not necessarily indicate the authenticity of his striving for Torah-based self-nullification. It may be that he is motivated by the logic of martyrdom: the thought that he has more to gain by dying than by living, some advantage greater than his mere physical survival.

Self-sacrifice based entirely upon logic and intellect can also exist among non-Jews. The individual experiencing self-sacrifice believes that his act will be to his advantage; his martyrdom will enhance his image. Expressed negatively, his

---

18. See *Torah Or* 99b; *Likkutei Torah*, Leviticus 4c; *Likkutei Sichot*, vol. 18, p. 300
19. *Berachot* 5b.
20. See *Minchat Chinuch*, Mitzvah 137.

logic dictates that if he does not achieve a certain goal, then life becomes meaningless. Thus, a person gripped by profane passion, or a soldier obsessed with military victory, or a warrior king completely fixated with the idea of conquest, may all do so to the point of self-sacrifice.

In contrast with the above, the true meaning of *mesirat nefesh* is to *give over one's soul*, an act beyond all reckoning of intellect and emotion, total self-nullification in which one's own being and will are subordinated to G-d's.

FAITH BEYOND REASON

It is therefore possible to say that this manifest, ultimate *mesirat nefesh* was the unique quality of the *Akeidah*, surpassing the ordeal of Ur Kasdim.

The self-sacrifice of Ur Kasdim consisted of the fact that Abraham endangered his life to promulgate faith in G-d. We might therefore suppose that his action was based upon spiritually-motivated *intellect*. His certainty of the need to illuminate a world groping in darkness[21] was so intense that he completely disregarded any difficulties and courageously imperiled his life.

However, in the trial of the *Akeidah* the only aspect necessary was Abraham's faith beyond reason, as indicated in G-d's word to Abraham *after* the *Akeidah* that he was "G-d-fearing."[22] It was this profound inner faith that gave Abraham the selfless courage to make this ultimate sacrifice.

But, perhaps, that Abraham (at the *Akeidah*) was motivated by the rational wish to spread the knowledge of G-d to the world and to convey by his actions the profound loyalty necessary for commitment to G-d. This is not so, however, for as Ibn Ezra states, the *Akeidah* took place under highly secluded circumstances. No one else was aware of what was taking place

---

21. See *Bereishit Rabbah* 2:3.
22. Genesis 22:12.

when Abraham bound his son (for the offering), not even the youths accompanying them.[23]

This action seems, for that matter, to contradict his striving to spread the knowledge of G-d, for in offering Isaac as a sacrifice, the elementary principle of belief in G-d, which Abraham taught to humanity, would have been uprooted. There would be no successor and spokesman to carry on and extend this radiant awareness to all mankind.[24]

The sole reason for the *Akeidah* was that G-d *willed* and asked this of Abraham, who then submissively compiled. This was Abraham's singular accomplishment: his willingness to undergo this extreme self-sacrifice was absolutely not based on reasoning and intellect, but only on his submission to G-d's will; ultimate self-nullification to G-d.

THE *AKEIDAH* AND ABRAHAM'S EARLIER SACRIFICES

We can now understand the words of the Talmud that the Almighty used the term *nah* (please) to Abraham when He asked him to obey His Will in the *Akeidah,* lest it be said that "the earlier trials had no meaning."

If Abraham had not passed the test of the *Akeidah,* then it could have been said that his motivation in overcoming the nine earlier trials was his intellectual comprehension, his power of human reasoning. His willingness was based upon the intellectuality of holiness. It would not be that clear that his acts in the earlier ordeals represented authentic self-sacrifice, derived from the innermost aspect of his soul. Hence the ordeal of the *Akeidah* sheds light *retrospectively* upon the earlier ordeals as being rooted in total self-nullification.

A SPIRITUAL HERITAGE

This, therefore, is the explanation of why the "opening of the channel in the world" for martyrdom and self-sacrifice occurred during the *Akeidah* and not as a result of the test in Ur

---

23. Ibn Ezra on Genesis 22:1.
24. See *Likkutei Sichot,* vol. 18, p. 322.

Kasdim. (Our Patriarch Abraham endowed all future generations of the Jewish people with a spiritual heritage: the capability for *true* self-sacrifice, expressing the innermost core and will of their spiritual selfhood, "in accordance with their authentic, essential will."[25]) Therefore, when a Jew gives his life for G-d, even if it should externally appear that his act is based upon reason or on a motive of selfish gain, in truth it is really the giving over of his total selfhood to G-d, transcending reason and logic, as exemplified by the *Akeidah*.

The influence of this basic event is so far-reaching that Rabbi Schneur Zalman, the Alter Rebbe, states in his *Shulchan Aruch* (Code of Jewish Law),[26] "It is fitting to recite the Torah portion of the *Akeidah* every day…in order to subjugate his will to the service of G-d, just as Isaac offered his soul." How can we compare our spiritual subjugation to serve G-d, to Isaac's willingness to give over his soul which was an act of self-sacrifice in its purest form?

We can justify the comparison by remembering the singular relationship between the event of the *Akeidah* and all future generations of Jewish existence. For Abraham opened the channel for actual self-sacrifice for every Jew who is a descendant of Abraham, a son and inheritor of the spiritual "heritage of the congregation of Jacob."[27] He is thus able to subordinate his personal inclinations in order to serve G-d "just as Isaac offered his soul." In periods of uncertainty and self-doubt, when external threats to our Judaism evoke anxiety and fear, we must remember that we possess this great inner spiritual treasure, the heroic heritage of *Akeidah* faith and courage. With this unique quality we shall overcome these ordeals and challenges of exile. May G-d grant that through this inner spiritual strength we merit the collective return of the entire Jewish people to *Eretz Yisrael* and most particularly to the

---

25. See Maimonides *Hilchot Gerushin*, end of ch. 2.

26. *Orach Chaim*, first version, ch. 1, sec. 10.

27. Deuteronomy 33:4

place of the original *Akeidah*, the mountain of Moriah, the Temple Mount, and the rebuilding of the *Beit Hamikdash* through *Mashiach* speedily and in our times.

(*Likkutei Sichot*, vol. 20, pp. 72-78)

YOM KIPPUR

GARMENTS OF LINEN—
GARMENTS OF GOLD

On Yom Kippur, the entrance of the high priest into the Holy of Holies with simple white linen garments exemplifies the essential relationship between a Jew and G-d. The golden garments are worn only outside of the Holy of Holies, representing Man's utilizing gold charitably for the betterment of the community by supporting Torah and *mitzvot*. However, the high priest and each individual Jew on Yom Kippur should strive for the "pure white clothing" of a "a pure cleansed heart and a pure mind," whether to a greater or lesser degree. This will evoke divine compassion for a good and blessed year.

THE TEN DAYS OF REPENTANCE AND YOM KIPPUR

The term *Aseret Yemei Teshuvah* (Ten Days of Repentance) includes the two days of Rosh Hashanah and the day of Yom Kippur,[1] since the intervening days between Rosh Hashanah and Yom Kippur only total seven. The fact that all ten days are referred to with one term—*Aseret Yemei Teshuvah*—indicates that all of these days are actually one entity, commencing with Rosh Hashanah and concluding on Yom Kippur. It is therefore evident that preparation for Yom Kippur starts from the very first moment of Rosh Hashanah.[2]

The unique mitzvah of Rosh Hashanah is *shofar*[3]; the pivotal effort of Yom Kippur in the days of the Temple was the special service of the *Kohein Gadol*—the high priest. During the

---

1. *Likkutei Dibburim*, p. 692.

2. *Moreh Nuvuchim*, ch. 45.

3. *Shemot Rabbah* 55:3.

entire year, the Temple rituals were also performed by other priests, but on Yom Kippur the *Kohein Gadol* alone performed all of the special Temple rites connected with the holy day.

The service of the *Kohein Gadol* on Yom Kippur consisted of two parts. While fulfilling the first, the *Kohein Gadol* wore garments which also contained other materials, but which were called "garments of gold." During the other part of the services he wore *bigdei lavan*—simple, white linen garments.

There were three separate sections to the Holy Temple: the *Azarah* (Temple court), the *Heichal* (the sanctuary) and the Holy of Holies. The *Kohein Gadol* performed the services in the *Heichal* and *Azarah* wearing the vestments of gold while during the service of the Holy of Holies he wore the white linen garments.

EVERY JEW A *KOHEIN GADOL*

When the Temple was destroyed, only the physical edifice, the stone and gold and silver were lost. However, the spiritual Temple, within the soul of each Jew, continues to exist and shall eternally remain in a state of indestructible wholeness. A Jew is incapable of destroying his inner spiritual edifice; all the more so, a non-Jew has no power to destroy it.

Rabbi Yosef Yitzchak Schneersohn, the sixth Lubavitcher Rebbe, stated: only our physical bodies were cast into physical exile and subjected to external authority; our souls were not driven into exile nor given over to alien dominion.[4]

The spiritual temple abiding within each Jew is also subject to the dimension of time—to the various phases of the year. When Yom Kippur arrives, every Jew, the "*Kohein Gadol* in his own individual temple," must perform all the temple rituals himself and not rely upon another person. This labor consists of two parts: the service in the Holy of Holies garbed in white and the other rituals wearing the golden priestly garments.

---

4. *Likkutei Dibburim*, vol. 3-4, p. 1383

THE SPIRITUAL MEANING OF THE GARMENTS

Maimonides in explaining the use of sumptuous priestly clothing, including the garments of the *Kohein Gadol* on Yom Kippur, states that sanctity requires the use of that which is most aesthetically impressive and qualitatively superior. Gold is highly significant and precious to Man, evoking awe and reverence. Hence, the rationale for the golden garments is understandable.[5]

Yet, how is this concept to be reconciled with the wearing of the simple white linen garments in the Holy of Holies? The Holy of Holies was of greater sanctity than the other precincts of the Temple. Why not require the use of golden garments there?

The underlying concept here is that each individual must serve G-d with the sum total of his own unique capabilities. When an affluent person is approached for charity, he cannot assert that he will fulfill his responsibilities with Torah study, and intensive prayer. He must know that service in the Temple requires garments of gold.

On the other hand, there must be the awareness that one's obligation is not solely discharged with "garments of Gold"—i.e. with sustaining *yeshivot* etc. Garments of white linen are also required—spiritual pursuits that are pure and utterly removed from the corporeal and material.

Each set of garments must be appropriate for its locale. The services outside the Holy of Holies required garments of gold. As the *Midrash* declares: No one would merit the use of gold; "it was created solely for the Holy Temple."[6] The creation of gold primarily for use in the Temple explains why it is also available throughout the world. It should therefore be self-evident to every Jew that uses of lesser significance should not be substituted for the primary purpose of gold—it is meant for spiritual purposes.

---

5. Shavuot 39a; *Sanhedrin* 27b.

6. *Shemot Rabbah* 55:3.

Nevertheless, in the precincts of the Holy of Holies within each Jewish soul, gold is not utilized. The Temple tasks must be performed in pure white clothes, for here everyone is equal.

BEGINNING WITH THE *SHOFAR*

We may now understand the purpose of the Ten Days of Repentance, starting with the sounds of the *shofar* on Rosh Hashanah and concluding with the service of the *Kohein Gadol* on Yom Kippur.

At the beginning of the Ten Days of Repentance we sound the *shofar*. The *shofar* is the horn of an animal and the sounds it produces are not particularly musical; they are the simple sounds of *Tekiah, Shevarim* and *Teruah*. Similarly, when a Jew places himself before G-d, it is with authentic simplicity devoid of cleverness and ingenuity. His link with G-d is expressed by a simple, intense, heartfelt outcry. He cries out from the depths of his heart that he is G-d's child and that G-d is his Father, and he beseeches his Father to bestow upon him a good and sweet year.

The end of the Ten Days of Repentance is marked by the service of the *Kohein Gadol* divided into the aforementioned two parts, expressing the commitment to serve G-d both in garments of gold and of linen.

Regarding those matters external to the Holy of Holies, the individual becomes aware that since G-d has given him wealth and instilled within him a Jewish soul, he cannot conceal himself in white linen garments. When asked for financial aid, he cannot claim that the aid of others should be sought since he is pious and pure and concerned solely with spiritual matters. He is fully aware that the Temple, the *Yeshivah*, and the Synagogue require gold, which he himself is obligated to give.

However, as regards the Holy of Holies, he is equal to all others; he does not wear vestments of gold but rather garments of white linen, untainted by the material and corporeal. He is fully aware that there was nothing in the Holy of Holies, not even the show bread; nothing but G-d, the Torah of the Ten Commandments, the ark, and the *Kohein Gadol*.

CONSTANT CHANGE

The moral implication for every Jew is as follows: The commencement of spiritual service at the onset of the year, must be the simple, sincere outcry to G-d, human expression beyond reason. After that, the person himself must perform the service of the inner temple—which is complete even in our times—garbed in garments of gold and linen.

If he performs the service successfully, he will then possess both the physical and spiritual, as did the *Kohein Gadol*. In the times of the Temple the ritual did not merely require the donning of garments of gold and then of linen; the high priest constantly changed from one to the other. First the garments of gold, then of linen, subsequently gold again, then back to linen, and then once again garments of gold—all to signify that in the life of the Jew, the material and spiritual are not distinct and separate, but coexistent.

THE SANCTUARY WITHIN

On Yom Kippur, a Jew reflects and prepares himself for entrance into his own inner Holy of Holies. And what is its significance?

The Holy of Holies contained only the ark, which contained the tablets of the Ten Commandments. The Torah, represented by the Ten Commandments on the tablets, consisted of engraved letters, intrinsic to the object upon which it is engraved. Similarly, within the Holy of Holies in the heart of each Jew, the bond of a Jew with Torah is in the manner of hewn letters.

When Yom Kippur arrives and a Jew must enter the Holy of Holies, he may worry: "How can I possibly enter into the innermost precincts when I am devoid of the outer adornments of Torah and good deeds?"

The divine reply to this is that entrance into the Holy of Holies requires no garments of gold, no ornamentation or bright colors; all that is needed is pure white clothing, a pure cleansed heart, and a pure mind. This quality is possessed by every Jew on the day before Yom Kippur after his immersion in the *mikveh*, an immersion which cleanses away all stains and blemishes.

The *Kohein Gadol*, after his lengthy and sacred service, would recite a short prayer, which would elicit a good and blessed year for himself, his tribe, and all Jews throughout the world, both materially and spiritually.[7] So too, every Jew, when he performs his own personal spiritual service in the Holy of Holies of his soul, can also, by means of a few chosen words, evoke joyousness for all the days of the entire year.

Just as the *Kohein Gadol* prayed for all Jews, so too, the prayer of each individual Jew on Yom Kippur, dressed in white garments—a pure heart, and sincere devotional thoughts, arouses divine compassion for a good sweet year both spiritually and materially, not only for himself and his family, but for all Jews—because "All of Israel are responsible for each other."[8]

(Likkutei Sichot, vol. 2, pp. 411-414*)*

---

7. See *Yoma* 53b.
8. *Shevu'ot* 39a.

YOM KIPPUR

THE REPENTANCE LADDER—
TWO VIEWS ON *VIDUY*

The present *sicha* is concerned with a dispute among the Sages as to
the manner of reciting *viduy*—the confession of sins on Yom
Kippur. According to Rabbi Yehuda ben Beteirah, one is to
enumerate, in detail, all the sins committed while Rabbi Akiva
maintains that a general statement is sufficient. The resolution of
the apparent conflict involves the division of the repentance process
into stages: a preliminary repentance based on fear, and a deeper,
more profound repentance based on love. Ultimately, however,
"there inheres, even on the lowest level of repentance, an inner
spark of the loftiest level of *teshuvah*, based on Man's love of G-d
and the intense desire to return to Him."

DETAILED ENUMERATION OR GENERAL STATEMENT?

There is a dispute among the Sages at the conclusion of
Tractate *Yoma*, in the Jerusalem Talmud, as to the proper
manner of reciting *viduy*—the confession of sins during the
Yom Kippur services. According to Rabbi Yehuda ben Beteirah[1]
one is required to enumerate all transgressions individually,
while according to Rabbi Akiva, a general statement of *viduy*
suffices. After continuing its discussion, *Yoma* ends with the
quote: *"Mikveh Yisrael Hashem"* etc.,[2] which means that G-d is
mikveh—the hope of Israel. Another meaning of the word
mikveh is a gathering of water for ritual purification. The
Talmud then explains this passage Midrashically and states:
"Just as the *mikveh* purifies the impure, similarly G-d purifies
the Jewish people." The text cites a further verse: "I [G-d] will

---

1. The Babylonian Talmud states "ben Bava." See *Yoma* 86b.
2. Jeremiah 17:13.

cast upon you pure waters and you will be purified from all your impurities, and from all your abominations will I purify you."[3]

What is the link between the passage about *viduy* and the concluding statement of the Talmud? Superficially, the ending in the Talmud is an extension of the preceding *Mishnah* which has these quotations, and it is also placed here at the end of this tractate in accordance with the practice of concluding with words that are "positive." Thus, it is not actually related to the above-mentioned dispute. However, it is a well-established fact that the entire Torah is written with rigorous precision. It is therefore logical to presume a conceptual theme uniting the discussion of *viduy* with these two verses.

THE "TIME" CONTROVERSY

We are confronted by another problem. The preceding *Mishnah* states, "Rabbi Akiva declared: Praised be you, Israel! Before Whom are you purified and Who purifies you? Your father in Heaven, as Scripture tells us, 'And I will cast upon you pure waters...' And it is said, 'G-d is the *mikveh* of the Jewish people.' Just as the *mikveh* purifies the impure, similarly G-d purifies the Jewish people." The verses in the Talmud are cited in a reverse sequence from those of the *Mishnah*. Apparently, this significant change is linked to the dispute about *viduy*, whether a general statement of confession is adequate or whether the transgressions must be detailed.

To clarify the matter, we must determine the rationale for this dispute. The opinion that the sins must be specified is based on Moses' plea for G-d's forgiveness for the Jewish people: "This nation has sinned a great sin and they have made for themselves idols of gold."[4] However, Rabbi Akiva's position that a general statement of *viduy* confession is adequate is based on the verse "Blessed be he whose iniquity, sin, is forgiven,

---

3. Ezekiel 36:25.
4. Exodus 32:31.

whose sins is concealed."[5] The *Tosafot*[6] commentary states that this is related to the statement in the Jerusalem Talmud[7] that the individual recitation of sins is "because of shame…that he should be ashamed of his sin." Rabbi Akiva's opinion is based on the concern "lest this cause others to suspect him of every other transgression."

This dispute itself, of the primacy of shame or the fear of even greater suspicion, would seem to be rooted in another concern. Chronologically, shame is related to the present experience of repentance—the experience of the searing anguish for one's sins. Therefore, the remorse for the past and one's acceptance for the future are more profound and sincere.

Rabbi Akiva's concern to avoid the stigma of being viewed by society with suspicion regarding other sins is a concern for the future—the fear of an eroded future reputation and impaired credibility. Moreover, such a suspicion may well lead the spirituality insensitive to mock him with the taunting cry, "Remember your early misdeeds!"[8]

The debate is thus connected to the famed "time" controversy[9]—should concern for the present override future consequences, or do the results in the future supersede and determine the present situation? The opinion requiring specific statement of sins is related to the *present* profound experience of repentance, regardless of future consequences. Rabbi Akiva however, states that our primary focus is upon the *future*. His vision of the present is based essentially upon how events develop and affect the future. Thus, despite significant results in the present, Rabbi Akiva is mainly concerned with future repercussions.

---

5. Psalms 32:1.
6. *Gittin* 35b.
7. *Nedarim* 5:4.
8. See *Mishnah, Bava Metzia* 58b.
9. See *S'dei Chemed, Klalim, Ma'arechet* 7, *Klal* 1 , etc., and see *Likkutei Sichot* vol. 15, p. 453 and ff.; vol. 16, p. 398 and ff. Vol. 19, p. 70 and ff.

Superficially, it seems that Rabbi Akiva's opinion requiring a general *viduy* applies only when the individual speaks aloud and enables others to hear him. But when speaking softly and privately, even according to Rabbi Akiva, he should state his transgressions. However, from the unqualified statement of Rabbi Akiva, it appears that his law of a general *viduy* applies even to inaudible confession. This gives us deeper insight into Rabbi Akiva's view that future consequences prevail over the present.

FEAR AND LOVE

There are different levels in the manner of repentance, which can generally be divided into two categories, as stated in the Talmud: Repentance based upon fear, and repentance based upon love.[10] The need for a general or specific *viduy* may also be significantly affected by these two modes of repentance.

In the case of repentance based upon fear, it is logical to specify one's past sins to avoid the pain of heavenly punishment: The greater the sin, the more intense the punishment. It is therefore necessary for a person to state the specific sins to effect a heightened consciousness of his past transgression, with a lesser or greater degrees of remorse corresponding to the seriousness of his sins. Indeed, in the absence of focused and clear awareness of the specific aspects of his past actions, his repentance is flawed and incomplete.

In contrast, repentance based upon love does not focus on the fear of punishment, but rather on the person's love and bond with G-d. The essence of love is closeness and unity. There is a common quality related to all the person's sins, making all of them equal in their severity, for even the lightest sin causes him to be separated from G-d, and through his sins Man is distanced, alienated, and exiled from G-d. Therefore, no need exists for mentioning and differentiating his sins. One dimension of his profound repentance based upon love is his

---

10. *Yoma* 86a, b.

awareness that *all* sins, whether great or small, distance him
from G-d. He rejects *totally* all evil aspects of his past, so that his
repentance based upon love can be perfectly sincere. This further broadens our understanding of the dispute between Rabbi
Akiva and Rabbi Yehuda ben Beteirah.

A Two-Runged Ladder

The word *teshuvah*, loosely translated as "repentance,"
actually means "return."[11] The innermost point of *teshuvah*,
even for a person on the lowest level, is that he will ultimately
be enabled to completely return to G-d. Indeed, *teshuvah* can be
seen as a two-rung ladder; the lower rung is repentance based
upon fear of punishment. This then permits a person to ascend
to the higher rung of repentance based upon love, and in this
way become united spiritually with G-d.

With penetrating insight, Rabbi Akiva sees the innermost
core of *teshuvah* as the ultimate aspiration to move from the repentance of fear to that of love. According to his future-focused
opinion, there exists the potential and the striving for the
teshuvah of love, despite the present appearance of an individual
corrupted and on a lowly level undergoing the *teshuvah* of fear.
In that *teshuvah* all sins are equal: They have a common
hindering quality, blocking Man from G-d, and therefore a
general *viduy*, not a specific enumeration of sins, is called for.

Rabbi Akiva's opinion prevails, as a rule, in disputes with
his colleagues.[12] However, Maimonides in his *halachic* work,
Mishneh Torah,[13] states that "one must enumerate individual
sins," which is contrary to Rabbi Akiva's opinion. The
commentaries are quick to point out: if the law is in accordance
with Rabbi Akiva, why does Maimonides cite the other
opinion?

---

11. See *Likkutei Torah, Rosh Hashanah*, beg. *Parshat Ha'azinu* and elsewhere.
12. *Eiruvin* 46b.
13. *Hilchot Teshuvah* 2:3.

The commentary *Kesef Mishnah* ascribes Maimonides' opinion to the Babylonian Talmud,[14] which discusses two verses that seem at variance with each other: One states, "Blessed be he whose iniquity is forgiven, whose sin is concealed,"[15] indicating the hiding of sins. The other states, "He who conceals his iniquities shall not succeed."[16] Rabbi Yehuda in the name of Rav, resolves this problem by stating that the verses deal with two kinds of sins. When the sins are known to others, the individual should publicly declare his remorse and desire for repentance. To publicly proclaim private sins, however, is in effect to imply a lack of appropriate deference and submission to G-d.

Thus, the Babylonian Talmud implies agreement with the position of Rabbi Yehuda ben Beteirah, who requires enumeration of specific transgressions. However, according to Rabbi Akiva, even those sins widely known should not be cited individually. It is for this reason that Maimonides states that the proper recitation of *viduy* means enumeration of each sin, which appears to be in accordance with the view of Rabbi Yehuda ben Beteirah.

This teaching of Rav is *not* cited in the Jerusalem Talmud, and since Rabbi Akiva's opinion prevails in disputes with his colleagues, the Jerusalem Talmud indicates that we follow Rabbi Akiva's opinion. On the other hand, Maimonides rules according to the other opinion, for *halachah* follows the Babylonian Talmud when it conflicts with the Jerusalem Talmud.

THE TWO TALMUDS

We have already stated on previous occasions that the Babylonian and Jerusalem Talmud differ in a general approach and outlook:[17] In the Babylonian Talmud present concerns are

---

14. *Yoma* 86b.

15. Psalms 32:1.

16. Proverbs 28:13.

17. See *Likkutei Sichot*, vol. 4, pp. 1337-8; vol. 15, p. 453 and ff.; Vol. 24, p. 173 and ff.

primary and outweigh any future consequences, and in the Jerusalem Talmud future results prevail.

There is a well-known distinction between the style of the Jerusalem and the Babylonian Talmud. The intricate and profound discussions in the Babylonian Talmud are described as "in the darkness"[18]—its final conclusions are only determined after long and difficult analysis. The Jerusalem Talmud, on the other hand, is compared to one who is "in the light"—its discussions are brief, and conclusions are determined quickly. In the Babylonian Talmud, the primary consideration is the present, for the present "darkness" beclouds the future. In contrast, the radiance of today's light in the Jerusalem Talmud illuminates and provides a vision of the future, causing it to prevail over the present.

In our present discussion, the Babylonian Talmud's emphasis on the present causes the law to be according to Rabbi Yehuda ben Beteirah's opinion. However, from the vantage point of the Jerusalem Talmud, the future outweighs the present and the law is in accordance with Rabbi Akiva.

"I WILL CAST UPON YOU PURE WATERS"

The above discussion provides insight into the concluding text in the Jerusalem Talmud and its relation to how *viduy* is recited. In the Midrashic explanation of *"Mikveh Yisrael,"* G-d is referred to as the purifying *mikveh*—the pool of water which cleanses impurity. The text then continues with G-d's declaration that the purification of the Jewish people will take place because "I will cast upon you pure waters."

Based on a number of commentaries, two modes of purification can be discerned here: G-d's declaration that "I will cast upon you" expresses His aid in initiating the sequence of events that will end in the Jew's repentance, while *"Mikveh Yisrael"* describes the effort of the Jew himself to repent.

---

18. *Sanhedrin* 24a; see at length *Sha'arei Orah.*

Precisely as in the actual use of the *mikveh*, the Jew, through his own initiative, must exert the effort to immerse himself.

This can explain the *Mishnah* which begins with the verse, "And I will cast upon you, etc," and then declares that G-d is the "*Mikveh* of Israel," for this is the actual sequence of the repentance process.

Prior to his return in *teshuvah*, the Jew is distant from G-d; evil is a barrier. Thus, the prophet states, "Your iniquities *separate* between you and G-d."[19] Generally, in such a situation it would be profoundly difficult for an individual to begin the *teshuvah* transition with his own effort. G-d must aid him from Above to begin the process. This nuance is implied in the verse "And I will cast upon you pure waters": G-d's "casting of waters" instills from Above thoughts of repentance. But, the intention is not that the *teshuvah* remain totally on this plane, rather, it is with the anticipation that effort and striving on the Jew's part will follow to effect his own cleansing and purification. The *Mishnah* then cites the verse regarding *mikveh*, implying the Jew's personal journey—his own effort to immerse himself in the purifying *mikveh*.

One can now understand the Talmudic passage, which cites the verses in a reverse order: First "*Mikveh Yisrael*" and then "I shall cast." For "I shall cast" can also be seen as a continuation of Man's commencing effort, which indeed can uplift him to an even higher level of *teshuvah*. G-d's declaring, "I shall cast" can be viewed in the context of the highest level of a Jew's ritual purification. In Jewish law the sprinkling of "living waters" is specifically required for purification from the most severe impurity, which is caused by different forms of contact with a dead person.

The Talmud implies that first there must be the intensive effort on the part of the Jew in the initial phase of self-immersion in the *mikveh*. Then G-d completes this process, elevating him to a surpassingly higher level of *teshuvah*, G-d

---

19. Isaiah 59:2.

"casting" upon him the spiritual waters of purification, similar to the lofty purification accomplished only by "living waters."

This is thematically related to the earlier Rabbinic dispute. Rabbi Akiva states that one need not enumerate individual sins. There inheres, even on the lowest level of repentance, an inner spark of the loftiest level of *teshuvah,* based on Man's love of G-d and the intense desire to return to Him.

In practice, we act in accordance with the opinion of Rabbi Yehuda ben Beteirah, and *viduy* requires the specific enumeration of sins. Nevertheless, the opinion of Rabbi Akiva provides a deep understanding of the ultimate goals of *teshuvah.* A Jew must, in full consciousness, focus on and regret past transgressions, but he must not remain obsessed with dark memories of past events. This is merely the lowest rung of the teshuvah ladder. From there he must advance and ascend to higher levels. Motivated by love, he undergoes the purification of both "*Mikveh Yisrael*" and G-d's casting upon him "pure water," so that he can finally merit the statement indicated by the phrase "before G-d you are purified." This applies to the Jewish people both individually and collectively. And the collective *teshuvah* of the Jewish people, when fully actualized, will culminate with the G-dly revelation of Messianic Redemption speedily and in our times!

(Likkutei Sichot, vol. 24, p. 239 - 245)

YOM KIPPUR

RATZO VESHOV—
THE LOVE AND FEAR OF G-D

On Yom Kippur morning during the *Shacharit* service, we read from the Torah about the service of the *Kohein Gadol* (high priest) on Yom Kippur in the holy *Beit Hamikdash* (Temple). This portion begins with a description of the death of Aaron's two sons resulting in their performing this service in an inappropriate manner.

The Rebbe explains the unique aspect of their service and derives from it spiritual implications for all Jews. Nadab and Avihu, the two sons of Aaron, were overwhelmed by the profound emotion of *ratzo* "running forward" or love for G-d, and oblivious of the necessary subsequent *shov*—"withdrawal"—or fear of the Almighty.

Ratzo, the entrance into the Holy of Holies, should be performed with the awareness that this spiritual service will culminate in *shov*, a return to the realm of the material and the mundane. It is only after the high priest's departure from the Holy of Holies that he prays for the material sustenance of the Jewish people.

THE DEATH OF NADAB AND AVIHU

The Torah states: "And G-d spoke to Moses, after the death of Aaron's two sons, while sacrificing before the Lord, they died."[1] The redundancy of the words "they died" after the earlier phrase "the death of Aaron's two sons" requires explanation.

The *Midrash* enumerates the following reasons for which the two sons of Aaron were punished: they entered the innermost chamber, the Holy of Holies, where only the *Kohein*

---

1. Leviticus 16:1.

Gadol was allowed on Yom Kippur[2]; they were not garbed in all of the priestly ritual garments required for the performance of their duties[3]; they had never married; they had no children. All of these details are included in the quoted verse if only by allusion: we must understand, however, exactly how they are implied.

We must also understand how it was possible for Nadab and Avihu to sin. Our Sages state that Moses said to Aaron, "Aaron, my brother, I knew that the sanctuary would be sanctified through those who are beloved and close to G-d. I now perceive that Nadab and Avihu surpassed both you and myself."[4] If that is so, how is it imaginable that they should commit such a transgression?

EXPIRATION OF THE SOUL

According to the teachings of *Chasidut*,[5] the transgression of Aaron's two sons was not a simple matter:[6] Their sin consisted of permitting their intense emotions of longing for G-d to cause their actual death, an expiration of the soul caused by great love of G-d. This is the significance of the phrase, "While sacrificing before G-d, they expired." The Hebrew word *korban* (sacrifice) is derived from the word *karov*—to draw near.[7] The manner of their drawing near was considered a sin. Of course, one should strive to reach a level wherein his service will ultimately achieve "divestment of the corporeal."[8] When, however, he has reached this level of the outpouring of the soul—*ratzo*—surging forward motivated wholly by love of G-d, it is simultaneously demanded of him that he evoke *shov*, the

---

2. *Vayikra Rabbah,* 20:6.
3. *Vayikra Rabbah* 20:9; *Tanchuma* loc cit.
4. *Rashi, Leviticus* 10:3, based on *Torat Kohanim, Shemini,* and *Zevachim* 115b.
5. See *Sefer Ham'amarim 5649,* p. 250 and ff.; *Sefer Hama'amarim* 5722, p. 199 and ff.
6. See *Or Hachaim,* Leviticus 16a.
7. See *Sefer Habahir,* ch. 46.
8. See *Tur, Orach Chaim,* ch. 98, *Shulchan Aruch* of R. Schneur Zalman there and his *Hilchot Talmud Torah* 4:5.

withdrawal and return to perform the service of a soul vested in a body, in this world. As our Sages declare, "Contrary to your will do your exist[9]; Man's purpose is to create an abode for G-d precisely in the realm of the mundane.[10] There must not be a complete departure from worldliness, but rather the transformation of the world into an abode for the Almighty. The sin of Nadab and Avihu was that their service was characterized by *ratzo*, a wholly spiritual love without the subsequent *shov*, or return to worldliness.

The verse's repetition, "they expired," is, thus, an explanation of why the two sons of Aaron perished. Their sins were caused *bekarvatam*—"in their coming close"—in sacrificing before G-d, they expired. Their closeness to G-d was in a manner of *ratzo*, spiritual surging love that reaches expiration, without *shov*, the return to worldliness.

RATZO WITHOUT *SHOV*

We can now understand how the precise words of the verse refer to the details of Aaron's sons' transgressions as enumerated in the *Midrash*. The primary concept underlying all the reasons given is the aspect of *ratzo* without *shov*. "They entered the innermost chamber"—They strove and ascended to the loftiest realm without concern for their return below to the mundane. "They were not wearing all of the priestly garments required for their labor"—Garments in *Chasidut* refer to the garbs of the soul,[11] namely the six hundred and thirteen *mitzvot*, many of which are vested in material matters. Thus, they did not preoccupy themselves with the *mitzvot* which are fulfilled with material objects, in order to refine the world. Their sole desire was to depart from worldliness and achieve union with ultimate spirituality. "They had no children," and "they had no wives"—they did not involve themselves in the Biblical

---

9. *Pirkei Avot* 4:22. And see *Tanya*, end ch. 50.

10. *Tanchuma, Naso* 15. *Tanya*, ch. 36.

11. See *Tanya*, ch. 5. *Igeret Hakodesh*, ch. 29.

commandments of "Be fruitful and multiply,"[12] which bring about the descent of souls into bodies; their service was in a diametrically opposed manner—to depart from the physical.

Rashi states that the commandment (to the *Kohein Gadol*) "...and he shall not come at all times into the Holy of Holies...in this manner shall he enter"[13] is meant specifically as an admonition that the sacred service should not be similar to the actions of Aaron's two sons. It is necessary to understand how this command warns against and negates the service of *ratzo* devoid of *shov*.

In order to comprehend this point, we must first clarify how a person is in the lofty state of *ratzo* can achieve *shov*, return. The state of *ratzo* is characterized by a love for the Almighty to the degree of *bechol me'odecha* (with one's whole being)[14] —without limitations. As long as any hindrance exists and the individual is still restrained, whether by intellect or other factors, he has not achieved the status of *bechol me'odecha*. Consequently, when an individual reaches the state of *ratzo*, devotion without any limits, how can he avoid a complete expiration and outpouring of his soul? How is it possible at this peak of religious emotion to experience and actualize *shov*?

In reality, *shov* must exist at the very onset of *ratzo*. A person's closeness to G-dliness must occur not because he has worked to achieve *ratzo* for his own benefit and gratification, motivated by the knowledge that the closeness to G-d is "good for *me*"[15] that such proximity to G-d would be a source of joy to him. Rather, he must strive for *ratzo* in order to fulfill the will of the most High, the command of the Holy One Blessed be He, "And you shall love...with your allness" or "total being." He does not seek to fulfill his own will, but G-d's will, and he realizes that the G-dly intention of creating the world is that it

---

12. Genesis 1:28.
13. Leviticus 16:2, 3.
14. Deuteronomy 6:5.
15. Psalms 73:28.

should have sustained existence—"He did not create the world to be void. He formed it to be inhabited."[16] Consequently, the *ratzo* is established initially in such a manner that the movement of *shov*, or return, should inevitably follow.

FOUR WHO ENTERED THE *PARDEIS*

Accordingly, we can understand the narrative in the Talmud of the four who entered the *Pardeis*, the "garden" of Jewish mysticism. "Ben Azzai gazed and expired...Rabbi Akiva entered in peace and returned in peace."[17] Initially, it seems that the sole distinction between Rabbi Akiva and his colleagues was in the *emergence* from *Pardeis*, in the fact that Rabbi Akiva "returned in peace." There seems to be no distinction in the manner of their *entrance* to *Pardeis*. Why, then, does the Talmud also say that "Rabbi Akiva entered in peace"? ·

Ben Azzai's "gazing and expiring" was due to the devotion of *ratzo* without *shov*. His entrance into *Pardeis* was in the manner of *ratzo* to the Almighty with an "outpouring of soul," utterly without *shov*. The reason was that initially he did not *enter* in peace. However, Rabbi Akiva's entrance was to fulfill the will of the most High, "to create peace in the host of heaven and the host of earth," to cause the joining of the spiritual with the material and to unite the world with G-dliness. Since he entered in peace, he emerged in peace.

This explains the admonition of "He shall not enter at all times into the sacred precincts"[18] and "he shall atone for himself and for all the members of his household"[19]—the rejection of spiritual endeavor consisting of *ratzo* without *shov*. "*Ve'al yavo bechol eit el hakodesh*"—simply, this means "He shall not enter at all times into the sacred precincts." Interpreted by *Chasidut*: by means of *Al*—"non-being"[20] or self-nullification, not the

---

16. Isaiah 45:18.
17. *Chagigah* 14b.
18. Leviticus 16:2.
19. Leviticus 16:6.
20. See *Hayom Yom*, 27 Adar II.

satisfaction of one's desire for closeness to the Almighty, but rather for fulfillment of His most exalted will—"shall he enter the sacred precincts."

This is also the meaning of *"Bezot yavo Aharon el hakodesh,"*[21] literally: "In this manner shall Aaron enter the sacred precincts." The *Zohar* interprets the word *"bezot"* as meaning fear and self-nullification[22]—"this is the gate for ascent."[23] If there exists the precedence of *"zot,"* fear and self-nullification, then even Aaron's *entrance* into the sacred precincts, *ratzo*, shall in no way hinder or nullify the achievement of "forgiveness for his household." The word *"beito"* (household) is explained in the Talmud as referring to the high priest's wife.[24] His presence in the Holy of Holies in no way contradicts the *shov* to matters of the mundane world. On the contrary, a high priest, if not married, is forbidden to enter the Holy of Holies. The purpose of *ratzo* is its culmination and realization in the state of *shov*. It was the same when the high priest departed from the Holy of Holies. Immediately upon his emergence from the Holy of Holies, this very same high priest recited a prayer for the "sustenance of your nation the house of Israel"—material and economic sustenance.[25]

EMERGING FROM THE HOLY OF HOLIES

All narratives of the Torah provide guidance not only for special individuals, but for all Jews. At first glance, the teaching derived from the narrative of Nadab and Avihu is related only to the few, to those who have reached the level of *ratzo*, the actual expiration of soul. It is they who must be admonished to take heed lest they succumb to *ratzo* without subsequent *shov*. What instruction may be gained for the major part of Israel, or

---

21. Leviticus 16:3.
22. *Zohar* III:108a.
23. *Zohar* I 8a.
24. *Yoma* 2a.
25. *Yoma* 53b, according to the text as quoted in the *Seder Ha'avodah* in the *Siddur* of Rabbi Schneur Zalman of Liadi.

for those Jews at the nethermost limits, lesser in degree than even the majority of their fellow Jews?

There are times when every Jew is spiritually awakened and inspired. This occurs particularly on those occasions which are a time of mercy from Above, as for example, Shabbat and the Holidays. This is even truer of the days "when He is to be found" and "when He is near,"[26] the Ten Days of Penitence[27] in general and Rosh Hashanah and Yom Kippur in particular. For at that time a Jew stands on a higher level, far beyond his mundane concerns, completely removed from the worldly matter with which he is normally preoccupied.

At the time that an individual—a soul garbed in a body and at the same time above worldly matters—stands in a manner of *ratzo*, he must know that *ratzo* must be united with *shov*. The entrance into sanctity may not be separated from the emergence from the Holy of Holies. The emotion of the most sublime soul-yearning, occurring on the holy day of Yom Kippur, should not remain isolated and remote from the world, but translate into a firm resolve to actualize and unite this emotion with one's daily life. "He entered in peace"—at the time of entrance into sanctity there must be the fulfillment of G-d's intention in creation: peace and harmony by means of uniting the world with G-dliness, that all worldly matters should be done for the "sake of heaven,"[28] till one achieves the level of "know Him in all your ways."[29]

Uniting the entrance into sanctity with the subsequent departure involves not only the spiritual elevation of material matters upon one's emergence from the Holy of Holies; the worldly matters of a Jew are themselves related to the entrance into the Holy of Holies. For everything of import to a Jew, even material abundance, i.e., children, life and abundant

---

26. Isaiah 55:6.
27. *Rosh Hashanah* 18a.
28. *Pirkei Avot* 2:12.
29. Proverbs 3:6.

livelihood, are received from the Almighty. The Torah states, "If you shall proceed in My statutes and observe My commandments," then "I shall give your rains at their appropriate time."[30] A Jew can receive the "rains at their appropriate time" only by means of his fulfilling Torah and *mitzvot*.

The reckoning that "I shall have peace for I shall go after the longing of *my own heart*"[31] is not derived from sanctity. This thought can only exist for a short while because, ultimately, the life-power of a Jew must be directly united with G-dliness.[32]

This is also suggested by the relationship between the entrance and emergence from sanctity. Only through the entrance of the high priest into the Holy of Holies was it possible for him upon his emergence to utter a special prayer and thereby evoke economic sustenance. At that time his prayer is of greatest significance, for the evocation of material blessing occurs in great measure, without limitation, when it derives from the Holy of Holies.

As stated, the entrance of the high priest into the Holy of Holies on Yom Kippur is linked to his wife. The high priest's entrance into sanctity must be in a proper manner, one that will cause his "departure in peace," which is the very purpose of his entrance—and all this is contingent on the Jewish woman.

Even when the husband is *within* the innermost precincts, his "household" (which the Rabbis tell us specifically refers to his wife) is considered related to his lofty degree,[33] both then and in the future. This means that it is the privilege and responsibility of Jewish women to influence their husbands and children that their entrance and departure from sanctity are constantly united.

---

30. Leviticus 26:4.

31. Deuteronomy 29:18.

32. *Kuntreis Uma'ayon, Ma'amar* 10.

33. See *Chiddushei Agadot Maharsha, Shabbat* 118b.

Jewish women should not fear that their husbands, by praying an hour or more beyond the normal length of prayer, or studying an hour or more beyond the time set aside for study, will cause an inadequacy in material matters; they should similarly understand that if a child is educated to study Torah the entire day, he will not lack primary needs later. On the contrary, they should set the standard and clarify to their husbands and children that only increased efforts in Torah and *mitzvot*—"If you will go in My statutes and observe My commands"—will cause bountiful increase in the blessing of "I shall give your rains in their time."

(Likkutei Sichot, Vol. 3, pp. 987-993*)*

SUKKOT

THE *LULAV*—
SYMBOL OF THE TORAH SCHOLAR

The following *sicha* focuses on the unity with G-d achieved specifically through the study of Torah. Since "G-d and the Torah are one",[1] it follows that the scholar primarily immersed in Torah study achieves the highest level of unity with G-d. The *lulav* is symbolic of Torah study. This explains why when we recite the blessing over the four species on Sukkot, the blessing is primarily on the *lulav*: "*al netilat lulav*"—"to take the *lulav*." The Rebbe's analysis of the role of the *lulav* eventually leads to a deeper appreciation of the unification of all Jews exemplified by the taking of the four species, one of the major themes of the holiday.

THE REVELATION OF SUKKOT

The verse "*Tiku bachodesh shofar bakesseh leyom chagainu*"[2] is literally translated as: "Blow the *shofar* on the new month, on the day designated for our festival."

Chasidut explains that the biblical phrase "*bakesseh leyom chagainu*" refers to those matters "*bakesseh*," which are in a state of concealment on both Rosh Hashanah and Yom Kippur, and which are revealed, "*leyom chagainu*," on the day of our rejoicing, Sukkot.[3] Both Rosh Hashanah and Yom Kippur serve as a unifying force for all Jewish souls. During these holidays, Jews serve G-d with the inner aspect of the soul, as indicated by the phrase, recited during these days, "*Bakshu panai*."[4] Although

---

1. See *Likkutei Amarim Tanya*, ch. 4.

2. Psalms 81:4.

3. *Likkutei Torah*, Deuteronomy 48b; *Siddur Im Dach* 235b.

4. Psalms 27:8.

literally translated as "seek My (G-d's) face," this is interpreted in *Chasidut* as the quest for finding one's own *penimiyut*—inner spirituality.[5]

Within this inner spiritual realm, all Jews are equal to each other.[6] Thus, G-d declares: "You stand before me all of you," from "the hewer of wood to the drawer of water."[7] This unity of all the Jewish people emerges from its concealed state (as do all other concealed aspects of Rosh Hashanah and Yom Kippur) and is revealed on Sukkot.

This motif of unity is reflected in the *Midrash's* comment[8] that "the four species"—*etrog* (citron), *lulav* (date-palm branch), *aravot* (willow), and *hadasim* (myrtle)—ritually used by Jews on Sukkot hint at four different kinds of Jews. The *etrog* refers to the Jewish people. Just as the *etrog* possesses taste and smell, so does the Jewish people have individuals who possess taste (Torah) and smell (virtuous deeds). *Ta'am*—taste—is equated with the intellectual knowledge of Torah because Torah requires "taste"—comprehension and mastery gratifying to the laboring scholar. The more subtle sense of smell is equated with *mitzvot*, the fulfillment of G-d's commands. Here the primary emphasis is not upon understanding, but upon *kabbalat ol*—submission to G-d's will. Palm branches refer to the Jewish people. The date tree has a taste (the dates) but no scent; similar to those Jews who possess Torah knowledge but are lacking in scent—good deeds. The myrtle branch possesses a scent but has no taste. Similarly, among the Jewish people there are individuals who have virtuous deeds but who are devoid of Torah. Finally, just as willow branches have neither taste nor scent, similarly, the Jewish people includes individuals lacking both Torah and virtuous deeds. The *Midrash* concludes, "And G-d declared, let them all be tied together in one bond, and they shall atone for each other."

---

5.   *Likkutei Torah*, Deuteronomy 44b, c.

6.   See *Tanya*, ch. 32.

7.   Deuteronomy 29:9.

8.   *Vayikra Rabbah* 30:12.

The unity of Sukkot surpasses that of Rosh Hashanah and Yom Kippur. On both of these holidays, the unity of these four categories remains latent. In the blowing of the *shofar* on Rosh Hashanah and the repentance on Yom Kippur the equality of all Jews is discerned. The differences among all the categories are *"bakesseh"*—concealed. However, on Sukkot, the individual qualities of the four categories emerge and are clearly perceived. Indeed, the mitzvah consists of taking four distinct species and binding them into one cohesive mitzvah entity—one unity.

WHY *AL NETILAT LULAV*?

The *Midrash* indicates that the *etrog* is the superior of the "four kinds," since it has both qualities of taste and scent, and it therefore refers to the foremost category among Jews—those possessing both Torah and *mitzvot*. If the *etrog* is superior, then why does the blessing of this mitzvah conclude with the phrase *"al netilat lulav"* ("to take the *lulav*") which indicates the *lulav's* primacy? One answer[9] is that the *lulav* is the tallest object of the "four kinds." Yet, outward physical appearance, especially of a mitzvah, corresponds and reflects its spiritual dimension and source. The very fact that the *lulav* is the tallest of the objects indicates its superior spiritual quality compared to the other three. Viewed superficially, however, why should the *lulav*, possessing only taste, surpass the *etrog*, having both taste and scent?

To solve this problem, we must be clarify the distinction between Torah and *mitzvot*.[10] *Mitzvot* are described as the "organs of the King;"[11] regarding Torah it is stated: "G-d and the Torah are one."[12] The organs of the body are not completely one with the soul. Though they are subordinated and nullified to the soul to the extent that they naturally fulfill the soul's desire, they are not the soul itself. Similarly, a Jew's

9. *Sukkah* 37b.

10. See *Tanya*, ch. 23. *Kitzurim Veha'arot Letanya*, p. 104 and ff.

11. *Tikkunei Zohar, Tikkun* 30.

12. See *Zohar* I 24a; *Tanya* ch. 4, beg. ch. 23.

performance of *mitzvot* indicates and expresses his self-nullification and submission to the divine will. Nevertheless, as he performs the mitzvah, he retains his own independent selfhood and he does not, as it were, become wholly merged with the oneness of G-d. But in the study of Torah with comprehension and understanding, the mind grasps, as it were, the "wisdom of G-d" to the degree that Man's intellect becomes a Torah intellect—thus he is united with the wisdom of G-d, and "G-d and His wisdom are one."[13]

Since the advantage of Torah study is the resultant unity with G-d, it is obvious that the more a Jew strives to study and comprehend Torah, the more he will achieve this unity. Therefore, one wholly dedicated to the study of Torah, excluding all other concerns, is described as a *lulav* "possessing only Torah and without any virtuous deeds."

The phrase "without virtuous deeds" must be clarified. A person learned in Torah obviously performs *mitzvot* and virtuous deeds, or we would be referring to a Jew who does not practice what he learns. About such a person the Torah states, "And to the evil man G-d says: What is it to you to speak of statutes?"[14] Even one who avoids transgressing any prohibitions of the Code of Jewish Law through inaction, but does not strive to perform additional virtuous deeds is in the category of "one who declares that he possesses only Torah, also lacks Torah itself."[15] Thus, it is apparent that additional good deeds are required.

The "*lulav*" personality is one who observes *mitzvot* and indeed has additional virtuous deeds, but only in accordance with the minimal level necessary to abide by all the obligations of the *Shulchan Aruch*—The Code of Jewish Law. The remainder of his primary concern and preoccupation is with Torah study.

---

13. See *Tanya*, ch. 5.

14. Psalms 50:16; *Hilchot Talmud Torah* of the Alter Rebbe 4:3.

15. *Yevamot* 109b.

His unity with G-d surpasses, therefore, the personality described as an *etrog*, one who is dedicated to the dual endeavor of Torah and *mitzvot*. Since the *etrog* is involved in other efforts besides Torah study (despite the fact that these actions are the fulfillment of G-d's exalted will), he is linked and unified with G-d in *mitzvot*, which are the "organs of the King," a lower level than the unity effected with G-dliness through the assiduous study of Torah.

Thus, in the mitzvah of taking the "four species," the quality of the *lulav* is emphasized in the *berachah* since it exemplifies the total unity with G-d accomplished through dedicated Torah study. The purpose of the "four species" is to express the unity of all Jews with each other, and this in turn is derived from the elemental unity of Jews with G-d.

THE SIGNIFICANCE OF SHAKING

In light of this we can better understand the ritual of *na'anuim*—"shaking" the *lulav*. Although the extending and drawing close to the "six points"—the four directions, above and below—is done with all "four species," the actual "rustling" is done only with the *lulav*. This is emphasized by the custom of the leaders of *Chabad* that after every ritual extending of the *lulav* they would shake it, and only then would they pull it in. The particular significance of shaking of the *lulav* is reflected by the fact that the required length of the *lulav* is four handbreadths—one handbreadth longer than the myrtle and willow branches. The extra length facilitates the ritual shaking.[16]

Souls in the spiritual worlds are described as stationary[17] since they always remain on one level (even their advance is limited). However, when a soul descends into a body, through Torah and *mitzvot*, the soul progresses and ascends in an unlimited manner. This distinctive quality of spiritual advancement can only be accomplished when the soul is vested in the physical body.

---

16. See *Sukkah* 32b.

17. *Torah Or* 30a; *Likkutei Torah*, Numbers 38d.

The swaying, or shaking, which traditionaly accompanies Jewish prayer and Torah study, expresses this unlimited ascension of the soul. The *Zohar*[18] explains the verse, "The soul of Man is the flame of G-d"[19] as follows: The soul is similar to a flickering flame which strives constantly to ascend and be reunited with its spiritual source.[20] Thus, the soul "shakes" at the time of Torah study, indicating that through Torah the soul strives toward and is united with G-dliness. However, comprehension and understanding entails undistracted tranquility of thought. Such a state is the very opposite of the "shaking" activity. Nevertheless, "shaking" is necessary during Torah study to indicate that even Torah as vested in human intellectuality is the wisdom of G-d. Even at the very moment of one's intellectual comprehension of Torah, the inner nature of his endeavor must be apparent: he is uniting himself with G-dliness.

A Jew's capability for unlimited advancement derives from his being united with G-d, Who is truly infinite. Since true unity with G-d is accomplished through the study of Torah, as explained previously, Man's capability for infinite spiritual advance is primarily through Torah study. Thus, the ritual shaking is fulfilled with the *lulav*, which exemplifies the Torah scholar. This unity of Torah also causes "forward movement" in the performance of *mitzvot*—which corresponds to the concomitant shaking of the other three species due to their closeness to the *lulav*.

TWO ASPECTS OF TORAH STUDY

The connotation of the "shaking" of Torah is not limited to the infinite advance accomplished through Torah study. It also refers to a twofold process necessary for Torah study itself:

---

18. III 218b.

19. Proverbs 20:27.

20. *Tanya*, ch. 19.

a) Torah study must be in a manner of "daily increase in the knowledge of Torah."[21] The person studying Torah must constantly add to his knowledge. This is one of the distinctions between the spiritual endeavor of prayer and that of Torah study. The same prayers are recited every weekday, with standardized variations for Shabbat and holidays. But Torah study requires a constant augmenting and increase.

b) "A person does not acquire true mastery of Torah without initially succumbing to error."[22] In order to correctly understand a matter of Torah there must be a *shakla vetarya* (weighing and shaking), a preliminary process of intense intellectual analysis marked by alternation from one rationale to another. Each idea must be explored, revised, possibly only to give way to another rationale, which itself might be ultimately abandoned for a third point of view. Thus, in a *lulav*-like manner, the reflecting mind "shakes" and explores to all "six points," every vantage point being analyzed, until the person finally reaches the true understanding of the concept.

WHY A PALM *BRANCH*?

The *Midrash* states that the *lulav* alludes to Torah scholars because the date "possesses taste but has no scent." Consequently, when performing the mitzvah it would seem that we should hold the *fruit* itself, since it is the fruit that has the actual taste. Why is it that we take the palm *branch*?

This can be clarified as follows: The holding of the "four species" expresses the unity of all Jews. Prior to this unity each Jew must experience a sense of humility, since vanity and self-esteem impedes the bond linking one Jew to another.[23] This humility must be expressed materially, not just spiritually. In every one of the "four species" there must be some element of humility which facilitates the total merging of the "four species" into one entity. Thus, the *etrog*, the most superior of

---

21. *Zohar* I 12b.

22. *Gittin* 43a.

23. See "*Heichaltzu*," ch. 4 (*Sefer Hama'amarim* 5659, p. 50).

the "four species," having both taste and scent, has in its very name letters which are an acronym for the phrase reflecting King David's humility: the initials for "*al tevo'eini regel ga'ava*"[24] ("let not the foot of pride come upon me").[25]

As previously mentioned, the *lulav* possesses a quality surpassing even the *etrog* in that it only has taste—the quality of Torah study. Similarly, the *lulav* also requires some hint of *bitul*—the quality of self-nullification. Thus, we take the palm branch and not its fruit.

THE SIGNIFICANCE OF LEAVES

Torah compares Man to a tree,[26] and intellect, the unique quality within Man, to fruit, the superior product of the tree. The *Midrash* states that the taste of the date is comparable to Torah. The function of leaves is to protect the fruit they grow with.[27] This is also true regarding intellect. The conceptual trial and error are similar to protective "leaves," assuring the goodness of the "fruit"—the final, true understanding of the concept.

It is the nature of Man to derive intellectual gratification upon reaching a final conclusion to a problem. A person experiences no delight while still occupied with the problem solving process. The very reverse is true: beleaguered with questions and contradictions, he is in distress. He is not content during this mental process, nor can he feel a sense of self-sufficiency. Instead, he experiences a humbling sense of inadequacy and his own intellectual limitation.

This is the humbling experience, the *bitul* in the use of the *lulav*, the palm leaves. A person should always perceive himself as being on the level of the "leaves." No matter how great or profound his understanding, he should be mindful that his

---

24. Psalms 36:12.

25. *Panim Yafot, Parshat Emor.*

26. See Deuteronomy 20:19; *Ta'anit* 7a; *Likkutei Sichot*, vol. 4, p. 1114 and references there.

27. *Chulin* 92a.

knowledge is less than a drop from the sea, for Torah is "longer than the land and broader than the sea,"[28] and that the ultimate truth of Torah is "concealed from the eyes of all living beings."[29]

This steadfast awareness prevents the vanity and self-esteem that can accompany Torah erudition. On the contrary, the awareness of one's remoteness from the ultimate truth of Torah evokes a sense of self-nullification and humility.

This, too, is hinted at in the words "*kapot temarim*" (palm branches). The word *kapot* is related to the word *kafut* (bound)[30]—by means of self-nullification he is bound up and united with G-d. It is specifically through exemplifying this quality of self-nullification that the *lulav* merits being the highest of the "four species." Only to the extent that a person experiences self-nullification can he approach and truly comprehend Jewish Law. Our Sages state that the school of Hillel were "patient and enduring,"[31] and therefore they merited that the law is ruled in accordance with their opinion.

THE LESSON OF THE *LULAV*

One must be wholly committed to Torah study, in a manner of *lulav*, and while engaged in this unity with Torah be totally undistracted by any other matter. This does not pertain only to *yeshivah* students or to scholars whose sole occupation is the study of Torah. Indeed, every one of the "four kinds" should be merged into a new unifying identity, integrated to such an extent that each individual "kind" should possess not only its own unique quality, but also the advantages of the other "kinds" of Jews. This means that even those Jews in the category of *aravah* (willow branches), devoid of taste and smell, should elevate themselves to the extent that they too will, at

---

28. Job 11:9.

29. Job 28:21.

30. *Sukkah* 32a.

31. See *Eiruvin* 13b; and see *Sefer Hama'amarim* 5627, p. 276 and ff.; *Likkutei Sichot* vol. 21, p. 115 and sources cited there.

certain times, be in the realm of the *lulav*, studying Torah in a manner of total unity with G-d.

These periods of Torah study in the aforementioned manner will so influence the individual as to liberate him from his former level and influence all other aspects of his life, just as the shaking of the *lulav* causes the shaking and movement of the three other "kinds." Thus, there is a sustained advance in the observance of *mitzvot* as well. They continuously influence the everyday aspects of a person's life until they are also characterized by "know Him in *all* your ways"[32]—the devotional awareness of G-dliness in all of one's daily activities. This will, thus, become a progressively ascendant spiritual dedication.

This spiritual endeavor begins with intensive concentration in Torah study "to master in greater measure," advancing every day to a higher degree of Torah knowledge. G-d has given His assurance that this intense effort of "you shall strive" will inevitably result in "you shall find."[33] The word "find" indicates that G-d's reward will be far beyond the measure of effort expended, just as the process of discovery, of "finding" something occurs in a totally unanticipated way. This will ultimately result in the revelation of the inner teachings of Torah through our righteous *Mashiach*, whose advent will also be in the manner of "finding." Thus, G-d declares, "I have *found* David My servant."[34] This "finding" refers to the *Mashiach*, who will come in a "wholly unanticipated manner."[35] Those aspects of Torah which have required intensive effort and hitherto have only been understood in the *galyah*—the external aspects of the Torah—will then be revealed to us in their full profundity with the imparting of the concealed aspects

32. Proverbs 3:6.
33. *Megillah* 6b.
34. Psalms 89:21.
35. *Sanhedrin* 97a.

of the Torah[36] at the time of the coming of our righteous
Mashiach, speedily and in our times.

(Likkutei Sichot, vol. 4, pp. 1159-1165)

---

36. See Rashi, Song of Songs 1:2.

SUKKOT

THE LOFTY ASPIRATION
OF YOUTH

On *Simchat Beit Hasho'eivah*—the celebration accompanying the water libation of the holiday of Sukkot—the young priests would take large jugs of oil, climb up steep ladders, and place them in the gold menorahs of the *Beit Hamikdash* and thus illuminate *all* of Jerusalem.

The Rebbe points to the difference between this climb and that of the high priest's on the ramp of the Temple altar. The high priest ascent is gradual, in contrast to the steep climb and advance of the younger priests, which entails greater inner struggle. But it is particularly through the efforts of the high priest on Yom Kippur, and particularly in the Holy of Holies, which opens the spiritual channels to enable the young men to climb to the menorah and thus illuminate *all* of "Jerusalem"—the external mundane world.

SIMCHAT BEIT HASHO'EIVAH

The festive event of *Simchat Beit Hasho'eivah*, the drawing and pouring of the water of the altar of the *Beit Hamikdash* on Sukkot, is described in the *Mishnah* and Talmud.[1] Young priests—the *pirchei kehuna*—would take large jugs of oil, each jug containing 30 *lug*, and carry them up tall ladders to the top of the gold *menorot* that stood in the *Beit Hamikdash*. After the *menorot* were filled with the oil and kindled, the brilliant light illuminated even the most remote house in Jerusalem, to the extent that the women could use the light to sort grain.

Maimonides[2] writes that every person who is moved to spend his life serving G-d is comparable to that of a *kohein*. The

---

1. *Sukkah* 52b.
2. Maimonides, *Hilchot Shemitah Veyovel* 13:13.

priestly task is fulfilled primarily by those who bring the light of Torah and its commandments into Jewish homes so that there is "light in their dwelling places."[3] This light should be bright enough so that a woman "can select from the kernels of grain"[4] — that is, even matters which are inherently mundane, such as the sifting of grains, should be illuminated with the light of Torah.

YOUNG STRENGTH

Just as the young men were the ones to kindle the *menorot* at the time of the Temple, so too are contemporary youth particularly obligated to spread the light of Torah. They will thus bring radiance into their entire environment, and G-d will repay them generously, causing "light in all their spiritual and material endeavors."

The Talmud[5] relates that the task of the priestly youth was more arduous than that of the strongest adult priest in two ways: the weight of their burden was far greater than the heaviest weight borne by an adult priest, and the older priests would ascend to the altar on an inclined plane, while the young men would ascend on a steep ladder.

According to Maimonides' concept of priesthood, cited above, which would include all those inspired to serve G-d, the most powerful priest in the spiritual sense would be the high priest. Distinguished and more sanctified than his fellow priests, he was privileged to enter the most sacred precincts of the Temple, the Holy of Holies. Nevertheless, the young priests surpassed him in the two aforementioned qualities.

The high priest's task was to effect pardon, forgiveness, and cleansing on Yom Kippur for the Jewish people's transgressions of the past year. Although this was the ultimate level of "spiritual might," the young priests' task was characterized by a

---

3. Exodus 10:23.

4. See *Yevamot* 63a.

5. *Sukkah*, ibid.

superior quality in relation to *Simchat Beit Hasho'eivah*—the bringing of light into Jewish homes.

This seeming paradox can be explained in the following way: the high priest had already completed his own spiritual labors to the extent that he was deemed worthy by divine Providence of his lofty spiritual status. Consequently, his "burden was not overly heavy." Having achieved nullification of his material desires, he was no longer engaged in conflict with his evil inclination. Rabbi Schneur Zalman, the Alter Rebbe,[6] defines the term "servant of the L-rd" as one who has "completed his task of struggle against the evil within him," and has thereby achieved the status of a "servant of G-d." Since the burden, that is, the conflict with the evil inclination, is no longer heavy, the consequent reward which is always in accordance with the effort expended[7] is likewise not that great.

The high priest's ascent on the gradual slope of a ramp implies that there is only a slight distinction between the beginning and conclusion of his ascent. For even at the very onset of his daily labors, the high priest has already achieved a lofty plane by virtue of his unique spiritual office. The high priest strives unceasingly in the service of G-d, and must constantly ascend higher. His daily spiritual ascent, however, is marked by a comparatively moderate advance in his exalted spiritual devotions, with no great contrast between the beginning and end of each day's labors.

The priestly youths, on the other hand, have not yet refined their bodies and animalistic souls; they are still tied to the physical and material. Their burden is exceedingly heavy, for they must struggle with their material inclinations.

Though they are on a lower spiritual level, their labor is not hindered by limited gradations. They ascend on steep ladders and are obligated to utilize their ability to the maximum extent and at every moment on the steep path leading upwards.

---

6. *Tanya*, ch. 15.

7. *Pirkei Avot* 5:26.

MAKING THE MOST OF EACH DAY

The significance of time, its passage and maximal use is two-fold. Firstly, time, when lost, can never be regained, as it is written, "Days were created, and not one amongst them."[8] Each individual has been given a specific amount of days and minutes on earth to fulfill the tasks assigned to him. "And not one amongst them"—if he should lose one day, it is an irreplaceable loss. Secondly, his labor on the first day affects the significance of his efforts on the next. As our Sages state: "He who possesses a hundred coins desires two hundred coins, and he who has three hundred coins desires four hundred."[9] Similarly, having ascended by means of his toil on the first day to a higher level, his desire, goal and manner of striving on the second day are increased.

These, then, are the unique qualities of the priestly youth. They bear exceedingly heavy burdens and climb upon high ladders. Theirs is a great ascent from the beginning of their labor until they reach their ultimate goal.

One need not fear that the burden is too great. The Almighty "does not come to overburden His creatures."[10] Each individual has been endowed with adequate strength and ability to fulfill his designated task.

The labor of the high priest on the Day of Atonement effected pardon, forgiveness and cleansing before G-d for all Israel, and thereby evoked the manifestation of the "time of our Joy"—Sukkot. On Sukkot, the "priestly youths" are endowed with the strength and ability to succeed in their labor and to perform the task incumbent upon them—to bring brilliant light, the light of Torah, into every corner,[11] so that the most

---

8. Psalms 139:16. See *Likkutei Torah*, Numbers 52a. Also see *Sefer Hama'amarim Yiddish*, p. 82.

9. See *Kohelet Rabbah* 1:13.

10. *Avodah Zarah* 3a.

11. This echoes the point made at the beginning of the *sichah* that the light from the menorot would illuminate the "even the most remote house."

mundane task is illuminated with its radiance—and to do this with "joy and gladness of heart."

(Likkutei Sichot, vol. 4, pp. 1365-1367)

SUKKOT

SERVING G-D WITH JOY

This *sicha*, the Rebbe derives an original concept following a detailed analysis of Maimonides' textual formulation (in *Mishneh Torah* of the mitzvah of *simchah* – rejoicing—on Sukkot in the Holy Temple.[1] He states that, in essence, the obligation of "You shall rejoice before the L-rd you G-d"[2] is not a separate mitzvah, but rather an intensification of the general obligation of *simchah*, related to all Jewish festivals, as stated in the verse "And you shall rejoice on your festival."[3] Indeed, Maimonides, in his *Sefer Hamitzvot*, does not count the *simchah* of Sukkot as a separate commandment but subsumes it under the general obligation of "You shall rejoice on your holiday."[4]

In the excerpt, which follows, the Rebbe then focuses on Maimonides' description of those participating the joyous festivities of the Holy Temple.

THE IDENTITY OF THE REJOICERS

Maimonides[5] writes regarding *Simchat Beit Hasho'eivah*, the special rejoicing that took place in the Temple:

There is a mitzvah to increase in the observance of this festivity. This was not done by the unlearned or anyone merely wanting to do so. The participants were eminent Jewish Sages, heads of the Talmudic academies and of the *Sanhedrin* court, men of piety, elders, and men of virtuous deeds. These were the

---

1. Maimonides: *Hilchot Lulav* 8:12.
2. Leviticus 23:40 on Sukkot.
3. Deuteronomy 16:14.
4. Maimonides: *Sefer Hamitzvot*, Positive Commands, Mitzvah 54. See also Maimonides *Hilchot Yom Tov* 6:17.
5. *Hilchot Lulav* 8:14.

individuals who danced, clapped, sang and encouraged joyousness in the holy Temple during the Sukkot holiday. However, the remainder of the populace, men and women came to see and hear.

The source for Maimonides' description is from the *Mishnah*, which cites only two groups: "The men of piety and men of virtuous deeds who danced before all those gathered."[6] The Talmud adds a third group, *Baalei teshuvah*—penitent individuals.[7] Maimonides, in his enumeration, adds individuals seemingly not mentioned in the *Mishnah*. However, he also omits citing *Baalei teshuvah* explicitly mentioned in the Talmud.

Maimonides continues:

> The joy that an individual should experience in the performance of *mitzvot* and in the love of G-d, Who commanded the *mitzvot*, is a profound service of G-d. And everyone who humbles himself, making light of his body and the like, is a distinguished, honored individual serving G-d on the level of love. Indeed, thus did King David declare (regarding his fervent dancing in front of the holy ark upon its return): "And I will make light of myself to an even greater degree and I shall be humble in my eyes."[8]

The command for an "increase in joy" is, in essence, not a separate commandment, but rather, a heightening of the general command of joy on Sukkot. Thus, it's expression is dependent on the feelings of joy felt by each individual on his or her level. It is for this reason that those eminent individuals, having reached a higher spiritual level with acknowledged piety, rejoiced in an animated manner of "dancing and clapping," etc, while the "entire populace, men and women, expressed their joy by coming to see and hear."

---

6. *Sukkah* 51a.
7. *Sukkah* 53a.
8. II Samuel 6:22.

The Rejoicing of the Sages

The Babylonian[9] and Jerusalem Talmuds[10] cite the names of several *Tanaim* (Sages of the Mishnah) and relate how they acted or what they said on *Simchat Beit Hasho'eivah*. We can be certain that all the *Tanaim* who lived in that era participated in these festivities. Why are only these specific individuals cited? We must assume that they represented all the different categories of those involved in the rejoicing.

a) The Talmud states, "Rabbi Yehoshua ben Chananya said: 'When we rejoiced on *Simchat Beit Hasho'eivah* we did not experience sleep...the participants would doze on each other's shoulders.'"

Regarding the uniqueness of Rabbi Yehoshua, we are told that he debated with the elders of Athens, famed as wise men, and was victorious.[11] Prior to his passing, the Jewish Sages asked him what would become of them "at the hands of the heretics," and he reassured them that the heretics would not prevail.[12] Here we see that he was numbered amongst the preeminent Jewish Sages. This appears to be the source for Maimonides' mentioning the involvement of "eminent Jewish Sages."

b) "It was said regarding Rabbi Shimon ben Gamliel, when he rejoiced on *Simchat Beit Hasho'eivah* he would juggle eight fiery torches and they wouldn't touch one another."

Rabbi Shimon ben Gamliel was the head of the *Sanhedrin*, as stated in the Talmud.[13] Maimonides states, "The great *Sanhedrin* was composed of seventy-one members. The preeminent one amongst them was designated as their leader. He was the head of the *Sanhedrin* academy and is referred to as the *Nasi* in every instance..."[14]

---

9. *Sukkah* 53a.

10. *Sukkah* 5:4.

11. *Bechorot* 8b.

12. *Chagigah* 5b.

13. *Shabbat* 15a.

14. Maimonides: *Hilchot Sanhedrin* 1:3.

This is the source for Maimonides' statement that the *Sanhedrin* participated in the festivities of *Simchat Beit Hasho'eivah.*

c) "It was said regarding Hillel the Elder…"—the emphasis on the title "Elder" in this context (despite the fact that he is cited in many instances in the Talmud without it), conveys that he exemplified this unique quality at the *Simchat Beit Hasho'eivah,* and it is from here that Maimonides derived the participation of "elders."

d) The Jerusalem Talmud[15] adds "Ben Yehoztadak, who was praised for his leaps." When Rabbi Shimon ben Yehoztadak is mentioned in the enumeration of *Tanaim,* no distinctive quality is related regarding him. We are therefore compelled to say that his uniqueness is inhered in his title, *Rebbi Shimon.* The *Tosefta*[16] states that "He who has students is called '*Rebbi.*'" That being the case, Rebbi Shimon ben Yehotzadak was the head of an academy. Hence the source for the statement of Maimonides that heads of Torah academies rejoiced on *Simchat Beit Hasho'eivah.*

This need clarification: If he is mentioned to his title "Rebbi," why then is he mentioned here only as the *son of Yehoztadak* without his own name and title? We can answer that the word "[he] was praised" is written in the reflexive form. Rabbi Shimon ben Yehotzadak is actually describing his *own* behavior, priding himself on his vigorous participation in the *Simchat Beit Hasho'eivah.* In describing his own virtues, and to dispel the slightest nuance or suggestion of vanity, he refers to himself merely as "ben Yehotzadak," totally nullifying himself to his father. We find a similar mode of modest self-reference in the instance of Rabbi Yochanan ben Zakkai, who refers to himself merely as "ben Zakkai."[17]

---

15. *Sukkah* 5:4, cited above.
16. Conclusion of *Eduyot.*
17. *Berachot* 34b.

THE DEFINITION OF A *CHASID*

The rationale for Maimonides' omission of *Baalei teshuvah*, repentant individuals, cited in the *Beraitah*, is that he sees the *Beraitah* as an elaboration on the *Mishnah*. He perceives the term *Chasidim*, pious men, in the *Mishnah*, as inclusive of both those virtuous their entire lives, and of those who have repented. This is in contrast to Rashi who defines the term *Chasid* as referring to an individual who maintained pious behavior during the entire course of his life.[18] Maimonides, however, declares that "He who does not merely follow the middle path but goes to some extent beyond, this is a *Chasid*."[19] Therefore, Maimonides' citation of *Chasidim* among the participants of *Simchat Beit Hasho'eivah*, includes *Baalei teshuvah*, as well.

Maimonides concludes his description of *simchah* on *Simchat Beit Hasho'eivah* by speaking of the significance of serving G-d by performing all *mitzvot* with joy. This provides for us a new insight regarding this endeavor.

The joy of *Simchat Beit Hasho'eivah*, being an intensification of an already existing joy, is easy to engender. The joy of doing a mitzvah in general, however, required at all times and for all *mitzvot* without regard for one's emotional state at the time, is, as Maimonides puts it, a particularly "profound service," entailing greater effort. Accordingly, Maimonides cites the intensely animated joy of King David,[20] which conveys the necessity for *simchah* generically in all *mitzvot*, even though it is a formidable challenge to awaken this emotion.

This has very practical implications. People could see themselves arouse the vibrant emotion of joy during festive holiday seasons, "times of our joy." But how can this permeate all mundane, day-to-day activities? To that end, Maimonides imparts to us that only after *Simchat Beit Hasho'eivah*, does the "profound service" of *mitzvot* performed with *simchah* begin.

---

18. *Sukkah* 53a.

19. Maimonides, *Hilchot Dei'ot* 1:5.

20. II Samuel 6:16.

For even during the normal weekdays, every action of a Jew must be linked to the service of G-d on whatever level he may be; a Jew's simple performance of a mitzvah, the higher level of "All your deeds should be for the sake of heaven,"[21] or beyond that: "Know Him (G-d) in all your ways."[22] Whatever gradation, the mitzvah should be done with the intention of *fulfilling* "Serve G-d with joy."[23]

Though our Sages admonish "It is prohibited for a person to fill his mouth with laughter in this world,"[24] with regard to the performance of *mitzvot* the very reverse is true. It is obligatory and necessary to perform *mitzvot* with joy. And this will bring about the evocation of "laughter" in the spiritual realm—that "He who abides in the Heavens shall laugh."[25] G-d will laugh derisively at all those attempting to oppress the Jewish people, and ultimately fulfill the prophetic assurance that "Then shall our mouths be filled with laughter,"[26] with the coming of our righteous *Mashiach* speedily in our time.

(*Likkutei Sichot*, vol. 17, pp. 267-275)

---

21. *Pirkei Avot* 2:12.
22. Proverbs 3:6.
23. Psalms 100:2.
24. *Berachot* 31a.
25. Psalms 2:4.
26. Psalms 126:2.

SUKKOT

ETERNAL *HAKHEL*—
A DYNAMIC DIMENSION FOR
JEWISH ACTIVISM

Mitzvot are both specific as well as eternal. In a narrow sense, *mitzvot* have specific details and requirements for their valid, legal fulfillment. On the other hand, since the Torah is divine and eternal, its *mitzvot* are eternal, with profound implications and teachings for all places and times. This especially apparent in connection with the mitzvah of *Hakhel*, a large public assembly, which in Biblical times involved the participation of the entire Jewish people.

The Rebbe explains that the essential goal of the gathering was the strengthening of faith and commitment to Torah and *mitzvot*, a goal shared by contemporary public gatherings.

"GATHER THE NATION"

In describing the mitzvah of *Hakhel* Maimonides writes:

It is a positive commandment to assemble the entire Jewish nation, men, women and children, and to read to them from the Torah selections that will positively influence their performance of G-d's commandments and strengthen [their hands in] the true faith; as it is written: "At the end of every seven years, on the holiday of Sukkot of the Sabbatical Year ... gather the nation ... in your gates, etc."[1]

Maimonides' usual style is to first describe the particular mitzvah under discussion with great brevity, then only after this initial definition does he permit himself chapters to clarify

---

1. Maimonides, *Hilchot Chagigah* 3:1; Deuteronomy 31:10.

specifics, and relevant details. Why, in this case, does Maimonides describe the topics and goals of the Torah readings, rather than simply stating the mitzvah briefly in his usual style: "to read before them selections from the Torah"?

Another question: Maimonides enumerates details of this mitzvah (the time, place, etc.) not in the first paragraph, as he usually does, but in the third one: "When was it read? On the night after the first day of Sukkot ... and the King should read in the Women's Section of the Temple." He also enumerates the verses that are read, even though these are already enumerated in the cited text. However, inherent concepts are not included here; the text only declares "You shall read this Torah, and yet Maimonides finds it necessary to emphasize the inspirational impact of *Hakhel* at the very beginning of these laws.

Near the conclusion of his discussion of this mitzvah, Maimonides states:

> Converts to Judaism who do not understand (what is being read) are obligated to heed with their heart's devotion, and to listen attentively with awe and fear, rejoicing and trembling, like when the Torah was given at Sinai. Even great sages who are familiar with the entire Torah are obligated to hear with great devotion and concentration. One who is unable to hear should focus his thoughts on the reading, for it was enacted solely to strengthen true faith. One should feel as though he had just been commanded these laws from G-d Himself, for the King is an emissary causing the word of G-d to be heard.

Once again the problem arises: Why does Maimonides mention all these facts at length? This is totally at variance with Maimonides' stated purpose of his work *Mishnah Torah*, which is to teach "*halachot, halachot*"—the practical rulings.

Thus, Maimonides' opinion in this case seems to be that strengthening the true faith is not merely a *reason* for the mitzvah or a result of it, but the very essence of the mitzvah. "The strengthening of the true faith" *is actually the* mitzvah *itself.*

(This gives insight into the Torah's stating in *one verse* both the commandment and the reason, "Gather the nation, the men, women and small children and the stranger in your gate *so that they may hear,* and *so that they may learn* and fear G-d your L-rd and they shall take heed to fulfill," etc. This contrasts with the mitzvah of *sukkah,* which is expressed in *two separate* verses: "You shall sit in Sukkot," etc., and the next verse, "so that your generations should know."[2] The reason the mitzvah of *Hakhel* is stated in one verse is that the actual law and the reason for it are not two *separate* matters, but one concept, the evocation of profound fear of G-d in the entire Jewish people.)

This is the reason why Maimonides states at length, and at the very beginning of his description of *Hakhel,* "To read to them from the Torah selections that will positively influence their performance of G-d's commandments and strengthen [their hands in] the true faith." This statement is distinctive from the other details of the *Hakhel* mitzvah, i.e. the time, the specific place, the identity of the person reading. These are details related to the *manner* of fulfilling this mitzvah; the "alerting and strengthening in the true faith" is its very essence.

Now we can gain insight into Maimonides' elaborating in paragraph six, about converts who may not understand what is being read, and Torah Sages who know the entire Torah, who are still obligated to listen.

If "strengthening of the true faith" were merely a result and consequence of the *Hakhel* Torah readings, then it is not possible to *obligate* and *require* that each individual gathered there should "...direct [his] heart, and listen attentively." However, since the mitzvah itself is "to strengthen the true faith," it is self-evident that the attention and involvement of each participant at that time is part of the mitzvah.

---

2. Leviticus 22:42, 43.

We can thus understand Maimonides' subsequent statement, "And he should perceive himself as though he were being commanded now, at this time, hearing these words from G-d himself." Since "strengthening the true faith" is an ongoing, sustained occurrence extending to the present, a nuance implied in the Biblical verse "to fear G-d all the days,"[3] the obligation includes "perceiving [oneself] as being commanded *now, at this time,* hearing these words from G-d Himself." Only such fear and awe of G-d have the power to influence and achieve a "strengthening of true faith, all the days"—for all time—as a result of a profound religious experience like that of the Jewish people at Mt. Sinai. That is why Maimonides explains the rationale for the mitzvah right at the start, because its intent and purpose are actual parts of the mitzvah, while in other instances, the mitzvah and its rationale are two separate entities.

The mitzvah of praying to G-d to fulfill one's needs is similar, for its primary purpose is that Man "beseech" and ask G-d for his needs. This intense plea is not extrinsic or an additional condition to prayer, but the very essence of the mitzvah itself, and without it, prayer is emptied of its essential content.

The same can be said of *Hakhel*: If the assemblage hearing the Torah reading does not have the devotion and intent discussed above, it does not mean that the performance of the mitzvah is imperfect in some detail, but that the fulfillment of the essence of the mitzvah is lacking.

ETERNAL HAKHEL

This gives us a profound insight into the eternal relevance of *Hakhel*:

It is a well-known concept that the inner dimension of the Torah is eternal and relevant to all times and places. There are *mitzvot* related to specific times, places, and even particular

---

3. Deuteronomy 31:13.

individuals, such as the priests and Levites. The mitzvah of *Hakhel* itself must take place on the Temple site, and includes other specific conditions. There is also a higher dimension, a spiritual content to *mitzvot* as they inhere to the soul of Man, and these have enduring relevance to all times and places. All *mitzvot* encompass the three aspects of thought, speech, and deed. Though we cannot, at the present time, fulfill certain *mitzvot* in actual deed, as for example, the offering of sacrifices, nevertheless the levels of thought and speech can still apply. Prayer is the service of the heart on the inner level of thought. The details of our daily prayers were enacted by the Rabbis to correspond to the rituals of sacrifice, and through our sincere prayers, we fulfill the intent of sacrifice through thought. Similarly, regarding speech—the verbal utterance of Torah passages describing the details of Temple sacrifices is viewed as though we have fulfilled the requirement for bringing the sacrifices. The Sages have taught that one who is preoccupied with the study of the laws of *olah* (whole offering sacrifice) is considered as actually having brought that sacrifice,[4] to the extent that this idea is expressed in the Biblical words "we shall render the (animal sacrifices) through the utterance of our lips."[5]

The Biblical laws of *shemittah*, letting the fields lie fallow every seventh year, has as its inner spiritual content the fact that all of "creation is owned by G-d."[6] It is self-evident that this awareness is eternally linked to all places and all times, even at a time when according to the Torah the actual mitzvah is not obligatory, even in a non-*shemittah* year.

The eternal relevance of *mitzvot* in general is usually connected with some particular aspect of detail of the *mitzvot*, not to their very essence. In the cases of sacrifices or the

---

4. *Menachot* 110a.
5. Hosea 14:3.
6. *Sefer Hachinuch,* Mitzvah 328.

shemittah-year, these *mitzvot* themselves cannot be observed in our time.

This is not so in the case of *Hakhel,* for the inner core of the mitzvah, i.e. "to strengthen the true faith" and the devotion of the heart, combined with fear and awe evoked by the assemblage of the Jewish people, is itself the mitzvah. Since these factors relate to all times, the eternal dimension of this mitzvah is manifested and revealed to a far greater extent than for other *mitzvot.*

"THESE DAYS ARE REMEMBERED AND DONE"

The famed Kabbalist, Rabbi Yitzchak Luria[7] interprets the phrase in the book of Esther, "These days are remembered and done"[8] to mean that if, on the anniversary of a holiday, its events are remembered in a proper way, this results in their being "done," i.e., we elicit from the very same divine source from which they were derived the first time, bringing about their actual occurrence in our lives as perennial and collective experiences. This implies the awakening of similar spiritual influence even if the observance is only partially fulfilled because of the absence of certain requirements or details.

Hakhel can occur both inwardly and externally. Each individual should strive to observe and fulfill *Hakhel* inwardly, within the bounds of his own soul, integrating the qualities and faculties of the soul toward the service of G-d. Communally, *Hakhel* can also be fulfilled in a Jew's immediate environment, family, neighborhood and city—to assemble men, women and children with the intention "that they may hear and learn, and fear G-d their L-rd and to heed and observe all of the teachings of this Torah," and "strengthen the true faith."

Moreover, and this is perhaps even more crucial, whoever participated in a modern-day *Hakhel,* even though the assemblage may have been a small one and on an ordinary day,

---

7. Ramaz, *Sefer Tikun Sovevim.* See *Sefer Leiv David* of the *Chidah,* ch. 29.
8. Esther 9:25.

could plainly see that the Jewish heart is awake, conscious and receptive to the true faith. The success and inspiration of innumerable Torah gatherings irrefutably proves that this practice should be pursued whenever feasible. Moreover, the absence of effort may lead to further communal disintegration and individual alienation from Torah values.

May it be G-d's will that a great initiative be set in motion in this *Hakhel* project, with imaginative efforts far exceeding the goals delineated above. This includes influencing others to become *Hakhel* activists, with as many as possible serving as inspirational rallying personalities for their communities. This applies not only to the past post-*shemittah* year of *Hakhel*, but also to all future years. Motivated by *Ahavat Yisrael*, it is our hope to witness the ultimate *Hakhel*—the gathering of the "scattered" and "dispersed," when "A great assemblage shall return here."[9]

May it also be the will of G-d that the above efforts hasten and accelerate the coming of *Mashiach*. At that time the mitzvah of *Hakhel* will be fulfilled in total conformity with the Biblical obligation: in the Holy Temple, with *Mashiach* reading for the entire Jewish people those Torah segments "which alert them to the performance of *mitzvot* and strengthen their hands in the true faith."

Then, as Maimonides declares, "The entire Jewish nation will be great Sages, knowledgeable in Torah mysteries and of their Creator ... as it is stated: 'For the earth will be filled with the knowledge of G-d as the waters cover the sea.'"[10]

(*Likkutei Sichot*, vol. 34, pp. 211-216)

---

9. Jeremiah 31:7.
10. Maimonides, Conclusion *Hilchot Melachim;* Isaiah 11:9.

SIMCHAT TORAH

THE *BAAL TESHUVAH* AND THE JOY OF SIMCHAT TORAH

There is a well-known question concerning why the celebration of the Torah occurs on Simchat Torah rather than on Shavuot. On Shavuot G-d gave us the Ten Commandments which, as our Sages tell us, quintessentially contained the Torah in its entirety. Thus, we could commemorate G-d's giving us the Torah in its entirety rather than the conclusion of the yearly cycle of reading the Torah. The answer involves the distinction between two modes of G-dly service, that of *tzaddikim*—the wholly righteous—and that of *baalei teshuvah*—penitents. The particular advantages of the service of *baalei teshuvah* are associated with Simchat Torah, which follows the penitence of the whole Jewish people on Yom Kippur, the time of the giving of the second tablets.

THE TORAH READING OF SIMCHAT TORAH

Maimonides states:[1] "Moses ordained that the appropriate Torah portion which describes the laws related to each holiday be read on that holiday." He cites the various holidays and the specific Torah section read. For the two concluding festival days of Sukkot he writes, "On the first day, Shemini Atzeret, *Kol habechor* is read and the following day, Simchat Torah, *Vezot haberachah*."

Machzor Vitri explains that "*Vezot haberachah*," the last section of the Pentateuch, is read on the last day of Sukkot in order to link the joy of concluding the Torah to the joy of Shemini Atzeret, since the term *simchah* (joy) is repeated by the

---

1. Maimonides, *Hilchot Tefilah* 13:8 and ff.

Torah when referring to Shemini Atzeret, and finishing the reading of the Torah further enhances the joy of the festival.[2]

However, the fact that Maimonides enumerates "*Vezot haberachah*" in the *festival* cycle, rather than in connection with the conclusion of the sequence of the *weekly* Torah reading, seems to indicate that "*Vezot haberachah*" is related in its very theme to the last day of Sukkot.

SIMCHAT TORAH AND SHAVUOT

In various Chasidic discourses[3] a question is raised about the reading of "*Vezot haberachah*" on Simchat Torah: since the Torah was given on Shavuot, why do we observe Simchat Torah—the joy of the Torah—on Shemini Atzeret? Shavuot would seem to be a far more appropriate occasion for expressing this joy. The answer given is that the joy of Simchat Torah expresses our happiness at receiving the Ten Commandments for the second time, an event which occurred on Yom Kippur. For this reason we rejoice at the end of Sukkot, "for it is the last day of holiday observance after Yom Kippur."

It is a self-evident truth that the inner teachings of the Torah, "the soul of the Torah,"[4] and the revealed teachings of the Torah, "the body of the Torah," are not, heaven forbid, two separate entities, but rather comprise one complete, perfect Torah. The very terms "soul" and "body" indicate to us their inseparable organic unity. From this it can be understood that every aspect of the "inner teachings" of Torah must correspond to and harmonize with the "outer *teachings*" of Torah. Why, therefore, is this question raised, being that the Code of Jewish law explicitly states the rationale: "For the reading of the Torah is then concluded and it is appropriate to rejoice on the occasion of its conclusion"?[5]

---

2. *Machzor Vitri*, sect. 385.

3. *Or HaTorah*, p. 1779 and ff. *Sefer Hama'amarim 5698*, p. 56 and ff.

4. *Zohar* III:152a.

5. *Tur, Orach Chaim*, ch. 669, and see *Rema*.

A simple explanation is that *Chasidut* focuses on the reason for the very arrangement of the original sequence of Torah readings. Why indeed did our Sages initially ordain that the annual public reading of the Torah begin on the Shabbat after Sukkot, extend through the year, and end in joyous festivity at the conclusion of Sukkot? It would seem far more appropriate that the cycle of reading begin and end on Shavuot, the holiday commemorating the date when the Torah was originally given. *Chasidut* resolves this problem by explaining that the second giving of the Tablets of Ten Commandments occurred on Yom Kippur, about which it is said, "'On the day of his wedding,' this is the giving of the Torah."[6] These second Tablets are described as "double strength"[7] in comparison to the first Tablets—hence it is their giving that specifically express the essence of joy.

THE QUESTION INTENSIFIES

Actually, the question posed in *Chasidut* applies even to our present custom of ending the Torah reading on Simchat Torah and not on Shavuot. Since Shavuot is the time of our receiving the Torah, it would seem appropriate to fix the day of joy at that time, in observance of "the conclusion of the Torah." This is underscored by Rashi's quotation[8] from the *Azharot* of Rav Sa'adia Gaon that the Ten Commandments contain all 613 *mitzvot* in capsule form. Thus, at the time of the giving of the Ten Commandments, there was also a completion of the Torah in a sense, since it was given completely. That day, therefore, should be observed as the time of the "conclusion of the Torah."

Actually, this form of encapsulated Torah is similar to the event from which we learn that one celebrates completing the Torah more than the completion of the reading cycle. The

---

6. Rashi, *Mishnah, Ta'anit* 26b (quoting Song of Songs 3:11).

7. *Shemot Rabbah* 46:1.

8. Exodus 24:12.

Midrash states,[9] "G-d said to Solomon: 'You have asked wisdom for yourself...By your very life, wisdom and intelligence are given to you...' Immediately, Solomon awakened and it was a dream. Rabbi Yitzchak declared, the dream was fulfilled. A donkey brayed, and he understood its braying; a bird twittered and he understood its twittering. Immediately, he came to Jerusalem and stood before the ark of G-d's covenant. And he brought sacrificial whole offerings and peace offerings and made a feast for all his servants. Rabbi Elazar states: 'From here we learn that a feast is made for concluding the Torah.'"

Only the Ten Commandments themselves were given in a revealed form. Nevertheless, the complete Torah was actually given to Israel at that time. This concept of potential knowledge, latent in Torah, that must be discovered, is reflected similarly in the word of our Sages: "Delve intensively in the study of Torah, for all is to be found therein."[10] At Shavuot all Torah knowledge existed potentially within Torah. The fact that Israel received the Torah in its entirety would be an adequate reason for making Shavuot a time for rejoicing, and for designating this day as a time of festivity marking the "conclusion" of the Torah.

It is well-known that every time a Jewish holiday is observed, the spiritual revelations of the past recur, and their spiritual effects extend and exert their influence, even in the present and in the realm of human existence.[11] Thus, it is apparent that on every Shavuot the Torah is received anew. This is reflected in the reading of the portion describing the giving of the Torah and the Ten Commandments—the conclusion of the giving of the Torah in commandment form. Again, this seems to be the occasion most appropriate for commemorating the "concluding of the Torah?"

---

9. *Shir Hashirim Rabbah* 1:1 (9). And see *Beit Yosef, Tur, Orach Chaim*, end ch. 669.

10. *Pirkei Avot* 5:21.

11. See *Sefer Leiv David* of the *Chidah*, ch. 29.

THE ADVANTAGE OF PERSONAL ACCOMPLISHMENT

The question can be answered in the following way:

The Ten Commandments were given to the Jewish people as a gift from Above.[12] This is in direct contrast to the situation on Shemini Atzeret, when the Torah is concluded, i.e., when Jewish people have studied Torah during the course of the entire year and have finally completed its study by their own intensive effort.

This is precisely why Shemini Atzeret rather than Shavuot marks the conclusion of Torah. True and utter joy at the receiving of something can only occur when it is not "shameful bread"—something unearned.[13] The joy of Shemini Atzeret expresses our gladness for our own actual study of Torah, mastered by virtue of our own effort and striving. This joy relates even to those who merely read the words of Torah without understanding its true meaning. They, too, participate in the festivities of Simchat Torah, for though they do not "understand," their spiritual service and faithful commitment to G-d are asserted by means of the written Torah which they have uttered with their lips and which is regarded as Torah study in the eyes of G-d.

The same is not true of Shavuot, even though it also entails the conclusion of the Torah (and though it might appear that the divine revelation from Above at the time of giving the Torah would be far superior in value to the human study of Torah). Nevertheless, since the Torah was given as a gift and bestowal from Above, without study or effort by Israel below, the joy is incomplete.

The Talmud states: "An individual prefers one measure of grain derived from his own effort rather than nine measures given to him gratuitously by a friend."[14] When someone receives something which he is utterly incapable of achieving

---

12. See *Shemot Rabbah* 41:6; Rashi, Exodus 31:18.

13. See Jerusalem Talmud, *Orlah* 1:3; *Likkutei Torah*, Leviticus 7d.

14. *Bava Metzia* 38a.

on his own, he will, of course, experience joy. However, it is not as complete as the joy in something obtained through his own efforts. Something a person can acquire on his own but which he receives as a gift, is "shameful bread." His joy is thus mingled with pain because he has not exerted the effort enabling him to take pride in his own accomplishments.

This concept is especially pertinent to the matter under discussion, for the Torah was given on Shavuot with G-d's intention that the Jews should subsequently learn and delve into the Torah. For this reason, the day of the "conclusion" of the Torah, Shavuot, is not observed with unusual festivity, for at that time it was a "gift from Above."

It is also self-evident that since Simchat Torah is related to every Jew, with men, women, and children participating in its joyful observance, the reason for Simchat Torah must also be understood by all—it must be comprehended even by the very young child.

A child asks the same question as well: Why wasn't Shavuot designated as the day of Simchat Torah? He is also aware that this is the "time of the giving of the Torah." The answer can be illustrated by two contrasting experiences of the child himself. Every Jewish child "receives" the Torah from earliest childhood, for "The Torah which Moses commanded us is a heritage of the congregation of Jacob,"[15] meaning that the Torah is the personal inheritance of every Jew, even the smallest child. Nevertheless, the child does not yet comprehend or grasp its contents. With the passage of time, however, growth and intellectual maturity will enable him to understand the Torah. These two contrasting factors—Torah which is a heritage of the child, and Torah which requires great personal effort for its understanding—awaken within the child two opposing emotions: joy for his present link with Torah, and pain because he does not yet understand it. Thus his joy in his Torah heritage is still imperfect.

---

15. Deuteronomy 33:5.

THE SECOND TABLETS

The above explanation accords with the concept cited in the various Chasidic discourses that Simchat Torah occurs at the time of Shemini Atzeret[16] because the second Tablets were given on Yom Kippur, and this event is commemorated on Shemini Atzeret, which occurs immediately afterwards. Thus, the concluding reading of the Torah is established on Shemini Atzeret, for at that time Man, by his own intense efforts, has concluded the study of the written Torah.

The general distinction between the first and second set of Ten Commandments[17] is that the first Tablets were "the word of G-d" and the "writing of G-d;"[18] the second Tablets, though also the "writing of G-d" were nevertheless hewn by Moses.[19] This is the reason for the difference in the effects they exerted within Israel and the world.

Our Sages tell us[20] that "If the first Tablets were not broken, then Torah would never have been forgotten by Israel...and no nation or tongue could prevail upon Israel." With the giving of the second Tablets, however, came a new dimension—the need to undergo intense effort in attempting to master Torah. In the giving of the first Tablets, Israel received the Torah as it is derived from Above, in the mystical manner of "Direct Light."[21] In this "revelation from Above," they

---

16. More specifically, the second day of Shemini Atzeret in the Diaspora.

17. See *Sefer Hama'amarim 5689*, p. 57 and ff.

18. Exodus 32:16.

19. Ibid. 34:1.

20. *Eiruvin* 54a.

21. DIRECT LIGHT–RETURNING LIGHT. There are two primary modes in which energy (for want of a better term) can reach its intended recipients: a) the energy is radiated "downward" from the source to the recipient. However, in order for the recipient to absorb it, the energy must be reduced to a level where it can be assimilated by the recipient on its level; b) the recipient rises up to the level of the source of energy in order to receive from it. Here the source remains unchanged. It does not reduce itself to accommodate the needs of the recipient; rather it remains as it is until the recipient has reached the level of the source. Only then does it transfer its energy to the recipient.

surpassed the later Tablets. However, with the receiving of the second Tablets, we were granted a dimension of great spiritual significance—the labor and endeavor in Torah based upon Man's own efforts in the category of "returning light." Only Man's striving in Torah, can evoke and reveal far more exalted levels of Torah than that manifested in the magnanimous giving of the first Tablets. We therefore rejoice on Simchat Torah, which is the culmination and conclusion of the giving of the *second* Tablets on Yom Kippur, and this day is the primary occasion for the "rejoicing in the Torah."

TZADDIKIM AND BAALEI TESHUVAH

In the Chasidic discourses referred to above,[22] another reason is cited for the designation of Simchat Torah to coincide with Shemini Atzeret.

The first Tablets correspond to the spiritual service of *tzaddikim*—spiritually righteous people devoid of evil. The Torah tells us, "And Israel camped there," at Sinai, as "one person"[23]—united in their will to receive the Torah. Israel's intense willingness to receive the Torah found eloquent expression in their declaration "to do" and fulfill the Torah's

---

An analogy: In order for a teacher to convey a complex idea to his students who are unable to comprehend the idea on their own, the teacher must reduce the idea to more basic components. Each concept is then introduced to the student in a progressive way—from the simplest to the moderately difficult, to the complex, so that he can eventually understand the entire concept as a whole. This is an analogy for *Or Yashar* (direct, diminishing light), which reduces itself in order to radiate downward to the level of the recipient while investing itself in the vessels (the understanding, in our analogy) of the recipient.

Or Chozer (returning light) represents the efforts of the recipient to rise up to the level of the source in order to receive from it *at the level of the source*. In order to do this, the recipient must progressively divest himself of his limitations (in technical terms—the vessels) that prevent him from comprehending the source as it is. Thus *or chozer* depends upon the yearning of the recipient to reach beyond itself—to comprehend the source of the energy. But this can only take place when the source retains its state of concealment from the recipient, so that it is forced to rise up beyond itself if it wishes to receive at all.

22. *Or HaTorah*, ibid. And see *Sefer Hama'amarim 5689*, p. 57 and ff, p. 70.
23. Exodus 19:2 and Rashi there.

commands before "we will hear,"[24] even before they were instructed about its contents and teachings. When they initially stood before Mount Sinai they were cleansed and purged from the *zuhamah*—the coarse substance which debased mankind as a result of Adam's first transgression[25]—and they were all *tzaddikim*. The second Tablets, however, correspond to the level of *baalei teshuvah* (penitents) experiencing profound remorse for the sin of the Golden Calf. The occasion of their rejoicing was therefore specified for the time related to Yom Kippur, the holiday which reflects their status of *baalei teshuvah*. Indeed, the greatest joy experienced by the soul striving to serve and be close to G-d, is after the return from its exile and remoteness caused by sin and disobedience.

This concept of the bond between Simchat Torah as the time of the conclusion of the Torah and as an occasion related to *baalei teshuvah* can be further underscored by clarifying a twofold distinction between *tzaddikim* and *baalei teshuvah*.[26] The distinction applies to (a) Man's spiritual service in relation to himself; and (b) to the effect of his service in relation to the world:

A) In relation to himself: a Jew, by his very nature, cannot be separated from G-dliness. In the case of the *tzaddik* who is not subject to the control and darkness of the evil inclination, his service to G-d is derived from his very nature. He is also strengthened by the heavenly oath which the soul takes before its descent to this world: "You shall be a *tzaddik*."[27]

This is not the case for a *baal teshuvah* who has sinned, caused a spiritual defect, and deviated from the proper faith. For just as the deviation resulted from his very own actions, similarly his later observance of Torah and *mitzvot* must be based primarily upon his own intense efforts. Thus, we can

---

24. Exodus 24:7; *Shabbat* 88a.
25. *Shabbat* 146a; *Zohar* I 52b.
26. See *Likkutei Sichot*, vol. 9, p. 63 and ff.; vol. 10, p. 84 and ff.
27. *Niddah* 30b. See *Kitzurim Veha'ha'arot Letanya*, p. 57 and ff.

understand the description of the *baal teshuvah* as serving G-d with the intense effort of "surpassing valor."[28]

B) The effect of their service upon the world is similar: The service of the *tzaddik* in relation to himself is to reveal the inherent talents and qualities bestowed upon him from Above and to bring them from the potential to the actual. Similarly, the *tzaddik* creates an abode for G-d in the world by refining mundane matter to reveal its inner sanctity. Thus, the *tzaddik*, by his actions, does not actually transform or bring about something *new*; he only actualizes and discloses that which has already existed in the potential. His actions, therefore, do not wholly negate the concept of "shameful bread" in his spiritual service, because his efforts are primarily based upon the G-dly bestowal of spiritual qualities from Above[29] and the spiritual strength gained from the heavenly oath, "You shall be a *tzaddik*" prior to birth, which endows him with added spiritual capabilities. Concerning his effect on the world, he is not truly creative in revealing the light of G-dliness, since this light is already inherent in worldly existence.

In contrast to this, the *baal teshuvah* refines and uplifts even previous acts of intentional evil[30] so that they are transformed into acts of merit and goodness. Thus, his actions influence even that realm that oppose G-dliness, changing it into a vessel permeated with G-dly light. This service is not like that of the *tzaddik* who actualizes what is already potential. Thus, the service of the *baal teshuvah* is devoid of the aspect of "shameful bread," for this spiritual service, as it applies to his own self as well as to making the world an "abode" for the Divine Presence, is rooted in his own endeavor with exceeding "valor," till he finally accomplishes the transformation of actual evil into virtue and sanctity.

---

28. *Zohar* I 129b.

29. See *Tanya*, ch. 14.

30. *Yoma* 86b. See *Derech Mitzvotecha* 191a.

These two explanations, the importance of Torah acquired by personal effort, and Yom Kippur and Simchat Torah as a time for *baalei teshuvah,* are thus one theme. The greatest significance is attached to Man's actions when they are performed with his own initiative and effort. This factor results in the perfect joy of the "completion of the Torah" on Simchat Torah, the last day of Sukkot.

THE CULMINATION OF THE HOLIDAYS OF *TISHREI*

On the basis of the above reasoning, we can understand the relationship between the reading of "*Vezot haberachah*" and Shemini Atzeret.[31]

The first Tablets are discussed at the beginning of "*Vezot haberachah*": "G-d came from Sinai..."[32] Concerning this the Torah states, "The Torah which Moses commanded us is a heritage of the congregation of Jacob." This "heritage" is similar to the word "inheritance"[33]—something received and inherited, usually resulting from events external to the individual and not through his own efforts. The Talmud ascribes great significance to any concluding occurrence, with the statement: "All things go according to the way they are concluded."[34] Thus, at the end of "*Vezot haberachah*," we find the phrase, "Before the eyes of all Israel."[35] This passage refers to the shattered Tablets, as Rashi explains, "For his heart moved him to break the Tablets before their eyes, and G-d agreed to this, as it is written, 'that you have broken,'"[36] which the Rabbis explain means that G-d approved Moses breaking of the Tablets.[37] This passage subtly conveys the advantage of the second Tablets over the first. For it was by virtue of Moses' *own initiative* in breaking the Tablets before the

---

31. See *Likkutei Sichot*, vol. 9, p. 42 and ff.

32. Deuteronomy 33:2.

33. See *Likkutei Torah*, Deuteronomy 94d.

34. *Berachot* 12a.

35. Deuteronomy 34:12.

36. Exodus 34:1.

37. Shabbat 87a.

eyes of all Israel that the effort to do *teshuvah* was evoked within the *entire Jewish nation*, even those who had not sinned by serving the Golden Calf.

When their repentance was completely accepted, G-d gave them the second Tablets, thus manifesting to all humanity that G-d accepted their repentance and was completely in accord with them "in joy and in fullness of heart."[38] The giving of the second Tablets implied, that G-dly service based upon one's own initiative must exist within the realm of Torah study.

In the sequence of the religious holidays of the month of *Tishrei*, we ultimately reach Shemini Atzeret, the time when all the G-dly revelations of the sacred days are assimilated within the Jewish soul.[39] This includes the dimension of Torah that was given in the second Tablets, and we experience the true and perfect joy of learning Torah with our own effort.

For this reason after we conclude the Torah with the words "before the eyes of all Israel" we immediately again begin to read, "In the beginning G-d created the Heaven and Earth."[40] By virtue of the Jew's study of Torah with his own capabilities (which corresponds to the service of the *baal teshuvah* rooted in his own effort and personal initiative) the Jew becomes a partner with G-d,[41] adding to and augmenting the work of creation.

An authentic partnership exists when the partners are completely equal to each other. Thus, in the case of the *tzaddik* whose task is primarily to actualize the potential (in terms of his own capabilities as well as for the transformation of the world into an abode for G-dliness), the "partnership" is unequal, for G-d is the one Who created "being" from "non-being." But when the Jew's G-dly service is based upon his own creative capabilities, as in the case of the *baal teshuvah*, who actually

---

38. Rashi, Exodus 33:11.

39. See *Likkutei Torah*, Deuteronomy 88d.

40. Genesis 1:1.

41. See *Shabbat* 10a, 119b.

creates in so great a measure that he transforms that which is "undesirable to Me,"—abhorrent to G-d, into that "which is desirable to Me,"[42]—favored by G-d—he thus becomes comparable, if this can be imagined, to his Creator, a true partner in the act of creation. He creates a "new" heaven and earth in which "G-d, L-rd of Israel is King and His Majesty prevails over all existence."[43]

The Jew serving in the manner of the *baal teshuvah* is aided in an ascendant manner toward ever greater spiritual progress in the fulfillment of his task and purpose within the world.

(Likkutei Sichot, vol. 14, pp. 156-163)

---

42. *Bereishit Rabbah* 3:7.
43. High Holiday liturgy.

SIMCHAT TORAH

TORAH AND THE CUSTOM OF *HAKAFOT*

Whereas we might expect that the celebration of the completion of the yearly Torah-reading cycle on Simchat Torah would involve actual Torah-study, the distinctive mode of celebration on the holiday is dancing around the *bimah* with the Torah scrolls. The sixth Lubavitcher Rebbe writes[1] "The Torah desires to circle the *bimah*...the Jew serves as its feet, carrying it around the *bimah* just as feet walk and bear a person to his desired destination." "Dancing" symbolically conveys total faithful submission to G-d just as feet are subordinate to the mind. However, Torah study is a definite component of Simchat Torah. Thus, the dancing of *hakafot* is preceded by the recitation of verses of Torah and linked to the reading of Torah.

THE TORAH WHICH MOSES COMMANDED US...

In accord with the teachings of our Sages,[2] the first text which a Jewish child learns, as soon as he is able to speak, is the verse[3]: *Torah tzivah lanu Moshe morashah kehilat Yaakov*—The Torah which Moses commanded us is a heritage of the congregation of Jacob.

The verse describes the Torah as having been transmitted to the Jewish people by Moses and received by him from G-d at Sinai. This means that the Torah in its entirety, even "that which a student will formulate in the future," was given to Moses at Sinai.[4] This even applies to the inner, concealed

---

1. *Sefer Hasichot 5704*, p. 36.
2. *Sukkah 42a*.
3. Deuteronomy 33:4.
4. *Megillah 19b; Jerusalem Talmud, Peah 2:4*.

teachings of the Torah, which *Mashiach* will reveal. It is only in the different stages of the *revelation* of the Torah that there are different categories: some Torah teachings have already been revealed, and there are Torah teachings which will be disclosed in the future. Of course, those matters still to be imparted are not to be perceived as, heaven forbid, a "New Torah," but rather as part of the sustained, constantly ongoing, unfolding revelation of the Torah which was given in its entirety to Moses at Sinai.[5]

Thus, the phrase, "The Torah which Moses commanded us" means Torah in its totality—all that has been comprehended in the past and which will be understood in the future—all of this was "commanded to us by Moses." Torah is infinite in its profundity, and a student must always feel humble, no matter how great his scholarship, for he has grasped but a small segment of the boundless expanse of Torah knowledge.

It is therefore strange that we impart, or at least mention, so deep a concept to a child who stands at the threshold of his studies. The normal educational method is to proceed from the simple to the more complex. Applying principles of educational psychology, it seems inappropriate to discuss with a small child the concept that the Torah in its vastness is utterly beyond the grasp of the human mind and that all that one could possibly ever learn is but a small segment of infinite Torah. Why, then, is such a difficult concept taught to a child as soon as he can speak?

The answer is that the essential concept of Torah which was "commanded to us by Moses" is related to the *Jewish soul* and was given to every single Jew. It is therefore relevant to all Jews, even to a small child.

The education principle of proceeding from the simple to the more difficult cannot pertain to Torah, which far surpasses the capacity of human intellect. Within the essence of Torah,

---

5. See also *Likkutei Sichot*, vol. 19, p. 252 and ff.

G-d has given of His own selfhood, and by studying Torah, a Jew establishes a bond with G-d Himself.[6]

G-d has transmitted this unique ability to *every* Jew in his study of Torah. Every Jew is equal in this respect; the same concept of being united with G-d as He is vested in Torah applies to both the individual of lesser intellect and to the scholar endowed with great understanding. It is only by divine compassion that "He has chosen us from all the nations"[7] and given us *His* Torah. He, G-d, Who is all-powerful, has given us *His* Torah, the very same lofty Torah which preoccupies and concerns the Almighty Himself. And because G-d has given of Himself in the Torah, He has divinely endowed Torah with the unique spiritual quality of enabling both the mature scholar and the small child to be united with G-dliness. Whether in the profound Torah thoughts of the great Talmudic student or in the breath of the small child uttering words of Torah—there is a bond with absolute G-dliness.

Thus, the conclusion of the verse "a heritage of the congregation of Jacob" refers to something inherited[8] and not subject to the status and condition of the inheritor. "Even a small child, one day old can inherit,"[9] as long as he is the son of the individual leaving the estate.

Similarly, since Jews are G-d's children, our Torah heritage links us to G-d Himself. This "heritage" belongs to all Jews, even those described by the term "the congregation of *Jacob*," which is applied to individuals of relatively lower spiritual status.[6] They, too, by means of Torah, are joined with the essence of G-d.

THE DIVINE ELEMENT

Granted that we know that G-dliness is inherent to Torah, even in the text studied by a child, but why is it necessary to

---

6. See *Zohar* II 140b; *Tanya*, ch. 47.

7. Text of the blessing made before the Torah reading.

8. *Likkutei Torah: Vezot Haberachah* 94b.

9. *Mishnayot Niddah* 4:3.

share this particular knowledge with him? What difference would it make if he gained this awareness later, when he matured intellectually and could thoroughly grasp the concept? Until that time the child could concern himself with matters more easily understood?

The answer to this question is that every Jew must faithfully believe that the essence and truth of Torah are ultimately not subject to intellectual comprehension. The essence of Torah is comprised of the fact that "G-d and His wisdom are one."[10] Without this conviction, the entire foundation of Torah study is missing.

Furthermore, the awareness that G-d and Torah are one is not only a *detail* related to the study and comprehension of Torah; it is the essential point of the entire Torah commanded to us by Moses. It is the necessary foundation on which we can only later build the edifice—the study of Torah.

If we delay teaching a child this basic principle until he matures, then all the Torah he learns until that time will lack this basic element of faith. It will be difficult to instill this attitude later, since his initial study of Torah was based solely on reason and understanding. It is well known that reliance on logic and reason hinders the ability to apprehend absolute G-dliness, which is beyond the limited grasp of human intellect. Is is for this reason that we must imbue the student with this attitude when he is in his early childhood, and as a result, "Even when he ages, he will not turn from it."[11] True, study of Torah later on will be based on understanding, but it will be permeated with awe and fear of G-d and with submission to the heavenly yoke.

---

10. See Maimonides, *Hilchot Yesodei HaTorah* 2:10. Also see *Tanya,* ch. 2 and section 2, ch. 3.
11. Proverbs 22:6.

THE TORAH WRAPPED IN ITS MANTLE

It is a Jewish custom on the holiday of Simchat Torah—and "A Jewish custom is itself Torah"[12]—to take the Torah covered with its mantle, and to dance the *hakafot* around the table upon which the Torah is read.[13] Torah requires study and understanding. It would therefore seem more appropriate to express our joy with the Torah by concentrating that day on an intensified study of Torah. The intense effort of great and deeper study would bring the understanding that should awaken joy within us. Why, then, do we express our joy by dancing with out *feet* and with the Torah covered by its mantle, in a way that makes it impossible to even gaze upon the scroll for the purpose of Torah study?

It is true that one must have fixed times set aside for study on Simchat Torah, but this is part of our constant obligation to study Torah, not a special obligation through which to express the joyousness of the day. This is not the unique joy of Simchat Torah.

The true significance of Torah is its sanctity, not the intellect and understanding. That is why even unlearned persons may recite the blessing over the Torah;[14] all Jews have a relationship to Torah. Since, however, Torah must completely permeate an individual, and not remain external to him, it is therefore necessary to study and understand Torah, as well. The inherent unity that exists between the spirituality of Torah and the elemental aspect of the Jewish soul is evoked by comprehension, although this unity is actually beyond intellectual understanding.

This is the reason why the dancing on Simchat Torah is with the Torah concealed in its mantle, inaccessible to our eyes, i.e. beyond our understanding. Our rejoicing is not based on our understanding of Torah, but rather on the fact that through

---

12. See Jerusalem Talmud, *Pesachim* 4:1.

13. See *Sefer Hama'amarim* 5689, p. 57.

14. *Hilchot Talmud Torah* of the Alter Rebbe, 2:12.

Torah study, we relate to G-d as He exists in exalted sanctity, far beyond the grasp of human reason.

Our joy is therefore expressed in the dancing of our feet, because feet represent the quality of submission, total faith,[15] a wholly committed response to the will of a guiding intellect.

This rejoicing with the Torah concealed in its mantle takes place at the Torah portion of *Bereishit*, at the beginning of the year, after the period of repentance during *Elul*, and after Rosh Hashanah, the Ten Days of Penitence, Sukkot, and Shemini Atzeret. At the start of the New Year and its spiritual service, all Jews are like the small child whose education is commencing, and they, too, must begin with the awareness of "The Torah which Moses commanded us"—with submission to the heavenly yoke. This foundation, at the beginning of the year, guarantees that the Torah study—characterized by logic and understanding—during the course of the following year will be suffused with faith and wholehearted devotion to the fulfillment of G-d's Will.

THE "FEET" OF THE TORAH

This will explain the statement of the sixth Lubavitcher Rebbe, Rabbi Yosef Yitzchak Schneersohn, that on Simchat Torah, "The Torah desires to circle the *bimah* (the table on which the Torah is read), and since the Torah does not possess feet, the Jew serves as its feet, carrying it around the *bimah*, just as feet walk and bear the head of a person to his desired destination."[16]

What is the meaning of this strange phrase—that a Jew acquires the identity of feet in relation to the *Sefer Torah*? It implies that when a Jew dances on Simchat Torah, he submits himself totally to the Will of G-d, to the extent that he does not perceive himself as an independent being. He is like feet to the head, subordinate and instantly responsive to the mind's

---

15. See *Likkutei Torah*, Deuteronomy 63, 4.

16. *Sefer Hasichot*, ibid.

desire.[17] If feet were able to reflect whether they wish to comply with the mind's directives, if they had any kind of self-awareness, then this would be a sign of illness and malfunction.

"A Jew is like the feet of a *Sefer Torah*"—he accepts and firmly resolves that in the coming year he will completely subordinate himself to the dictates of Torah, fulfilling them instinctively so that they are inherent and natural to his personal conduct. And just as feet, by bringing the body and the head to a location they can not reach on their own,[18] bring fulfillment to the head, so do Jews, by accepting the yoke of Torah with joy, bring spiritual exaltation to the Torah.

This is the meaning of the plural expression, "The time of *our* joy": Jews rejoice with the Torah, and the Torah rejoices with the Jewish people, their rejoicing with the Torah causing an ascent in Torah.

THE INTELLECTUAL CONNECTION

Though the joy of Simchat Torah is primarily expressed by the dancing of feet, we must bear in mind that the dancers circle the *bimah* where the Torah is read. We thus link the joy of Torah with the reading and study of Torah. In addition, before the *hakafot*, we read "*Atah hareitah*"—a compilation of verses from the Torah. On the basis of our discussion, how can we reconcile the dancing feet, which express faith and submission, with circling the *bimah*, which symbolizes study and intellectual mastery?

Since *Tishrei* is the first month of the year, it possesses, in condensed form, all those spiritual qualities which inhere in the later fulfillment of our religious obligations—the study of Torah and the performance of *mitzvot* during the course of the entire year that follows.[19] Thus, *Tishrei* is unique in its twofold nature, having qualities specific to itself as well as being an

---

17. *Tanya,* ch. 23.

18. *Likkutei Torah,* Deuteronomy 44a.

19. See *M'amarei Admor Hazakein 5566,* p. 379; 5569, p. 238; etc.

inclusive, general source for all of our religious conduct during the coming year.

Tishrei thus includes not only the *foundation* for Torah study—faithful submission to G-d's Will as expressed by dancing feet, which relates to the specific nature of *Tishrei*—it also contains the *structure* which rests on the foundation, i.e. the study of Torah, derived from the general nature of *Tishrei,* which encompasses spirituality for an entire year. Since it is the very beginning of the year, we *concentrate* on the foundation—faithful commitment, expressed by dancing feet. The later study of Torah is, however, symbolized by the circling around the *bimah.*

Another more profound relationship exists between faithful submission and the actual study of Torah. In addition to sincere, supra-rational faith, a Jew must also have the kind of faith and submission to G-d's will which results from his understanding of G-dliness. Chabad *Chasidut* distinguishes between those aspects of Man's soul external to him and those inherent in him. Simple faith and submission to the heavenly yoke are praiseworthy attributes, but they are external to his intellect and other spiritual faculties. Consequently, those faculties are not permeated with G-dliness. It is only when his knowledge is also wholly pervaded with intellectual awareness of G-dliness that he is truly and completely unified with G-d. This consciousness encompasses not only Man, but also his entire physical environment. G-dliness and spirituality are thus apprehended even in mundane matters. Man perceives the entire world as permeated with inner G-dly radiance.

Thus the dancing of the *hakafot* is preceded by the saying of verses of Torah and linked to the reading of Torah. The study and understanding of Torah, wholly encompassing the total identity of a Jew, makes the dancing of *hakafot* completely appropriate.

This concept, that the point of faith beyond knowledge must be joined with intellectual understanding of Torah, is subtly alluded to in the verse recited before *hakafot*. We declare:

"It has been revealed to you [Israel] to know that G-d is the L-rd."[20] G-d has disclosed Himself so that each Jew may perceive G-dliness with experiential vision, a quality beyond intellect. Every Jew perceives that "G-d is the L-rd," "Nothing exists besides G-dliness." G-d revealed Himself to the Jewish people of His own will; no effort was required on their part. Sinaitic revelation resulted from the primary bond of Jewish souls with absolute G-dliness.

"It has been revealed to you" is immediately followed by, "to know," implying that there must be an extension from "vision" to "knowledge," that the mind may grasp by means of knowledge, understanding and comprehension. If Man does not strive to "know," then his perception of the revelation at Sinai is imperfect and unfulfilled! There is a defect in his unity with G-d. When Man is truly united with G-dliness, this awareness pervades and encompasses all his attributes, ultimately affecting his total environment.

At the time of *hakafot*, we also recite, "For Torah shall go forth from Zion, and the word of G-d from Jerusalem."[21] Zion—Jerusalem—is an actual city. How, one may ask, can the spiritual Torah and the "word of G-d" emerge from a specific physical place? But precisely herein is the unique transformative quality of Torah: it can extend from the awesome "vision" of Sinai—the perception of absolute G-dliness—to affecting all of Man's spiritual qualities through total involvement in the study of Torah, and finally exerting its influence on Man's physical environment. Man, through Torah, acquires knowledge of reality. The physical world becomes a *tzion* (a sign)[22] that the significance of the material world is not as an entity unto itself. Its true significance is in serving as a "sign" and "guidepost" directing Man to G-dliness. As a result of his Torah study, Man is infused with the knowledge that G-d

---

20. Deuteronomy 4:35.

21. Isaiah 2:3.

22. See *Torah Or, Mikeitz* 37b, 38a.

constantly sustains the world, and attains awareness that "Nothing exists aside from G-dliness." The material world is then transformed into *Yerushalayim* (Jerusalem), the name composed of the two Hebrew words, *yerei shaleim*—"perfect awe."[23] A Jew perceives that the entire universe is pervaded with "perfect awe" and submission to G-d's will. It is by means of Torah study, that Man gains the all-inclusive awareness of G-d's omnipresence; he perceives that even within the physical world "Nothing exists aside from G-dliness."

(*Likkutei Sichot*, vol. 4, pp. 1165-1171)

---

23. See *Bereishit Rabbah* 56:10; *Likkutei Torah*, Leviticus 4a.

Simchat Torah

Joy and the Inner Oneness of the Soul

The night of Shemini Atzeret 5738—1977, the Chasidic and Jewish world was traumatized to learn of the Rebbe's serious heart illness. Despite the severity of his condition and with selfless courage, he instructed that the observance and dancing of Simchat Torah should not be disrupted. Immediately on the night after Simchat Torah the Rebbe delivered the following *ma'amar* (discourse) in his room. The discourse discusses Simchat Torah as the culmination of the theme of oneness exemplified by the sequence of holidays of the month of *Tishrei*, enabling a Jewish person to extend the spirituality of the holidays, culminating in the joy of Simchat Torah, to the rest of the year.

THE CONCEPT OF SIMCHAT TORAH

The concept of Simchat Torah requires some explanation. There is a well-known Chasidic explanation regarding the joyous observance of the holiday, in which Jews dance with a Torah scroll as it is covered in its mantle. Though the Torah states that "this is your wisdom and understanding," etc.,[1] the rejoicing is not by study or textual analysis, but specifically through dancing. It is for this reason that the joyousness of this day is relevant to all Jews, even those who are extremely simple, uninvolved in the intellectual pursuit of Torah. Moreover, at the time of rejoicing and the circular *hakafot* processions, people are frequently drawn into the dance, although their connection and bond to the Torah are not discernible during the rest of the year. Dancing specifically with the Torah scroll, the written Torah, manifests the relevance of Simchat Torah to all Jews.

---

1. Deuteronomy 4:6.

For even an unlearned Jew, having no understanding of the Torah text, is required to recite the Torah blessing when he reads from the *written* Torah scroll. Indeed, the very fact that this individual recites a blessing on the Torah in conformity with the command of the "Torah of truth" indicates that what he is doing has genuine significance. Though he does not comprehend what he is saying, he nevertheless "draws down" G-d's infinite light, and even a revelation from the loftier level of G-d Himself (the giver of the Torah) in the very Torah that he is learning. The Chasidic explanation of the rationale for the fixing of Simchat Torah on Shemini Atzeret (in the land of Israel) and the second day of Shemini Atzeret (outside the land of Israel) is well known. For superficially, Simchat Torah, the day of rejoicing with the Torah, actually should have been on Shavuot, the time of the giving of the Torah.

A PARABLE

The explanation is given[2] based upon the *Midrash*:

It would have been fitting for the concluding day of assembly (Shemini Atzeret) to take place fifty days after the first day of Sukkot, corresponding to the interval between Pesach and Shavuot. However, since this is a time of transition from summer to winter, the time is not suitable for going and returning. This can allegorically be compared to a king who had many married daughters, some living nearby and some at a distance. One day they all came to visit their father the king. He said, "Those living nearby are able to arrive and return, whereas those coming from afar do not have adequate time to come and return. Therefore while you are all still here, let us make one festival day and rejoice with all the daughters."

Similarly, Shavuot, the *Atzeret* of Pesach (the culminating assembly day of Pesach), occurs at the transition time of the

---

2.   See "On the Day of Shemini Atzeret" 5689 and 5706.

winter to summer. G-d therefore says, "The Jewish people are able to arrive and return." However, concerning the concluding Shemini Atzeret of Sukkot, when summer passes into winter, G-d says: "There is not enough time to come and return. Since the Jewish people are all here, let us make one festival day and rejoice." For this reason Shemini Atzeret is designated as the day of Simchat Torah—rejoicing with the Torah. For on the "one day" (Yom Kippur) on which all the daughters come (the Daughters of Zion—these being Jewish souls[3]) to inquire as to the welfare of the King their father, the father later states, "Let us make one festive day and rejoice." This is the day of Simchat Torah, designated on Shemini Atzeret, "one festive day" corresponding to the other "one day" of Yom Kippur.

A PERVASIVE ONENESS

The above is to be understood in the context of a Chasidic discourse[4] which explains that all of the holidays of the month of *Tishrei* are in the category of "one." Regarding Rosh Hashanah, our Sages state that the "commandment of the day is the *shofar*"[5] This means that the uniqueness of the day lies in one single command—the mitzvah of *shofar*. Maimonides states that this commandment is a faith law beyond our understanding, for though the command hints to lofty matters related to *teshuvah* (repentance), as Maimonides goes on to note[6], the essence of *shofar* is a divine command beyond our understanding. Yom Kippur, the Day of Atonement, the concluding day of the Ten Days of Repentance, also has a unique oneness, and the three dimensions frequently discussed in Chasidic philosophy: time, place, and soul—temporal, spatial, and spiritual—are united within it. Since the priestly incense service is performed in a single unique locale, the Holy of Holies, it exhibits a oneness of "place." It occurs on the day

---

3. See *Likkutei Torah*, *Shir Hashirm* 6c; 22b.
4. *BaSukkot Teishvu 5738*.
5. *Mishnah, Rosh Hashanah 26b*.
6. See Laws of Repentance 3:4.

of Yom Kippur, described in the Torah as "once in the year,"[7] relevant to "time." Moreover, the service is fulfilled by the high priest, acting as the representative of the collective Jewish people, as the verse states, "and Aharon was separated to sanctify him as the Holy of Holies."[8] Thus, Yom Kippur also exhibits the unique oneness of "soul."

Similarly, in the mitzvah of *Sukkah* (which spans the entire seven days of Sukkot from the very first moment at the beginning of the holiday) the concept of the unity, the *oneness*, of the entire Jewish people is emphasized. As our Sages tell us, "the entire Jewish people are worthy of sitting in one *Sukkah*."[9]

A further parallel exists in the commandment of taking the "four kinds," which has as its purpose the eliciting and drawing down of the encompassing spiritual quality[10] (exemplified by "one *Sukkah*") and causing this quality to be internalized inwardly.[11] Each one of the four kinds possesses a unique quality of oneness, most particularly the *etrog*, (the citron fruit,) in which this quality is surpassingly expressed. Thus, in the sequence of the four kinds in the Torah—sequence in Torah also being part of Torah and conveying significant concepts— the Torah commences with enumerating the *etrog*, "the beautiful fruit of the tree." The word used to describe this fruit is *hadar*, usually translated as "beautiful." However, our Sages explain this as conveying that *dar*—it dwells or abides in the tree from year to year, thus enduring the four changes of weather during the course of the entire year—and not merely enduring, but thriving and developing from them. The oneness of the *etrog* affects the other three kinds as well. Thus, the concept of *hadar*—beauty—is *halachically* derived from *etrog* and applied to the other three kinds.[12] In addition to the fact that every one of

7. Leviticus 16:34.

8. Chronicles 23:13.

9. *Sukkah* 27b.

10. "*Makif*" in the original. See *Tanya*, Bilingual Edition, Glossary (Kehot 1981).

11. See *Siddur*, p. 265 and *Sefer Hama'amarim 5666*, p. 329.

12. See *Sukkah* 3a, and *Shulchan Aruch Harav* 645:2.

the four kinds conveys the quality of "oneness," the very mitzvah of holding the four kinds is to unite them all. Consequently, taking the four species, which have a spiritual quality which is linked to the four categories[13] of Jews, causes the actual unity of the Jewish people, "And they shall all be made into one collective entity to serve you wholeheartedly."[14]

THE POWER OF REPENTANCE

In order to create true and enduring unity among the four categories of the Jewish people mentioned above, it must be prefaced by *teshuvah*—repentance. Repentance transcends division and fragmentation; therefore, it can actually occur in one short interval of time, or even in one brief moment.[15] This is the distinction between the two sets of Tablets of the Law: The first represents Torah in itself, while the second Tablets represent Torah attained through *teshuvah*. In preparation for receiving the first Tablets, Moses was on the mountain forty days in addition to fulfilling G-d's prior command to count *Sefirah*, "seven weeks shall you count for yourself." This was not the case regarding the second Tablets, for in the concluding forty days that Moses was on the mountain, he was mainly concerned that G-d should re-accept the Jewish people wholeheartedly and with joy. And subsequently the second tablets were given in a short interval of time. The potentially instantaneous nature of *teshuvah* underscores the concept that repentance transcends the finite. This is because true *teshuvah* extends to the inner aspect and to the very essence of the soul, a realm beyond division, representing the category of oneness of the soul (paralleling the fact that *teshuvah* can occur in *one* brief period of time or in *one* instant). Thus, *teshuvah* accomplishes the oneness of all categories of Jews from "the heads of your tribes...to your wood choppers and water drawers.[16] Moreover,

---

13. *Vayikra Rabbah* 30:12.
14. Liturgy, *Rosh HaShana Amidah.*
15. *Zohar Chadash* 129a.
16. Deuteronomy 29:10.

this is in a manner of *nitzavim* (standing firm and steadfast) as in the expression "*nitzav melech*,"[17] meaning that the king is established with unwavering authority. Thus, the Jewish people become kings and masters of all existence in the world. This commences from their being inscribed and sealed for a good and sweet year with manifest and revealed goodness, below the "ten handbreadths" of mystical worlds, here in this physical world, i.e. also as regard to material matters. For in this mode of unity there can be no differentiation between the spiritual and the realms above and below, and this encompasses the entire descending chain of cosmological, spiritual, and physical creation as well as that which is above and beyond this chain.

This is the meaning of "*one* day they all came to inquire as to the welfare of their father the king...Let us all make *one* day of festivity and rejoice together." The "one day" (of their coming to inquire as to the welfare of the king) is Yom Kippur. This leads to, "let us all make one day of festivity together" — Simchat Torah—"one day" in the category of singular oneness.

"ALL OF YOU AS ONE"

The soul's "oneness," although sublime and transcending, infuses the multiple levels and diverse powers of the soul. (This is exemplified by the fact that that this awakening is related to physical action as, for example, sitting in the *Sukkah*, taking of the Four Kinds, dancing with physical legs.) This occurs after the Torah reading of *Atem nitzavim*—"You all stand firm and steadfast," etc., "all of you," etc., for the entire Jewish people are included in the unity of *kulchem* (all of you) as a result of the oneness within them. The Torah then enumerates the ten specific categories from the "head of your tribes" until the "wood choppers and those drawing water." The "oneness" quality of *kulchem*, of the entire Jewish people, must be discernible as they are in their diverse levels of identity. This "oneness" in terms of "soul" must also occur in "time." Thus, the quality of "one day" of Yom Kippur and Simchat Torah

---

17. I Kings 22:48 .

should affect and influence all the days of the year—commencing from the day immediately after the holiday that in all the details of one's actions ("in all your ways and in all your deeds") it is apparent that the Jew has just come from the "one day" of Yom Kippur and Simchat Torah. This state is subsequently sustained during the entire year. Though many days, weeks, and months have passed, nevertheless the manifestation of "one day" is not weakened. It endures in its full power, because it is derived from the realm that is above divisions and variations, from the lofty realm of "I, G-d, have not changed."[18] It is through the extending of the "one day," which is above division, into all the days of the year, which are characterized by division and variation, that an elevation occurs in the "one day" itself. This process parallels the concept described above that an *etrog* not only withstands the weather changes of the whole year, but thrives because of them.

May it be G-d's will that all of the aforementioned should be fulfilled in every Jew, that it should be a good and blessed year in manifest and revealed goodness "below ten handbreadths"—here in this physical world. May they all be blessed with children, life, and economic sustenance and all of them in an abundant manner. This applies to literal children, life, and sustenance as well as to spiritual children, life, and sustenance, the spiritual being the source of the physical. As we leave the festive days of joy and enter the material workweek in a mundane world, we embark on the spiritual service of "and Jacob proceeded to his way." Jacob's proceeding to his way after Yom Kippur is "his way" in terms of G-d's commandments, for on the four days between Yom Kippur and Sukkot the entire Jewish people are preoccupied with G-d's commandments.[19] In contrast, Jacob's "proceeding on his way" *after* Simchat Torah refers also to permissible, worldly matters. On every day, whether on weekdays and even more so on the Shabbat and

---

18. Malachi 3:6.
19. *Vayikra Rabbah* 30:7.

holidays (including Rosh Hashanah and Yom Kippur) his mundane matters are permeated with the innermost point of the essence of the soul, which is bonded with the inner dimension and essence of G-d.

JOY SHATTERS ALL BARRIERS

And since this occurs subsequent to the joy of Simchat Torah—for joy shatters all barriers, beyond limitation—it shatters and nullifies the barriers and limitations of inner exile and those of literal exile. And we will merit that in the actual near future there shall be fulfilled, "And our eyes shall see Your return to Zion in mercy" with the true and complete redemption through our Righteous *Mashiach*, may he come and redeem us in the literal near future. May he come and lead us upright to our land speedily and in our very days. And the Holy Temple shall be rebuilt in its place, and He shall gather in the dispersed of Israel, etc. "Then I [G-d] will transform (the nations) to speak out in pure language and to serve Him [G-d] with united oneness,"[20] "and kingship shall be G-d's."[21]

(*Sefer Hama'amarim Melukat*, vol. 1, pp. 259-263)

---

20. Zephaniah 3:9.
21. Obadiah 1:21.

SIMCHAT TORAH

THE CONCLUSION
OF THE TORAH

In the following *sicha* the Rebbe explores the relationship between the Torah reading of Simchat Torah and the Holiday itself. Since the last words of the Torah reading refer to the seemingly negative event of the breaking of the Tablets, a question arises concerning why the reading of *Vezot haberachah* was chosen for the culminating holiday of the month of *Tishrei*. The answer lies, as we have also seen in some of the previous *sichot*, in the advantage of the service of repentance.

THE RATIONALE FOR THE TORAH READING
OF SIMCHAT TORAH

Maimonides, based on Talmud sources, states that the Torah reading of every holiday is thematically linked to that holiday, for this was the procedure enacted by Moses. Maimonides then enumerates the Torah reading for the various holidays. Discussing Sukkot he declares, "And on the concluding days *Kol habechor* is read, and the next day *Vezot haberachah*.[1] Thus, it appears that there is a thematic link between the reading of *Vezot haberachah*, the conclusion of the Torah, and the second day of Shemini Atzeret (our Simchat Torah).

Various reasons are given by the commentators: "To connect the end of all holidays with the blessing given by Moses to the Jewish people";[2] or "to join the rejoicing of concluding the Torah with the joy of the holiday"; or "to link

---

1. Maimonides: *Hilchot Tefilah* 13:8 etc. See *Megilah* 31b.
2. See Ran on *Megilah* 31b.

the blessing of King Solomon (the *Haftorah* of Shemini Atzeret) to the blessing of Moses"[3] What, then, is the connection between the Torah reading of *Vezot haberachah* and the holiday of Shemini Atzeret?

THE SINGULAR NATION

The Talmud states that the sum total of seventy bullocks sacrificed during *Sukkot* correspond to the seventy nations of the world.[4] The single bullock brought on Shemini Atzeret is, however, equivalent to the Jewish people, the singular nation. Thus Shemini Atzeret expresses the uniqueness of the Jewish People, how they are *apart* from all other nations.

Superficially, one could attempt to explain the link between the Torah reading of *Vezot haberachah* and the holiday of Shemini Atzeret on the basis of a Midrashic commentary. The *Midrash*, commenting on the beginning verses of *Vezot haberachah* "G-d came from Sinai, etc.," states[5] that G-d offered the Torah initially to the nations of Esau, Ishmael, and indeed to all the nations of the world. They declined to accept the Torah because in each instance the Torah's high moral standards would have prohibited them from the improper behavior that they felt inhered to their national identity.[6] Only the Jewish people, the "singular nation," (as expressed by Shemini Atzeret), were willing to accept the Torah.

This rationale is problematic, however, for the Torah reading of the distinction created between the Jewish people and the nations of the world at the time of the Giving of the Torah would seem more appropriate for the holiday of Shavuot than Shemini Atzeret. Thus the statement that "G-d came from

---

3. See *Machzor Vitri*, section 385.

4. *Sukkah* 55b.

5. *Sifri*, Deuteronomy 23:2.

6. One objected to "Do not steal," another to "Do not commit adultery," etc. *Sifri* and Rashi on Deuteronomy 33:2; *Zohar* III 192b.

Sinai"[7] would seem related to Shavuot rather than to the time of Shemini Atzeret.

A NEGATIVE CONCLUSION?

This problem should be viewed within the context of the conclusion of the Torah, the end of *Vezot Haberachah*. There the Torah relates a number of significant qualities and praises of Moses. It then concludes with the words "which Moses did before the eyes of all Israel."[8] The *Midrash* explains this as referring to Moses' breaking of the Tablets with the Ten Commandments.[9]

This confronts us with a challenging question. The breaking of the Tablets was a tragic occurrence, to the extent that the death of *tzaddikim* is compared to it. Why, therefore, is this occurrence enumerated among the praises and positive qualities of Moses?[10] Indeed, Rashi adds in his comment of this passage the Midrashic statement that G-d praised Moses, saying "*Yasher koach*"[11] to him for breaking the *luchot*. This requires clarification.

The Talmud relates Moses' reasoning in the breaking of the *luchot*: If, concerning the Pesach sacrifice, which is only one of the 613 *mitzvot*, the Torah states that no non-Jew shall eat of it, the Torah in its entirety is here and the Jewish people are rebellious, how much more so [that they should not receive it].[12] It is understandable that Moses is praised for his defense of the Torah's honor in desisting from giving it to those who were "rebellious." However, as regards the Jewish people, his shattering of the tablets was a negation of their spiritual level.

We are confronted with a profound problem. *Vezot haberachah* commences with the uniqueness and merit of the

---

7. Deuteronomy 33:2.
8. Deuteronomy 34:12.
9. *Sifri* and Rashi, ibid.
10. See Rashi on Deuteronomy 10:6.
11. "*Yeyasher kochacha*" in the original.
12. *Shabbat* 87a.

Jewish people in their singular acceptance of the Torah in contrast with the nations of the world who declined to receive the Torah. This is by way of preface and rationale for the essential content of this Torah reading, the blessing with which "Moses blessed the Jewish people." Why, then, should this Torah portion conclude with a seemingly negative statement about the Jewish people, and specifically the shattering of the Tablets which was a result of their rebelliousness and thus seemingly unworthy of receiving the Torah? Moreover, why is this event, which occurred before the eyes of all Israel, cited at the very conclusion of the entire written Torah? The focus of the Torah is the Jewish people (thus the recurrent command, "Speak to the Jewish people," conveying that they preceded the Torah).[13] Why, then, does the Torah conclude with the very reverse of praise for the Jewish people, the distressing event of the shattering of the Tablets? We are therefore compelled to presume that the praise for Moses in the shattering of the Tablets also entailed praise in some sense for the entire Jewish people.

YASHER KOACH FOR BREAKING THE TABLETS

This can be understood in the context of G-d's praising Moses, "*Yasher koach*" for the shattering of the Tablets which took place forty days after that event, rather than at the time it occurred or on the very next day when he ascended Mt. Sinai again. Forty days later when G-d told Moses "Carve for yourself" the second tablets, only then did G-d declare this laudatory statement. Even more perplexing is the fact that Rashi does not cite this *Midrash* on the phrase "that you broke."[14] It is only at the conclusion of *Vezot haberachah*, occurring forty years later, that Rashi mentions this statement. A simple rationale for Rashi's comment at that point is because it is related to the concluding words of the Torah, "before the eyes of the entire

---

13. See *Bereishit Rabbah* 1:4; *Tanna D'vei Eliyahu,* ch. 14.
14. Exodus 34:1.

Israel." However, since all matters in the Torah are stated with rigorous precision, it is apparent that G-d's praise to Moses—said at the time when He instructed him to carve the second tablets—was *revealed* only at the end of Moses' life when, "Moses ascended Mt. Nebo."

THE POSSIBILITY OF REPENTANCE

The Talmud states regarding the event of the Golden Calf, "There was no purpose for the creation of the golden calf other than to create vindication for *Baalei teshuvah*"—the possibility of repentance.[15] G-d enabled the evil inclination to prevail against the Jewish people and to persuade them to make the golden calf so that they would later be able to achieve a higher spiritual level through *teshuvah*. Moreover, through repentance they would reach a lofty gradation surpassing their status before the sin.

This is true also concerning the shattering of the Tablets due to the sin of the Golden Calf. The actual divine intent was that the Jewish people should reach a new singular level of Torah knowledge with the second Tablets being "twofold in their spiritual power"[16] in relation to the first ones.

Similarly, Moses' motive in perceiving the Jewish people as rebellious and unworthy of receiving the Torah was not solely to protect the Torah's honor, but also to influence the Jewish people to return in repentance to G-d.

This is expressed in the Chasidic allegory of the prince who acts improperly. His provoked father banishes him from the palace and renounces his parenthood.[17] Specifically through this is the son's love for his father awakened to the degree of causing him to cry out with an embittered soul that he does not want to be separated from his father, under any circumstance, and most assuredly not that his father should renounce the name "father." Thus, the precise nuance of "And I broke (the

---

15. *Avodah Zarah* 4b.

15.   *Shemot Rabbah* ch. 46.

17. See *Or HaTorah, Va'era*, p. 123.

Tablets) *before their eyes*"—and as emphasized in the concluding words of the Torah, *before the eyes* of Israel, explained by Rashi as referring to the breaking of the Tablets. This was the unique distinction and praise of Moses that he shattered the tablets *"before their eyes"* and awakened their hearts to return in repentance.

THE TRANSFORMATION OF A FAST DAY

This will help explain how the seventeenth day of *Tammuz*, the day on which the Tablets were broken, will be transformed into a day of "rejoicing and happiness."[18] During the exile phase of Jewish history, when we perceive the vulnerability of the Jewish people with "alien nations prevailing against them," the day of the breaking of the Tablets is commemorated as a fast day. However, in the future, the lofty perfection of the repentance of the Jewish people for the sin of the golden calf will be revealed. This historical progression of repentance commenced with the shattering of the Tablets and the subsequent receiving of the second Tablets with their superior qualities, and it will culminate with the transformation of the seventeenth day of *Tammuz*, originally the time of the breaking of the Tablets, into a day of "rejoicing and happiness."

This is the reason that G-d's approval and affirmation of Moses' "power" (*Yasher Koach*) in the breaking of the Tablets was declared only at the time of the command for making the second Tablets. And this was finally revealed in the literal text only at the conclusion of *Vezot haberachah*. At that time G-d provided for Moses a landscape view of the future of the Jewish people, "till the most distant sea," which is explained Midrashically as the "end of days."[19] Thus, Moses had a panoramic view of what would later occur to the Jewish people. For only at the end of Moses' mortal life could the high spiritual level of repentance that Israel attained specifically through the breaking of the tablets be revealed.

---

18. Ezekiel 8:19.

19. *Sifri* and Rashi on Deuteronomy 34:2.

THE SECOND TABLETS

We can now gain insight into the link between the Torah reading of *Vezot haberachah* on Shemini Atzeret (which is Simchat Torah in the Land of Israel;) or its being read on Simchat Torah which follows Shemini Atzeret in the entire world outside the Land of Israel. *Chasidut* explains that Simchat Torah occurs after Sukkot rather than at the time of the Giving of the Torah, Shavuot, because our joy in receiving the Torah is for the second Tablets given on Yom Kippur. This bestowal is an occasion of great joy highly surpassing that of the first Tablets, because it indicated the acceptance of our repentance. Since Simchat Torah is the very last day of holiday observance, this is the time in which we express our profound joy for G-d's compassion and magnanimity. Therefore, the words "before the eyes of all Israel" which are related to and express the superior quality of the second Tablets, are conceptually linked to Simchat Torah. Nevertheless, the beginning of the Torah reading on Simchat Torah is "*Vezot haberachah*...G-d came from Sinai..." regarding the *first* Tablets, as will be explained.

CAUSING THE TORAH ITSELF TO REJOICE

The two sets of Tablets correspond to the two levels of divine service as reflected in the difference between *tzaddikim* and *Baalei teshuvah*, those naturally pious and those who have returned in repentance. The first tablets are equivalent to the level of *tzaddikim*, and the second tablets to that of penitent souls. The *tzaddik* acts in accordance with the obligations of Torah; however, the *Baal teshuvah* reaches a level *above* Torah.

It follows, then, that in the instance of the first Tablets the Jewish people are *receivers* of the Torah whereas the second Tablets involve the quality of repentance, which evokes and reveals the primary source of the Jewish soul. This source is G-d's thought of Israel—the collective Jewish soul which ascended in G-d's thought[20] and preceded Torah, being on a higher level than Torah.[21] Thus, Israel influences and bestows its spiritual influx *within* Torah.

This is the connection between the beginning and conclusion of *Vezot haberachah* and Simchat Torah. Two unique qualities inhere to Simchat Torah: 1) the Jewish people rejoice with the Torah, and are elevated to a higher degree; 2) the Jewish people cause joy to the Torah itself. These two themes are expressed in the Torah reading. Firstly: "G-d came from Sinai." The Jewish people receive the Torah and rejoice in it. Subsequently, they reach a higher level: "Before the eyes of the entire Jewish people" because they are above Torah and cause the bestowal and flow of joy within Torah.

"AND JACOB WENT ON HIS WAY"

The purpose of Shemini Atzeret and Simchat Torah—"the end of all holidays"—is to infuse the spiritual service of Torah study and mitzvah fulfillment during the entire year, with the inspiration of all the holidays. This service of G-d in mundane affairs after the holiday, is described in the phrase, "And Jacob went on *his* way." *This* very matter is also alluded to in the phrase, "before the eyes of the entire Jewish people."

One emerges within the *olam* (world)—this word being derived from *helem*, concealment[22]—he is gripped by fear caused by the thought, "How do I have the power to stand steadfast and prevail against the darkness of the world and perform the G-dly service demanded of me?" The Torah responds and provides guidance to cope with this challenge. Even in the concealment and hiddenness of the shattering of the Tablets, G-d affirmed the power and strength of Moses in this action. Similarly, a Jew has the ability to cope with adverse

---

20. *Bereishit Rabbah* 1:4; *Midrash Tehillim* 93, 2; see *Likkutei Torah, Shir Hashirim* 19b; *Sefer Hama'amarim 5666*, p. 385, and elsewhere.

21. *Bereishit Rabbah*, ibid.; *Likkutei Torah*, ibid.; *Sefer Hama'amarim*, ibid.

22. See *Likkutei Torah, Bamidbar* 37b.

challenges, resulting in self-elevation, to a level even higher than the level prior to his decline.

It is for this very reason that immediately after the conclusion of the reading of the entire Torah, "before the eyes of the entire Jewish people," the opening words of the Torah are immediately read: "In the beginning G-d created heaven and earth." This tells us that a Jew should not be discouraged or taken aback by the spiritual concealment of G-dliness. For since "a Jew and G-d are all one,"[23] whatever the conditions and circumstances of worldly existence, the Jew has the power to "create" a new world, a world wherein "every created being will know that You created him...G-d the L-rd of Israel is King and His Kingship reigns over all existence."[24]

(Likkutei Sichot, vol. 9, pp. 237-243)

---

22.   See *Zohar* vol. 3, 73a and 93b.

24. Rosh Hashanah liturgy.

SIMCHAT TORAH

PEACE AND UNITY—
ACTIVE AND PASSIVE
INVOLVEMENT

At the conclusion of *Vezot haberachah*, the Torah reading for Simchat
Torah discussed in the previous *sicha*, the passing of Moses is
described. We are told in connection with Moses' death that all the
men cried, while in connection with the death of Aaron we are told
that all the Jewish people cried. According to Rashi's explanation the
grief for Aaron reflected his admirable quality that he "pursued
peace...between one Jew and another...between husband and
wife..." Why, in a passage detailing Moses' greatness, does Rashi's
explanation stress his seemingly lesser status compared to Aaron?
The answer leads to a deeper appreciation of the mitzvah of *Ahavat
Yisrael* and the unique greatness of Moses.

WHY DID ONLY THE MEN WEEP?

The Torah text which describes the passing of Moses
essentially emphasizes his greatness: "His vision did not dim...
No other prophet comparable to him arose...All the signs and
miracles that the Almighty sent him to do in Egypt...the
powerful hand and great fear which Moses displayed...And the
sons of Israel, (the Jewish men,) mourned and wept for
Moses."[1]

When Moses' brother, Aaron, the high priest, passes away,
we are told that "the entire house of Israel"[2] mourned him.
Why this contrast? For Moses, only the men weep, while for
Aaron, *all*—men and women—mourn?

---

1. Deuteronomy 34:7-12.
2. Numbers 20:29.

One explanation given is that Moses' weeping for his brother Aaron evoked the tears of the entire Jewish people, because of the "honor and awe accorded Moses." However, after the death of Moses, "no one comparable in stature to Moses wept; therefore, only the men cried."[3]

According to another response, since Aaron "pursued peace, bringing about peace between one Jew and his fellow Jew, and between husband and wife, we are told of the grief of the *entire* Jewish people, men and women."[4]

The first explanation emphasizes the greatness of Moses, for no one was later comparable to him in stature, capable of evoking profound emotions and intense weeping of the entire Jewish people. However, the second rationale seems to convey that Aaron exceeded Moses in the ability to sow the seeds of interpersonal harmony between Jew and Jew and between husband and wife.

This second view requires clarification. Why should Aaron's ability to bring peace, one in which he seems to have excelled over his brother Moses, be cited when the Torah is describing Moses' greatness and his passing? This problem is further underscored in Rashi's explanation. Rashi, the preeminent commentator of the Bible, describes his commentary as follows: "I have only come to provide the literal meaning of the (Biblical) text."[5] Thus, it would be natural for Rashi to focus first on the variance between the phrases "the entire house of Israel" and "the sons of Israel," and explain that the former refers to both men and women, and the latter only to men. He should then describe Aaron's uniqueness as a peacemaker. But in fact, Rashi *first* describes Aaron's pursuit of peace. Thus Rashi's commentary: "'*The sons of Israel*'—this means the males"—mourned Moses. However, about Aaron, since he pursued peace and achieved peace between Man and

---

3. *Avot deRav Natan* 12:4; *Paaneach Raza* loc cit.

4. *Avot deRav Natan*, ibid; Rashi, Deuteronomy 34:8.

5. Rashi, Genesis 3:8.

his fellow man and between husband and wife, the Torah declares: "'the *entire house of Israel*'—this means the men and the women." It appears that Rashi wishes to emphasize the surpassing quality of Aaron as a peacemaker in relation to Moses, rather than simply interpret the two phases.

A further problem: Why, at the time of the passing of Moses, should Rashi dwell on the very reverse of Moses' greatness in relation to his brother Aaron? We cannot posit that the Torah seeks here to emphasize the unique importance of love for a fellow Jew, and thus teach us that despite the surpassing greatness of Moses in general, in regard to this specific trait we should try to emulate Aaron's conduct—this principle should have been enunciated in the earlier text, which discusses the passing away of Aaron. Here the primary stress should be on the unequaled spiritual greatness of Moses for all generations. There must be a compelling reason to underscore the quality of Aaron's love for a fellow Jew specifically in this context. This would also apply to the unusual manner in which Rashi first states Aaron's pursuit of peace and only then explains the phrase "the entire house of Israel."

A DIFFERENT MODE OF *AHAVAT YISRAEL*

We do not find any mention in our holy writings that Moses was instrumental in "bringing peace between a Jew and his fellow Jew and between husband and wife," as we do regarding Aaron. It is self-evident that Moses did not lack the quality of *Ahavat Yisrael*—love for his fellow Jews. On the contrary, the Talmud[6] clearly states that "Moses loved the Jewish people"; he was the "trustworthy shepherd"[7] of the Jewish people both collectively and individually, providing for all their needs.

Moses displayed concern for the spiritual needs of the Jewish people by teaching Torah "to the *entire* Jewish nation,"[8]

---

6.   *Menachot* 65a.

7.   *Tanya* ch. 42.

8.   *Eiruvin* 54a.

not only the Torah laws relating to personal conduct which every Jew must know, but also the profound *pilpula d'oraita,* the sophisticated, analytic study of Torah which was given specifically to Moses. In this matter, we are told, Moses conducted himself generously with a "beneficent eye and gave also this knowledge to the Jewish people."[9]

Moses also cared about the material needs of his people. The manna—the miraculous food that sustained the Jewish people in the desert for forty years—was provided by G-d in merit of Moses. Indeed, when Aaron and Miriam passed away, and both the clouds of G-d's glory which protected the Jews in the desert, given in Aaron's merit, and the wellsprings which traveled with the Jews in Miriam's merit, were withdrawn, they were then restored in Moses' merit.[10]

We must therefore conclude that Moses' mission on earth entailed a different mode of *Ahavat Yisrael* and "bringing peace" than Aaron's.

Our Sages tell us that Aaron effected peace between a Jew and a fellow Jew by "changing" the truth, Indeed, "It is permissible to modify the truth for the sake of peace."[11] On the other hand, Moses' unique spiritual attribute was that of truth;[12] he could not use this means in a quest to bring about peace.[13] Though legally justifiable, yet, an aspect of concealment of the truth still inheres in this conduct, not matching the personality of Moses. This mode of conduct related to Aaron, whose spiritual identity emphasizes the attribute of *chesed*—kindness.[14]

When Moses learned Torah with the Jewish people, he transmitted it in its entirety, including this principle of "It is permissible to modify the truth for the sake of peace." However, regarding Moses' personal spiritual level, and

---

9. *Nedarim* 38a.

10. *Ta'anit* 9a.

11. *Yevamot* 65b. It is worth noting here that the wording is to "modify," not to falsify.

12. *Shemot Rabbah* 5:10. And see *Sanhedrin* 111a and in many other places.

13. See *Binyan Yehoshua* on *Avot deRav Natan* ibid.

14. *Shemot Rabbah,* ibid.

mission in the world, it was inappropriate to apply this concept to himself.

We may speculate that this is so, because he could not descend to individuals on so low a level that the *only* way of bringing about them peace is to change the truth.

Since both modes of conduct are Torah prescribed, we may presume that each one possesses a distinctive quality not found in the other. Moses is unique in that there is not the slightest deviation from truth in his conduct. On the other hand, the uniqueness of Aaron is that his influence can extend to an individual on the lowest level, for whom it is necessary to "change" the truth.

We can now gain insight into why the Torah places emphasis on Aaron's unique spiritual trait at the time when Moses was departing from the physical world.

THE ATTRIBUTE OF TRUTH

During his life, Moses was preoccupied with accomplishing those spiritual goals particular to his identity. His actions were totally focused on acting truthfully. However, when "he ascended to the mountain of Nebo,"[15] when he had completed his divine mission in the world and prepared to leave it and advance to a loftier spiritual level, that time was appropriate for him to comprehend the great spiritual quality of Aaron's bringing about peace for *all* Jews.

—Relevant to this, we also find an unusual extent of self-evaluative introspection at the time of the passing away of Rabbi Yochanan ben Zakkai, who declared "I do not know in which path they will lead me."[16] This is very difficult to comprehend, for he was a preeminent *Tanna* whom our Sages praise many times,[17] as meticulously rigorous in his fulfillment of the Law and scrupulous in avoiding transgression. How could he possibly doubt his worthiness of the heavenly reward

---

15. Deuteronomy 34:1.

16. *Berachot* 28b.

17. See, for example, *Sukkah* 28a; *Rosh Hashanah* 31b; *Sifri*, end *Parshat Berachah*.

of *Gan Eden?* *Chasidut* explains[18] that although he was confident regarding the external faculties of his soul in their total purity and perfection in the service of G-d, he was nevertheless apprehensive about the *essence* of his soul. Had he fulfilled what heaven anticipated from him in the innermost aspect of his identity?

We are further confronted by the question of why this concern arose just prior to his death, and not at an earlier time. One possible explanation is that during the course of Rabbi Yochanan ben Zakkai's life, he was preoccupied with his essential mission in this world: studying and teaching Torah. He did not focus on ascertaining the true level of the essence of his soul. When he was about to pass away, to complete his task in this world, he felt it appropriate to reflect on the nature of his soul's essence, on whether he had accomplished G-d's purpose for the soul's descent within the earthly body.

Similarly, for Moses, having completed the formidable, G-d-given task designated for him, the time of his passing away was appropriate for reflecting on the difference between his spiritual service and Aaron's. It was then that he sensed the uniqueness of Aaron's level. For this reason, specifically in the Torah that Moses himself taught us, in the verses describing his death, we find mention of that aspect of Aaron's service of G-d which surpassed that of Moses. —

Yet this answer is problematic: Moses' primary spiritual trait was truth, which was constant, unvarying, and unchanging, whether during the course of his human existence or immediately prior to the ascent of his soul. Why, would he sense the superior quality of Aaron only at the time of his passing?

A SPIRITUAL ELEVATION

Viewed from the perspective of *Chasidut,* another answer may be advanced. The departure and ascent of Moshe are not

---

18. *Likkutei Torah,* Leviticus 50d; *Sefer Hama'amarim 5696,* p. 50 and ff.

to be understood solely in the sense of his soul leaving the body. At that time there also occurred a *spiritual* ascent and elevation, to a level far beyond that achieved during the course of Moses' physical existence. The Arizal explains[19] the ascent of Moshe on the mountain of Nebo: The name *Nebo* is comprised of the letter—*Nun*—plus the word *Bo*. During the span of his life, Moshe had reached the level of the forty-nine gates of *Binah*—understanding. But on the day of his passing away, he merited and ascended to the highest level, the fiftieth gate of understanding, *Nun*—the numerical equivalent of fifty—which was now *Bo*, which means *"within him."*

This may also be the inner meaning of the phrase, "And Moses ascended," etc. Mystically viewed, Moshe's task is to elicit spirituality from Above to below. He is described with the term *shushvina deMalka*[20]—the honor escort of the King—in the sense of escorting the majestic bestowal from Above to below. We say that he *gave* the Torah—"Moses received the Torah from Sinai and gave it over, etc."[21] Aaron, on the other hand, was the "honor escort of the Queen," expressing his service of *elevating* Jewish souls.

But on the day of Moses' passing, he was lifted above and beyond this level. The level of Aaron *within* Moses was revealed and thereby *"Vaya'al"*—he (Moshe) ascended (or was elevated) from below to Above—*elevation* from below to Above; he merited the "fiftieth gate" of understanding.

This gives us greater insight into the dimension of "love for a fellow Jew" and "accomplishing peace." Moses, on the day of his passing away, reached the level of *"Vaya'al,"* etc., because he encompassed the spiritual level of Aaron; he understood the surpassing quality of "bringing peace" which Aaron exemplified and which is related to *all* Jews.

---

19. *Sefer Halikutim Leha'arizal*, Deuteronomy 3:26.
20. *Zohar* I 266b; II 49b.
21. *Pirkei Avot* 1:1.

From all the aforementioned, we can gain an additional insight into the great measure of *Ahavat Yisrael*—love for a fellow Jew—possessed by Moses. According to the Sages, the concluding verses of the Torah, describing the passing of Moses, were actually written by Moses with divine prophecy. Yet, they speak of Aaron's virtues—all for the purpose of teaching the profundity of *Ahavat Yisrael*. Moses' great *Ahavat Yisrael* notwithstanding—which certainly flourished and grew during his lifetime—is not sufficient; we must learn to emulate Aaron, who "pursued peach, and made peace between a man and his fellow and between a wife and her husband."

(*Likkutei Sichot,* vol. 24, pp. 253 - 258)

TWENTIETH OF MAR CHESHVAN— BIRTHDAY OF RABBI SHALOM DOVBER SCHNEERSOHN

THE TEARS OF A JEWISH CHILD

The 20th of *Mar-Cheshvan* is the birthday of Rabbi Shalom DovBer Schneersohn, the fifth Rebbe of Lubavitch. The present *sicha* concerns a question that the Rebbe, as a boy of four or five, asked his grandfather: Why did the Patriarch Abraham merit G-d's appearance to him as a result of performing the mitzvah of circumcision on himself as an old man? An exploration of the significance of the young boy's asking of this question leads to a discussion of principles of Torah education which are applicable to every Jewish "child," in both the literal and spiritual senses.

A CHILD'S QUESTION

Rabbi Yosef Yitzchak Schneersohn, the sixth Lubavitcher Rebbe, once related[1] a Chasidic narrative about his father, Rabbi Shalom DovBer, in connection with his father's birthday, the 20th day of *Mar-Cheshvan*.[2] This narrative is related also to the Shabbat Torah reading of *Parshat Vayeira*.

When Rabbi Shalom DovBer was a small child, four or five years old, he came to his grandfather, the Tzemach Tzedek (Rabbi Menachem Mendel), to receive his blessings on the occasion of his birthday. Suddenly he burst into tears and plaintively asked, "We read in this week's Torah portion, *Vayeira*, that G-d revealed Himself to Abraham. Why has He not shown Himself to me?!" The Tzemach Tzedek replied: "When a Jew, a *tzaddik*, ninety-nine years of age, decides to

---

1. *Hayom Yom, 9 Cheshvan*; See *Likkutei Sichot,* vol. 5, p. 137.
2. In 5621. See *Chanoch Lana'ar; Sefer Hatoldot* of Rabbi Shalom DovBer (*Kehot* 1972).

circumcise himself, then he is worthy that G-d should appear to him."

A story about a *tzaddik* that is told publicly and then printed, indicates that it was told with care, and in precise detail because of its eternal relevance for all Jews. It is noteworthy that Rabbi Yosef Yitzchak emphasized the fact that his father was only four or five at the time. His intention was obviously not only to convey the rare spiritual sensitivity of his father, who even as a small child was moved to tears because G-d had not come to him, but the narrative, like any story so selected, was repeated because it has spiritual implications and meaning for every Jew, even for one four or five years of age.

This also applies to adults who are "four or five years old" spiritually, and like children of that age, have not yet prepared for the rigor and discipline of structured education. Such adults are circumscribed in their ability to respond to religious values and teachings. Nevertheless, even an individual of limited spiritual growth can demand with an inner resolution that G-d should reveal Himself to him as he did to our patriarch Abraham, and to be so deeply affected as to actually weep.

Moreover, the narrative refers literally to a four or five year old child, who can be educated in such a way that he will intensely and sincerely demand and weep that G-d should actually appear to him.

At first glance, it could be asked, how is it possible to generalize about the implications of this story for every Jewish child? The original story concerns a child who was saintly "sanctified from birth" a son of a Chasidic leader destined to be a Chasidic leader himself. Besides, even in his early childhood there were already indications of his potentiality for great spiritual stature. As the Talmud states, one can already perceive in children the "buds" of future greatness.[3]

Nevertheless, the fact that the Rebbe related this story publicly and then had it published indicates that it applies not

---

3. *Berachot* 48a.

only to a highly sensitive spiritual personality, even if only in early childhood, but to each and every Jew.

THE POTENTIAL OF A SMALL CHILD

In writing on teaching Torah to children, Maimonides[4] enumerates various kinds of motivation, each adapted to a different level of childhood development. The child should be given "those things beloved by him and in accordance with the child's developmental level." The different rewards are necessary because "due to his limited years and undeveloped intellect he does not understand the spiritual good inhering to Torah study." This narrative, in contrast, implies that even a small child can and should be affected and deeply moved by his education to the extent of intense weeping, not for a desire for material things, but for a yearning for G-dliness, and actually experiencing distress because "G-d has not revealed Himself to me." A child should be educated in a manner that evokes within him the longing to make G-dliness an actual part of his life, to the extent that he be greatly distressed that G-d does not reveal Himself to him.

This episode of the young Rabbi Shalom DovBer's weeping created groundbreaking dimensions in Jewish education, enabling us to sensitize our children to spiritual matters to the extent that they are moved to a profound desire to merit G-d's revelation. If a child is undisturbed by the fact that G-d has not appeared to him, this story conveys to us that it is not because this concept is beyond his understanding, but because his teacher failed to educate him in the devoted, dedicated way of "words that come from the heart will enter into the heart."[5]

RELEVANCE FOR EVERY JEWISH CHILD

The Tzemach Tzedek's reply also has special significance for every Jewish child. "When a Jew, a *tzaddik* ninety-nine years

---

4. Commentary on *Mishnah, Sanhedrin,* beginning of *Perek Chelek;* also see Maimonides, *Hilchot Teshuvah* 10:5.

5. See *Sefer Hayashar* of Rabbeinu Tam, *Sha'ar* 12; *Shelah* 69b.

of age, decides to circumcise himself, then he is worthy that
G-d should appear to him" is not to be understood as
expressing the uniqueness of Abraham, for he could have
replied that we cannot compare ourselves with Abraham.

The Tzemach Tzedek's answer is a Torah statement: On
whatever level a Jew may be, he must still focus on the spiritual
meaning of circumcision, which is the endeavor to remove the
barrier that obstructs and conceals the revelation of G-dliness
from worldly existence.

This feeling is related to all Jews. Although Abraham was a
tzaddik and ninety-nine years old," nevertheless he "opened this
channel"[6] for all other Jews. "Opening the channel" is a well-
known mystical concept: when someone strives intensively to
elicit and "bring down" a specific spiritual matter to this world,
his efforts also cause the opening of a channel for others and
they are able to accomplish the very same matter with much
less effort. This is particularly true of the historical period
following the giving of the Torah on Mount Sinai; a lesser
measure of spiritual effort is needed for us to accomplish that
which entailed great effort for the Patriarchs.

This is the meaning of the Tzemach Tzedek's reply as it
relates to the education of young children. After evoking within
the child the wondrous longing for G-d to reveal Himself to
the child, a proper education must also clarify for him the
means to effect such a revelation: one must always be
concerned with "circumcision," connoting constant and
progressive spiritual striving to remove the barriers and
concealments from worldly existence so that G-dliness can be
revealed.

Children should be taught not to be awed by the evil forces
that conceal G-dliness. They should be taught to be undeterred
by the values and societal norms of the world. Instead, the sole
criteria for personal conduct are the guiding illuminating
principles of Torah values. This resolve should be so firm and

---

6.   See *Sefer Hama'amarim 5678*, p. 283.

steadfast that "even when he grows old, he shall not veer from it."[7] As he matures from one level to another in his service of G-d, the need for self-circumcision, for the removal of the "wall" that stands between him and G-d should be deeply rooted within him. Consequently, even in childhood, G-d "will reveal Himself to him," bringing divine radiance to him and his entire surroundings, in the manner of "G-d shall be an eternal light to you."[8]

A Child's *Ahavat Yisrael*

Proper education for a Jewish child should, in addition to evoking an altruistic love of G-d, also instill within him ethical sensitivity in his relationship to his fellow Jews. Another narrative about the Rabbi Shalom DovBer illustrates this vividly:[9] When he was four years old, the tailor once brought a garment for his mother. As the garment was being scrutinized, the small child innocently extracted a piece of extra cloth from the tailor's pocket. The tailor was very embarrassed and apologetically tried to excuse himself, asserting that he had forgotten to return the piece of cloth. When the tailor left, his mother, the Rebbetzin, criticized her small son for having embarrassed the tailor. When he heard these words of criticism, he broke down in bitter weeping.

A few weeks later he asked his father, Rabbi Shmuel—the Rebbe Maharash—for a way to atone for the sin of having shamed someone. His father, Rabbi Shmuel, asked him the reason for the question, and the child answered simply that he would like to know the answer, without revealing details of the incident.

When his mother was told of this matter, she asked her son why he had not told his father the entire incident. He answered simply that embarrassing a Jew was enough of a problem, must

---

7. Proverbs 22:6.

8. Isaiah 60:19.

9. *Chanoch Lana'ar,* p. 9.

he complicate it further with the possibility of slander and gossip?

The child's original action was certainly innocent and devoid of malice. Nevertheless, he was distressed to the point of tears for having shamed another Jew. Though he could have rationalized revealing what had occurred, i.e. respect for his father, or to help determine the means for doing *teshuvah* and correcting the matter, he could, nevertheless, not endure speaking negatively about a Jew.

Since this story was also imparted to us with emphasis upon the fact of his young age, four years, it indicates to all of us that every Jewish child possesses the capability and sensitivity to be educated with these unusual spiritual qualities, even at this early phase of childhood.

EDUCATION A DAILY CONCERN

The above underscores the importance of exerting greater effort to provide a Jewish education for one's own children as well as for all Jewish children. Rabbi Shalom DovBer stated that[10] just as there is a Biblical command that every Jew put on *tefillin* daily, similarly it is the duty of every Jew to reflect half an hour every day on the education of his children, and to do all that is within his power, and even beyond his power, to see that they proceed upon the proper Torah path.

This concern should also extend to all other Jewish children whose parents have, for whatever reason, neglected this task. As stated by Maimonides[11] and Rabbi Schneur Zalman, the Alter Rebbe:[12] it is the task of "every single sage" to see that each Jewish child should receive a proper Jewish education.

Thus we establish a *Tzivot Hashem*—Army of G-d—that will depart very soon from the *galut* (exile), together with the

---

10. *Hayom Yom 22 Tevet.*

11. *Hilchot Talmud Torah 1:2.*

12. *Hilchot Talmud Torah 1:8.*

entire Jewish people "with our youths and elders...our sons and daughters"[13] led by our righteous *Mashiach*.

(Likkutei Sichot, vol. 15, p. 129)

---

13. Exodus 10:9.

NINETEENTH OF KISLEV—
LIBERATION OF RABBI SCHNEUR
ZALMAN OF LIADI

THE MIRROR LINK BETWEEN
TORAH AND HUMAN HISTORY

History can be divided into different eras based on differences in the revelation of Torah knowledge. Since "G-d looked into the Torah and created the world," the spiritual qualities of every era are revealed at their appropriate times as they derive from Torah. During the time of the first Temple the Jewish people were on a lofty spiritual level and consequently experienced material abundance. Later, after the destruction of the second Temple, there was a decline in both of these areas. This situation continued until a number of scholars began to reveal the teachings of Jewish mysticism. The Arizal in particular initiated the promulgation of *Kabbalah* study, until then only studied by prominent scholars, to a greater number of people and indeed, affirmed the widespread study of *Kabbalah*. Rabbi Israel Baal Shem Tov made these teachings even more accessible through the teachings of *Chasidut*. And the Alter Rebbe, Rabbi Schneur Zalman of Liadi, explained these teachings on the basis of Chabad *Chasidut*. Both the G-dly soul and animalistic soul of a Jew are elevated and transformed through the study of *Chasidut*, bringing about "the spreading of Chasidic wellsprings outward" and ultimately the era of Messianic Redemption.

THE NATURE OF TIME

Time should not be perceived as one continuous unity; different segments of time are characterized by individualized spiritual qualities. The *Zohar*, in speaking of the six days of creation states:[1] "Each day accomplishes its own unique task." Whatever was created on each separate day was inherently and

---

1. *Zohar* III:94b.

uniquely related to the inner spiritual quality of that day. Nachmonides,[2] in an overview of world history, states that the six thousand years of world history discussed in the Talmud[3] correspond to the six days of creation.

Rabbi DovBer, the Mitteler Rebbe, elaborates[4] on this relationship. He describes how the first thousand years are related to the first day of creation. On that day, light, which is linked to *chesed* (kindness) was created.[5] Thus, during the first thousand years the world was sustained solely by G-d's kindness and was not evaluated through the severity of G-d's divine judgment. The second thousand years correspond to the second day, when G-d's attribute of *gevurah* (strictness and rigor) prevailed. It was during this period that the flood and acts of judgment took place.

The third thousand years are in accord with the third day of creation, the day in which the phrase *"ki-tov"*—"(and G-d said) 'it is good'"—was stated twice.[6] This day is thus characterized by a twofold goodness. In this third millennium the Torah was given. The twofold quality of goodness is inherent in Torah, for it is both "good" for the realm of heaven and also for creatures on earth.[7] Torah unites G-dliness and created beings, and this is ultimate goodness.

TORAH—THE BLUEPRINTS OF CREATION

Every event in the world of necessity begins in Torah and then emerges into the world; as our Sages state, "G-d looked into the Torah and created the world."[8] Thus, the spiritual

---

2. See *Nachmonides*, Genesis 2:3.
3. *Rosh Hashanah* 31a.
4. *Torat Chaim*, Exodus 320b and ff.
5. Genesis 1:3.
6. Genesis 1:10, 12, and see Rashi, ibid 1:7.
7. See *Kiddushin* 40a; Commentary on the *Mishnah* of Maimonides on beginning of Tractate Peah; *Sefer Hama'amarim* 5709, p. 18.
8. *Zohar* II 161b.

qualities of every era are revealed at their appropriate times as they derive from Torah.

This concept helps us understand the era of exile and the destruction of the Holy Temple. At the time of the construction of the first Temple, the "moon was in its fullness."[9] The Jewish people are often compared to the moon,[10] and in that era they were on a lofty level of spiritual revelation. By the time of the second Temple they had regressed from that level. The second Temple was destroyed, and a great concealment of G-dliness occurred within the world. Applying the concept of the relationship of historical events and Torah, we know that concealment of G-dliness on earth is linked to those aspects of Torah knowledge which are also hidden within the Torah itself.

DIFFERENT ERAS IN TORAH KNOWLEDGE

In the beginning, all of the Torah was open and clearly revealed; there were no hidden aspects or obscurities, doubts or disputes. In cases of a Rabbinic difference of opinion, "they did not leave that place until a decision was reached, with the majority opinion prevailing."[11] There were only three *halachic* controversies between the famed Rabbis Hillel and Shammai.[12] The extensive disputes discussed in the Talmud started only later, between their *students*, between the *House* (i.e. school) of Shammai and the *House* of Hillel.[13]

A gradual and cumulative diminution of knowledge took place with the "diminishing of hearts."[14] The decrease in conceptual mastery made it necessary for Rabbi Yehuda *Hanassi* to commit the Oral Torah traditions to writing in the form of the *Mishnah*. Even for this quintessential document, further

---

9. See *Zohar I* 150a; *Shemot Rabbah* 15:26.

10. See *Sukkah 29a; Bereishit Rabbah* 6:3.

11. *Sanhedrin* 88b.

12. *Shabbat* 14b, 15a.

13. See *Sukkah 47b; Sanhedrin* ibid.

14. See Introduction of Maimonides to *Mishneh Torah.*

explanatory commentary was necessary, first the Jerusalem
Talmud and then the Babylonian Talmud. The latter, which is
very complex, is described by the phrase, "He has placed me in
darkness."[15]

The concealment of Torah light initiated an epoch of
proliferation of Talmudic questions, and in many instances,
lengthy Talmudic discussions, which ended with either a
question, a refutation, or *Teiku*—an acronym meaning that the
unanswered question will be answered in the Messianic era by
Elijah the Prophet. Nevertheless, even then, during the time of
the Talmud, the great and intense darkness which prevailed *after*
the redaction of the Talmud still did not exist. For up to the
time of Ravina and Rav Ashi, the editors of the Talmud, the
great and unbroken chain of *semichah* (ordination) from Rabbi
to Rabbi, which commenced with Moses, was still in force. But
in the time of Ravina and Rav Ashi the tradition of *semichah*
ceased, and the Talmudic era ended. Concurrent with the
increasing obscurity and concealment in Torah came a decline
in the material situation of the Jewish people and a worsening
of their trials in exile—a mirror reflection of the concealment
of Torah.

A GLIMMERING OF REDEMPTION

However, as the time of the final redemption of the Jewish
people approached, a significant transformation took place. Just
as the descent into exile began with the loss of Torah clarity,
the commencement of the glimmering of the light of
redemption started with the revelation of hitherto hidden
aspects of Torah: the revelation by the *Arizal*—Rabbi Yitzchak
Luria—and those who preceded him, of the teachings and
wisdom of *Kabbalah*.

Previously there had been constraints and prohibitions
regarding the teaching of this knowledge, but the *Arizal* began
to expound the study of *Kabbalah* to a significant degree.[16] This

---

15. See *Sanhedrin* 24a on this biblical phrase in Lamentations 3:5.

16. See *Tanya, Igeret Hakodesh*, ch. 26.

endeavor was later continued and expanded by those who followed him, until Rabbi Israel Baal Shem Tov revealed the teachings of *Chasidut*. Subsequently the Alter Rebbe, Rabbi Schneur Zalman, established the teaching of Chabad *Chasidut*. He formulated and explained profound and mystical concepts so that they could be grasped by the uninitiated. One of these teachings is that a Jew's soul has two aspects: a G-dly soul,[17] which desires and relates to the spiritual and holy,[18] and an animalistic soul[19] connected to the earthly and materialistic. The Alter Rebbe presented the profound concepts of Chabad *Chasidut* so they could be understood by the intellect of both the G-dly soul and the animalistic soul, with a resultant transformative influence upon the entire Jewish personality.

The primary revelation of this mode of *Chasidut* began on *Yud-Tet Kislev*—the nineteenth day of *Kislev*.[20] There was a significant difference between the *Chasidut* discourses given by the Alter Rebbe prior to his imprisonment in S. Petersburg and his discourses after his release on *Yud-Tet Kislev*. The earlier discourses "blazed" with intense spirituality; the post Petersburg discourses related more to immediate concerns, leant themselves more to intellectual comprehension, and were thus more relevant in their effect.[21]

These teachings were not merely for the elite; they were intended for all Jews, in fulfillment of the words, "When your wellsprings extend outward"—the famous answer[22] of *Mashiach* when asked by the Baal Shem Tov to reveal the exact time of the redemption of the Jewish people. The "wellsprings" refer to the Baal Shem Tov and his Chasidic teachings; these teachings

---

17. See *Tanya*, beg. ch. 2.
18. See ibid., ch. 19.
19. See ibid., ch. 1.
20. See *Sefer Hasichot, Torat Shalom*, p. 112 and ff.
21. See *Sefer Hasichot 5700*, p. 114.
22. Letter of the *Baal Shem Tov*—printed in *Keter Shem Tov* 2a.

"extend outward" when they burst all bounds and reach as many Jews as possible.

The revelation of the inner teachings of the Torah will be the major contributing factor in the revelation of divinity in the world with the coming of *Mashiach*.

It is thus, the primary spiritual effort and responsibility in our time is to bring the wellsprings of *Chasidut* to all others, and in this way to hasten the revelation of the true and complete redemption, speedily in our time.

(Likkutei Sichot, vol. 2, pp. 466-468)

TWENTY FOURTH OF TEVET, YAHRZEIT OF RABBI SCHNEUR ZALMAN OF LIADI

TORAH EDUCATION, ANSWERING THE CRY

Rabbi DovBer, the Mitteler Rebbe, was once studying and was so engrossed in his studies that he was oblivious to the cry of a child who had fallen from its crib. His father, Rabbi Schneur Zalman—the Alter Rebbe—living on a different floor, although also immersed in study, went to the room and placed the child in the crib.

In our own time there are many children who have "fallen from the crib," and who are utterly remote from any kind of Jewish education. In many instances they are unaware of the need to weep. The child must be "replaced in the crib." A Jewish education must be provided for every Jewish child under all circumstances to enable them to return to their Jewish heritage.

THE CRY OF A CHILD

The following story occurred at a time when Rabbi Schneur Zalman and his son and eventual successor, Rabbi dovBer, the Mitteler Rebbe, lived in the same house. The Alter Rebbe lived on the second floor. The Mitteler Rebbe still had small children at that time, including an infant. Once, as they were both studying in their respective quarters, the infant fell from its crib. The Mitteler Rebbe was so immersed in his studies that he was oblivious to what had taken place and continued studying. His father, the Alter Rebbe, although also deeply engrossed in studying on the upper floor, nevertheless heard the cry of the small child. He went down to his son's quarters, placed the infant in its crib, calmed it from its crying, and rocked it back to sleep.

The Alter Rebbe then spoke to his son and explained to him that to be so deeply involved in studying to the extent of being oblivious to the cry of a small child is an inappropriate mode of conduct.

ATTUNED AND SENSITIVE

The sixth Lubavitcher Rebbe, Rabbi Yosef Yitzchak Schneersohn, explained the general implications of this narrative. This story conveys to us that no matter how profoundly involved we may be in our own studies, we nevertheless must be attuned and sensitive to hear the cry of a Jewish child. One must interrupt from the significant efforts of study or prayer in order to still the crying of the small child. No matter how great the individual and how significant his preoccupation, he must still heed the cry of a fragile child calling. This is also true for an eminent scholar.

This concept has special relevance for our times, which has witnessed a general awakening of consciousness and concern as to Jewish religious identity by Jews in general and Jewish youth in particular. Broad segments of the Jewish population feel that they have finally arrived at the truth of authentic Judaism, and have been searching and yearning for a true Judaism devoid of dilution and compromise. This phenomenon further intensifies the obligation to provide a Jewish Torah education for all Jews in general and for Jewish children in particular—a religious education founded and based totally on our living Torah. We must hear, and respond to their cry.

This concern has priority over all other problems confronting the world Jewish community. The greatest effort must be made to enable *yeshivot* and Jewish educational institutions to provide a Torah true education and to have the capability to accept the maximal number of children possible. Unfortunately, the situation at present is such that many children remain on "the street," excluded because the *yeshivot* lack the economic funding to form additional classes or to hire more teachers.

In fact, the problem is even more severe. There are many Jewish homes in which the children are so removed from their Jewish identity that they are unaware that they lack something. In such cases, the obligation and task is even greater. That they do not weep is proof that their need for a Jewish education is even more urgent. This is one of the challenges that *yeshivot* must cope with directly.

Jewish educational institutions must accept children from all kinds of backgrounds without any limitation, not distinguishing between the child coming from a limited background but cognizant to some degree of his lack and void in Torah knowledge and the child totally unaware of the need to weep due to his total Torah ignorance. For all of these children, a maximal Jewish Torah education should be provided to enable them to advance on the path of life, thereby assuring them authentic happiness throughout their entire lives both materially and spiritually.

(*Likkutei Sichot*, vol. 3, pp. 802-803)

CHANUKAH

IN DAYS OF YORE...
AND IN OUR OWN TIMES

Although the kindling of the Chanukah menorah is linked to the kindling of the menorah in the Temple, there are some key differences. The menorah in the Temple was kindled within the edifice, the number of flames each day was constant, and they were lit during the day. Also, during the time of Moses and later King Solomon the Jewish people were materially prosperous and secure.

In contrast, in the present era we add a new flame to the Chanukah menorah each night, kindling it at nightfall, and the candles are placed to illuminate the outside. At the time of Chanukah, the Jews were under the tyrannical rule of the Syrian-Greeks, the Jewish army was small, and on the spiritual level, no pure oil was initially available, even for one night.

The above implies that when Jews have material abundance, then they can perform their spiritual tasks with ease. There is no need for special effort or self-sacrifice, and thus kindling a constant number of candles is adequate.

However, when spiritual darkness encroaches the Jewish community, as in our own times, there is a different mode of practice. We kindle the lights when the darkness is falling, direct the light to the outside world, and constantly increase the number of flames, thus conveying that we cannot sustain ourselves by remaining on the same level, but must progress and ascend until we shall kindle the menorah in the rebuilt Holy Temple.

THE CHANUKAH MENORAH AND THE TEMPLE MENORAH

The basic mitzvah of Chanukah is the kindling of flames. How is light created? One must take a physical substance, like oil, and heat it until it transforms from its original state into a flame which can illuminate the surrounding environment.

The lights of Chanukah are derived from the lights of the holy *Beit Hamikdash* (Temple), where the menorah was ritually kindled every evening. As is well-known,[1] when the miracle of Chanukah occurred, no pure oil was available for kindling the lights. G-d performed a miracle and a small jug of undefiled oil was discovered which bore the seal of the high priest. This oil should have been enough for only one day, but it burned for eight days, and in commemoration of this miracle we kindle lights all eight days of Chanukah.

Although the observance of Chanukah is rooted in the Temple menorah ritual, there are however several notable distinctions between the lights of Chanukah and those of the Temple:

a) In the Temple, the number of lights in the menorah remained constant, in contrast to Chanukah, when a new light is added each evening.[2]

b) In the Temple, the candles were lit during the day while there was yet light outside;[3] the lights of Chanukah are kindled in the evening, when darkness falls.[4]

c) The lights of the Temple were kindled inside, whereas it is necessary to place the lights of Chanukah to the outside of the entrance to the house.[5]

d) The times when the menorah was kindled in the sanctuary, and later in the Temples, were times of material abundance. This was particularly true during the period when Israel wandered through the desert under the leadership of Moses. The Jewish people were given all they required: manna from heaven for food, water from the miraculous well of

---

1. *Shabbat* 21b.
2. Ibid.
3. Exodus 30:8; and see *Sefer Hama'amarim Malukat*, vol. 2, p. 17 and note 12 there.
4. *Shabbat*, ibid.
5. Ibid.

Miriam, and the miraculous ability of their garments to grow along with them and always remain clean.[6]

Similarly, the era of King Solomon, who built the Temple, was an epoch in which abundance and peace prevailed. No one waged war against the Jewish people; on the contrary, many nations rendered homage by paying them tribute. It was an era of "each man under his vine and under his fig tree."[7]

The fact that the lights of the Temple menorah were kindled at times of peace and plenty for the Jews can also be understood in a spiritual sense. That is, when Man is free from material concern, he can dedicate himself wholly to the study of Torah and to the performance of *mitzvot*, occupying himself totally with spiritual matters.

In contrast, the lights of Chanukah were linked to a time when Israel endured the tyrannical rule of the Syrian-Greeks and the Jewish army was very small. This physical constraint was also true on the spiritual level; ritually pure oil was unavailable even for one night.

THE NEED FOR ADDITIONAL LIGHT

All of these distinctions, however, are interrelated. A time of material abundance, of prosperity, has a beneficial effect upon spiritual matters. For when a Jew possesses material means, he utilizes them with an open and generous hand for spiritual endeavors. Under such circumstances, there is no need for self-sacrifice; at such a time, kindling the same number of candles each day is adequate. Additional lights are not required for conditions that are stable and normal. Nor is extra effort needed to illuminate the external environment, since darkness does not reign in the world. The menorah burns in the Temple and, as a result, there is also light outside.

The period of the Hasmoneans, on the other hand, was filled with constant military conflict with the Syrian-Greeks,

---

6. See *Rashi, Deuteronomy* 8:4.

7. I Kings 5:5.

and internal conflict with Jewish assimilationists.[8] There were Jews who did not accord reverence to the Holy Temple, who were insensitive to the importance of religious independence, and who wished to assimilate into the Syrian-Greek culture.

Under such circumstances, intense self-sacrifice is required to illuminate our path. This, then, is the purpose of the mitzvah of Chanukah Lights. It is inadequate to illuminate only one's own home, for the outer darkness may penetrate within one's dwelling. Rather, one must bring light to the external world despite the great exertion required. We kindle the Chanukah lights specifically at the time of day when darkness falls, and do so at the door, thus implying that an intense effort must be made to spread light and banish darkness.

Nor is the number of lights kindled on past days sufficient, for we cannot be content with the fact that we have not declined spiritually, or that we have sustained ourselves continuously on the same spiritual level; rather we must be constantly progressing and ascending.

ILLUMINATING THE DARKNESS

At a time of great spiritual darkness one should not allow oneself to be frightened and overcome. On the contrary, this should actually serve as a challenge to evoke the qualities of *mesirat nefesh* (self-sacrifice) and one must make the utmost effort to illuminate the external darkness.

One should create additional light each day. Moreover, this should be done in the following manner: a person should not be content with the number of lights kindled the day before, but provide additional light every single day. Today one light, tomorrow two, and the next day three, and so on. Nor should one be satisfied with generating light in one's own home and thus indirectly illuminating the street outside. One must expend great effort for the specific purpose of creating light in the external world.

---

8.   See *Bava Kama* 82b.

This entire endeavor, furthermore, should be characterized by the quality of *mesirat nefesh* (self-sacrifice) of effort beyond the bounds of one's natural limitations, comparable to the supernatural miracle of the oil. If because of these efforts people look at a Jew askance and think him peculiar, he should not be perturbed; his only concern should be the fulfillment of the task designated for him by his Creator.

This manner of behavior is expected of *every* Jew. Every Jew should be aware that he or she is G-d's "ambassador," an emissary who is sent to "ignite" the material aspects of his or her own small world till it will finally result in the illumination of the entire environment.

One achieves this goal by not being content with past accomplishments, and realizing that every new day requires ever greater illumination. The knowledge of past accomplishment is necessary only in order to gauge how much one must increase one's present efforts.

When a Jew acts in this manner with *mesirat nefesh*, and is not content with past efforts, then he possesses the divine assurance that he will ultimately succeed. There will be ever-increasing light in the darkness of the external environment till its blackness will finally be banished completely. And there will then occur the great culmination, the bringing of pure oil for kindling the menorah in the *Beit Hamikdash*, may it be rebuilt speedily in our days.

(Likkutei Sichot, vol. 1, pp. 89-92)

Tenth of Shevat— Yahrzeit of Rabbi Yosef Yitzchak Schneersohn

Love and Concern for a Fellow Jew

The following is a segment of the *ma'amar* delivered by the Rebbe upon the occasion of the first yahrzeit of his father-in-law, Rabbi Yosef Yitzchak, the sixth Lubavitcher Rebbe. At that time the Rebbe formally accepted the mantle of leadership of the Chabad-Lubavitch movement, and this was the very first Chasidic discourse he delivered as such.

In this discourse, he interpolates narratives illustrating the *Ahavat Yisrael*—love of a fellow Jew—of the previous Chabad leaders. Seemingly, the Rebbe was conveying the impelling reason for his assumption of this leadership role and also projecting the focus of his future emphasis on dynamic outreach to the Jewish community in the entire world, aimed at bringing about a major return to the Torah tradition and the fulfillment of *mitzvot* and hastening the Messianic redemption.

These narratives are mentioned only briefly in the discourse. We have taken the liberty of adding the details of the stories, drawing on other sources, chiefly the *Likkutei Sichot* of the Rebbe and the *Sefer Hasichot* of his father-in-law.

Word and Deed

The Rebbe, my father-in-law, and the other leaders of Chabad, always practiced and fulfilled the *mitzvot* and good deeds which they expected of *chasidim*. This is consistent with our Sages'[1] interpretation of the verse,[2] "He relates *His* matters to Jacob": That which He does, He tells Israel to perform and heed; and that which He commands Israel, He actually does Himself. In a similar manner, whatever degree of devotion in matters of Torah and *mitzvot* the leaders of Chabad expected of those who followed and were loyal to them, they actually exemplified themselves. They revealed their deeds to us in order to instill the strength to perform these actions within us, and thus lessen the difficulties entailed.

This is beautifully exemplified in the mitzvah of *Ahavat Yisrael* (loving a fellow Jew). There are many narratives about the leaders of Chabad and the basic mitzvah.

a) The Alter Rebbe once interrupted his prayers on Yom Kippur. He removed his *talit* and went to the outskirts of the city in order to prepare food and drink for a woman who had just given birth, and who had no one else to care for her. One can easily recognize the unique significance of the Alter Rebbe's prayers on Yom Kippur; nevertheless, he interrupted his prayers in order to perform the mitzvah of kindness for a fellow Jew.[3]

b) It is told that a *Chasid* once came to Rabbi DovBer, the Mitteler Rebbe, for a personal audience and related in deep embitterment his various ethical shortcomings. The Mitteler Rebbe bared his arm and said to the *Chasid*, "Do you see how the skin of my arm is shriveled? All this is due to the transgressions of your youth." The spiritual greatness and uniqueness of the Mitteler Rebbe is a matter that is self-evident, particularly his remoteness from the coarse matters in which the *Chasid* had once been involved. Despite this, the bond with his disciples was so profound that improper conduct on their part was responsible for weakening his health, to the extent of causing his skin to dry up.

---

1. *Shemot Rabbah* 30:9; Jerusalem Talmud, *Rosh Hashanah* 1:3.
2. Psalms 147:19.
3. *Likkutei Sichot*, vol. 4, p. 1255.

c) Once, on a Wednesday, the twentieth day of *Elul*, Rabbi Menachem Mendel, the Tzemach Tzedek, was going to the synagogue and morning services. On his way there, he encountered Rabbi Pinchas, a member of the Lubavitcher community, who requested a loan of three rubles so that he could purchase merchandise in the market place, resell it, and with the profit buy some food for Shabbat. The Tzemach Tzedek agreed and instructed Rabbi Pinchas to come to his home after the morning prayers for the loan.

As the Tzemach Tzedek placed his *talit* upon his shoulders and prepared for prayer, he remembered Rabbi Pinchas' request, and also that it was a market day, so trade would begin at an early hour. He realized that in all probability Rabbi Pinchas needed the money immediately. The Tzemach Tzedek removed his *talit*, went home, took five rubles and gave them to Rabbi Pinchas, thereby enabling him to earn his livelihood. Only then did the Tzemach Tzedek return to his morning prayers.[4]

d) It is known that Rabbi Shmuel, the Rebbe Maharash, was extremely scrupulous regarding the use of his time. Even his Chasidic discourses were very brief, and there were instances when his morning prayers would be concluded at a very early hour. Nevertheless, he once undertook a lengthy journey and spent some time at his destination in order to benefit one single individual.

The Rebbe went to Paris accompanied by his two personal attendants, Rabbi Leivik and Rabbi Pinchas Leib, as well as the wealthy merchants Rabbi M. Monensohn and Rabbi Yeshaye Berlin. When they arrived in Paris, Rabbi Yeshaye asked the Rebbe Maharash his destination. The Rebbe replied that he desired to stay at the Hotel Alexander, an establishment frequented by royalty and aristocracy. The Rebbe added, "You are somewhat timid, and you do not speak French. Therefore, I will speak for us."

---

4. See *Sefer Hasichot, Summer 5700*, p. 98. *Igrot Kodesh Admor Mahorayatz*, vol. 4, p. 522; *Likkutei Sichot*, vol. 2, p. 403.

When they arrived at the hotel, the Rebbe Maharash requested a suite with a number of rooms. The orderly replied that one was available and that the cost would be 200 francs for each day of their stay. The Rebbe asked if more elaborate accommodations were available, specifically, a suite on the same floor as the halls in which the games of chance were conducted. A suite was available, but the price was very high. The Rebbe Maharash took the three-room suite; one room was to be for himself, and the other two for Rabbi Leivik and Rabbi Pinchas Leib. Rabbi Berlin and Rabbi Monensohn stayed at a nearby hotel.

A few hours after their arrival, the Rebbe emerged from his room and entered one of the gambling halls. He sat down at a table adjacent to a young man who was playing cards and who would occasionally take a sip of wine from the glass at his elbow. The Rebbe Maharash placed his hands on the young man's shoulders and said to him, "Young man, it is forbidden to drink non-kosher wine. Non-kosher wine makes one's mind and heart callous. Be a Jew!" Then, wishing him good evening, the Rebbe Maharash started to return to his room in a state of deep agitation. Rabbi Berlin later related, "I have never seen the Rebbe Maharash so deeply moved as on that occasion."

As there were no elevators at that time, it was the custom at the hotel for attendants to carry the guests from one floor to another on sedan chairs. Deeply disturbed, the Rebbe, upon leaving the game room, abstractedly sat down on one of these chairs. Only when the attendants lifted it in order to bear him did the Rebbe Maharash focus on his surroundings. He apologized and returned to his room on the same floor.

A few hours passed, and the young man who had been playing cards came inquiring about the rabbi who had spoken to him earlier. He was directed to the Rebbe Maharash, with whom he remained for a long period of time. The next day, the Rebbe checked out from the hotel and left Paris.

On a later occasion, the Rebbe Maharash declared that such a pure soul, as that of the young man, had not descended to this world for a number of generations. But it had been debased in the depths of impurity until the time of the young man's repentance. Indeed, he later became the head of a distinguished and pious family in France.[5]

e) At the outset of his leadership, Rabbi Shalom DovBer, the fifth Lubavitcher Rebbe, found it necessary to travel to Moscow in order to try to alleviate a harsh decree recently enacted against the Jews of Russia. His older brother said to the Rebbe "Since time is so precious to you, and you do not speak Russian,[6] I volunteer to go and act as your emissary; I will carefully comply with your instructions." The Rebbe refused to agree to this arrangement, undertook the journey himself, and was successful in his mission to help his fellow Jews.

THIS BEHAVIOR IS REQUIRED OF US

There are various incidents related about the Rebbe, my father-in-law, regarding his efforts to perform acts of kindness, even for individual Jews, whether in a spiritual or a material matter. This was done even to the neglect of his own material and spiritual concerns, and for persons utterly remote from his lofty spiritual degree. This very behavior is required of us as well. Abraham, the first Jew, sought nothing for himself, not even self-sacrifice.[7] He traveled to places where there was no knowledge of G-dliness, and taught them to "cry out the name of G-d."[8]

Each individual is required to know that if he desires for himself the ability to "call out G-d's name," then he must inspire others to do so. One is not required to provide knowledge for the other person, but must cause him to "cry out." This person may have been utterly ignorant, but one must

---

5. *Sefer Hasichot 5705*, p. 30 and ff.

6. See *Igrot Kodesh* of Rabbi Shalom DovBer, vol. 4, p. 245.

7. *Sefer Hama'amarim 5700*, p. 29 and ff.

8. Genesis 21:33; *Sotah* 10a.

see that he cries out...that G-dliness and the world are one, that G-d constantly animates and sustains all of created existence.

(Based on *Sefer Hama'amarim Melukat*, pp. 3-10)

Shabbat Shirah

Anguish and Rejoicing— Jewish Women and the Exodus

Rabbi Schneur Zalman, the Alter Rebbe, states that the joy of the women at the time of the Exodus from Egypt surpassed that of the men, as indicated by their rejoicing with "timbrels and dances." This is the reason why the *Haftorah* of the Torah portion of *Beshallach* is about a woman, Deborah the prophetess, and her song of prayerful triumph.

The Rebbe asks, why indeed was the women's joy greater, and states that since they endured the anguish of Egypt in the most painful manner—the decree that "every male child shall be cast into the Nile," their joy at the time of the Exodus surpassed that of the men.

Similarly, in our own time, women, as the ones principally involved in childrearing, are the ones most involved in fighting the decrees of the contemporary "Pharaoh," the forces of assimilation and alienation from our heritage.

The Songs of the Women

At a Chasidic gathering in the year, 5698,[1] Rabbi Yosef Yitzchak Schneersohn of Lubavitch, related that Rabbi Menachem Mendel, the Tzemach Tzedek, once posed the following question in the name of Rabbi Schneur Zalman, the Alter Rebbe: The Torah portion of *Beshallach*[2] recounts the exultant song of both Moses and his sister Miriam after the Jews' miraculous crossing of the Red Sea. Why does the *Haftorah* of the week which usually parallels a theme from the weekly Torah section, deal here solely with the song of a

---

1. *Sefer Hasichot* 5698, p. 277 and ff.
2. Exodus 15:1 and ff.

woman—Deborah's song of prayerful triumph against the enemies of Israel?[3]

The Alter Rebbe answered the question by stating that when the Jews left Egypt and miraculously crossed the dry path in the Red Sea, not only did the women sing G-d's praises, as did the men, but their joy surpassed the men's. This is indicated by the Biblical phrase which describes the women's rejoicing *"Betupim u'vimecholot"*[4]—with percussion instruments and dancing. Since the Torah gives witness to their great joy, we read for the *Haftorah* about a woman, the prophetess Deborah.

Why, however, wasn't the song of Moses and the men equally joyous? A simple answer can be given: something acquired without effort and pain can never bring the same sense of accomplishment which follows great personal effort and difficult struggle. The *Mishnah*[5] tells us that "the reward is commensurate with the pain." To the extent of one's striving and anguish will the subsequent joy be increased.

Moses and all the Jewish men could not apprehend the profound joy experienced by the Jewish women. The harshest aspect of Egyptians exile and the most oppressive edict occurred after the birth of Miriam[6] in the proclamation that "every male child shall be cast into the Nile."[7] The earlier hardship of difficult labor was totally incomparable to the command of casting the newly born children into the Nile. Additionally, the Sages relate the cruel event of Pharaoh's bathing in the blood of Jewish children.[8] Since, a mother is far more intensely sensitive to the suffering of her children than a father, when Israel was freed from Pharaoh and his oppressive laws, the joy of the women far surpassed the joy of the men.

---

3. Judges, ch. 5.
4. Exodus 15:20.
5. *Pirkei Avot* 5:21.
6. *Shir Hashirim Rabbah* 2:11.
7. Exodus 1:22.
8. *Shemot Rabbah* 1:34.

The Contemporary Pharaoh

All Torah narratives serve as a source of spiritual guidance. The description of the exodus from Egypt and the joyous song with musical instruments and dance by Miriam and all Jewish women provides spiritual direction for all future times, including our very own. This is implied in the verse, "And *all* the women went out after *her.*" *All* Jewish women till the end of time proceed after Miriam and declare, "Sing unto G-d for He is most exalted; the horse and its rider He has cast into the sea".[9]

G-dliness and holiness are expressed by the phrase "most exalted," the loftiest, unequaled level of sanctity. And those forces which are the very reverse of sanctity, which wage war with holiness—"the horse and its rider"—were "cast into the sea," not merely cast low, but thrown with powerful impetus into the nethermost sea, to the lowest abysmal depths.

We have already observed in another discourse[10] that the sinister intent of Pharaoh's command is to cast every male child into the sea in each generation and in every land, and thus also in our own era and environment.

When a Jewish child is born, it is appropriate to immediately provide an environment and education for him in accordance with the Torah and its commands. At that time, Pharaoh, the King of Egypt, appears—meaning the lifestyle and mores of the particular land and culture—and contends: a child has been born and in due course will marry and bear the responsibility of being the breadwinner for his family. He must therefore be immediately "cast into the Nile." The Nile was the primary source of food and economic sustenance for the Egyptians, so the child must be prepared for involvement in the surging competitive, economic mainstream. The child should immerse himself and be submerged in powerful materialistic currents, alien to Torah and its ethics. And what of Torah and

---

9. Exodus 15:21.
10. See p. 222-223.

its commands? To this Pharaoh provides the self-deceptive rationalization: there is a Sunday School.

On Sunday the bank is closed. The child is therefore taken the night before to the movies or provided with similar experiences. Since the parents wish to sleep in on the following morning, they are not perturbed about sending him to a Sunday School for an education that consists not only of singing and dancing, but even perchance the reading of Hebrew and the study of *Chumash*. They, the parents, can sleep placidly, sunk in a deep state of spiritual as well as physical slumber.

Parents should, from earliest childhood on, unite their child with G-d, He Who sustains the entire world with His goodness, grace and kindness. In actuality, this bond of a Jew with G-d is the only authentic way of achieving economic livelihood. Though other nations are economically dependent upon the natural laws which govern "the river Nile," concerning the Jews the Torah declares, "And you who *cleave* unto the L-rd your G-d *are alive* every one of you this day."[11] When the Jew is united with G-d, he can live and also receive economic sustenance. For "He Who grants life grants food."[12] G-d, Who bestows life will also provide the means of livelihood for the head of the household, his wife, and their children.

Instead of Torah commitment, however, they cast their children "into the Nile," thus severing them not only from spiritual life, but from life even in its literal sense.

Furthermore, just as in the Egyptian exile, prior to the giving of the Torah, all of the many cruel decrees were incomparable to the edict of casting all of the male children into the Nile, so in the present exile, none of the evil inclination's designs upon mature adults are comparable in their severity and harshness to its stratagems against small children. One should not, however, be awed by "Pharaoh," or the many voices of "good friends" and neighbors who contend that the ancient

---

11. Deuteronomy 4:4.

12. See *Ta'anit* 8b.

heritage of our Torah given in the desert is not in harmony with modern times, and does not represent "progress" and "culture," as distinct from "old fashioned" values.

At other times, Pharaoh envelops himself in a deceptive cloak of piety and argues that educating one's child toward the goal of great financial gain will provide a future philanthropist for the Jewish community, one who will be extremely generous in his donations to *yeshivot* and other religious institutions.

Actually, only Pharaoh derives benefit from these thoughts. A Jew must realize that this is a warped and self-defeating course of action, which has as its goal to first undermine the faith of the Jews in G-d, and then consequently their very survival. Pharaoh desires that there should be no remnant of Jewish souls, and he seeks the physical destruction of the Jewish people as well through these means.

Our ancient Jewish tenacity and courage must be used to nullify Pharaoh's decrees. The primary concern should not be to educate the child for economic ends, for though there are "many thoughts in the heart of Man," we must realize that only "the counsel of G-d shall endure."[13]·G-d is not only the Master of the heavens, but also of the earth, and of every home where husband, wife, and children are to be found. Strengthened with this knowledge, the Jewish woman should not be awed by her neighbor, but on the contrary, she should actually influence her neighbor to rescue her children as well from the grasp of Pharaoh.

In this manner, there shall be established thousands of Jewish children who will go forward to greet *Mashiach*, and may this occur very soon.

ANSWERING THE ANGELS

In the times of Moses and Miriam, when the Jews were freed from Pharaoh's despotic rule, the joy of the women, as noted, exceeded by far the joy of the men, because the Jewish

---

13. Proverbs 19:21.

mothers more profoundly experienced anguish than did the men. Similarly in our own times, both the decree of the present day Pharaoh—the pressure to conform to values that conflict with Torah and *mitzvot*—and the joy subsequent to the liberation from these oppressive influences, is more vividly experienced by Jewish women. It is they who are in the home during the major part of the day while the husbands are engaged in earning a livelihood. Even when home, the men are not as deeply involved with the education of the children as the wives. Consequently, the major war must be waged by the Jewish women against Pharaoh, no matter how clever his disguise or in whatever form of "good friendship" he chooses to appear.

In this struggle, they are certain of victory and of finally causing G-dliness, as revealed by the fulfillment of Torah and *mitzvot*, to be "most exalted," and that those who attempt to oppose sanctity will be "cast into the sea." This will bring the great joy of "*tupim u'vimecholot*," rejoicing women dancing and expressing their gladness with musical instruments. Then we can proceed from the *Sidrah Beshallach* to the *Sidrah* of *Yitro*— the receiving of the Torah—when the women can truly declare as did our ancestors:("Our children shall serve as guarantors for

the future observance of the Torah."[14])

We can thus understand the commentary of the *Midrash Tanchuma*,[15] describing Miriam's song on the verse, "*Vata'an lahem Miriam*"—And Miriam answered unto them.[9] Since Miriam sang out to the women, why in the Hebrew is the third person plural *masculine* used? "*lahem*," the feminine plural form, *lahen*, would seem to be more fitting. The *Midrash* relates that when the Jews passed through the sea and sang their prayerful song of gladness, the angels also desired to sing, but G-d declared that first the Jews would sing and only then the angels.

---

14. *Shir Hashirim Rabbah* 1:3.
15. Exodus 13. See also *Shemot Rabbah* 23:7.

The *Midrash* thus explains the unusual introductory word for the song of Moses, "*yashir*"—which can be translated either as an imperative command, "sing," or as in the future tense, "will sing," rather than *shar*, "he sang," in the past tense. This was G-d's command: Moses and Israel *will sing*, and only later can the angels express themselves in song.

Afterwards, when Miriam and the women gave voice to their song, the angels once again expressed their desire to praise G-d in song, before the song of the women. The *Midrash* cites two opinions: one view is that the plea of the angels was granted; and the second, the authoritative concluding opinion, states that the woman sang before the angels. Even according to the first viewpoint that the song of the angels preceded the song of the women, the angels were not permitted to say *shirah* until Miriam granted them this privilege. Therefore "*lahem*" is in the masculine form: Miriam addressed herself to the angels and consented to their request.

All the above is a source of spiritual guidance for every Jew. There is no need to fear either Pharaoh, his harsh decrees, or his Nile River. If a Jew proceeds with his characteristic tenacity and strength, then even if he lives in Egypt where Pharaoh reigns and proclaims his cruel edicts, the destiny of Israel's children will in no way be affected. The Jew will courageously guide his children in the way of Torah, the path that brings them life not only in the world to come, but even in this physical and material world. He will lead them on the path that will cause them to say, "This is my G-d and I will glorify Him; my father's G-d and I will exalt Him,"[16] and they will continue upon the very path of their parents. This is the greatest joy and gratification that parents can receive from their children.

This will bring the fulfillment of the subsequent verse in the *shirah*: "You will bring them and plant them on the

---

16. Exodus 15:2.

mountain of your inheritance,"[17] that Israel will merit the building of the third Temple, may it occur speedily in our day.

Furthermore, the Talmud[18] adds that one can learn of G-d's great love for Israel, for the Almighty did not wait for the occurrence of "You will bring them and plant them on the mountain of your inheritance," which refers to the Holy Temple, the eternal abode of G-d, but even while they were still in the desert He said: "And they shall make Me a sanctuary and I shall abide in their midst."[19]

The above also applies to our own era and the short interval remaining until the coming of the Messiah. The Jew, undaunted by Pharaoh's decrees, will by virtue of his courage be enabled to bring up "offspring blessed by G-d;"[20] "and they shall make Me a sanctuary and I shall abide in their midst"[21]— G-d will abide in every Jewish home. And since the Jewish home is in an abode of G-d, it is self-evident that this home shall be a worthy recipient of the G-dly bestowal of bountiful sustenance and health, and that the parents shall derive joy from their children and their children's children for many long, good, joyous, blessed years.

(*Likkutei Sichot*, vol. 1, pp. 139-144)

---

17. Ibid. 15:17.
18. *Kutubot* 62b.
19. Exodus 25:8.
20. Isaiah 61:9.
21. *Resishit Chachmah, Sha'ar Ha'ahavah*, ch. 6 , etc.

TU B'SHEVAT

"MAN IS LIKE THE TREE OF THE FIELD"

Since Man is described as "a tree of the field," the different components of a tree all have a particular significance. Roots represent faith, the source of a Jew's vitality, the trunk is equivalent to Torah study and mitzvah observance, and fruit corresponds to deeds. Just as the tree depends on its roots, deeds do not have full significance unless they are based upon faith. It is only thus that a Jew can assure Torah and mitzvah observance in the future generation with the seeds of his actions leading to perpetuation of the chain of Jewish existence.

THE LESSON OF *TU B'SHEVAT*

One can learn much from the current observance of *Tu B'shevat*—the New Year for Trees[1]—for if Man pays close attention to everything that occurs around him, then from everything which happens he can increase his wisdom.[2] This pertains to matters both between man and G-d and between man and man. Nor is this limited to an unusual occurrence, but also relevant to recurrent events. Thus, even from viewing a tree we can derive many concepts affecting our daily life.

The majority of growths in the vegetative category are comprised of three parts: the root, the tree itself (trunk, branches and leaves) and the fruit (the shell or peel, the fruit itself, and the seeds).

Each one of these parts serves a different function. It is only by means of the roots that the tree stands firm and upright. If

---

1. *Rosh Hashanah*, beg.
2. *Keter Shem Tov*, additions, sec. 127-128.

its roots are firmly imbedded in the ground then there is no danger that a strong wind will come and uproot the tree. And although the root is concealed from the eye of the viewer, the tree's primary vitality is derived through this source. In addition, there are other sustaining means, as for example, the leaves absorbing necessary nutrients from the atmosphere and assimilating warmth from the sun's rays, etc.

The trunk is the major part of the tree. With the passage of time the tree grows in mass, which also causes the increase of the branches and leaves. It is particularly through analysis of the tree's trunk that experts can determine the age of the tree.

However, the primary purpose of the tree is to bear fruit, and the tree's fertility is on the most part evidenced by means of the seeds taken from its fruit and planted to cause the growth of other trees in future generations.

The Torah states, "Man is like the tree of the field."[3] In many respects, including the spiritual sense, Man is similar to a tree. Here we can also perceive three categories.

The root is equivalent to the faith of the Jew. In this manner he is connected with the realm and source of his life, G-d. Even if one has matured to significant levels in the study of Torah and the performance of *mitzvot*, the vitality of a Jew is derived through his faith in G-d and his faith in the sanctity of the Torah.

The trunk of the tree connotes the study of Torah and the fulfillment of *mitzvot* (248 positive commands equal to the 248 limbs of a human body, and 365 negative commands corresponding to the 365 sinews within the body[4]), which ideally should constitute the major part of a Jew's deeds and accomplishments. On the basis of the quantity of Torah and *mitzvot* one can determine the "significant life span of an individual," those years of a Jew's life rich in Torah knowledge and *mitzvot*.

---

3. Deuteronomy 20:19. And see *Ta'anit* 7a.
4. *Makkot* 23b; *Zohar* I 170b.

The ultimate self-realization of a Jew's life is gauged by the "fruits" he produces. For in addition to fulfilling those tasks specifically related to him, he should also concern himself with influencing others. He should endeavor that these people in turn should be trees (individuals) fully developed in their Torah identity, possessing roots (the primary qualities of faith) and a trunk with branches (Torah study and virtuous deeds), and bearing fruit (benefit to others).

A CONTINUING CYCLE

In summation, the root of a Jew and the primary aspect of his identity is pure faith. Any element of weakness in faith represents a significant threat to the sustained spiritual life of a fully grown person. This is so even if the significantly major part of his life is characterized by a constantly progressive increase in virtuous deeds.

The perfection, or "wholeness" of an individual is in the act of "bearing fruit," in influencing others and in aiding them to live meaningful lives in which they fulfill their tasks and G-d's purpose in their creation. Thus, the actions of the individual bear fruit and this fruit in turn bears other fruit—this sustained sequence constantly progressing and bearing the fruit of Torah and *mitzvot* in future generations. And all of this results from the initiative of the individual who begins the sequence.

(*Likkutei Sichot*, vol. 6, pp. 308-309)

SEVENTH OF ADAR—BIRTHDAY
AND YAHRZEIT OF MOSES

PRIDE AND HUMILITY

The following *sicha* concerns an explanation by Rabbi Schneur Zalman, the Alter Rebbe, of the small *alef* in the word "*Vayikra*" at the beginning of the book of Leviticus. The *alef* represents Moses' humility in contrast, the Alter Rebbe explains, to the large *alef* with which the name of Adam is written in the book of Chronicles, exemplifying the awareness of his own greatness that led to his sin with the Tree of the Knowledge. Why, the Rebbe asks, does the Alter Rebbe introduce the contrast with Adam, unlike most of the commentators who have discussed only the small *alef* in Moses' name? Moreover, why is the large *alef* presented as something negative in relation to Adam, while in many sources it is seen simply as indicating his lofty qualities? The answer explores the special balance which a Jew must achieve between awareness of his good qualities and humility that derives from the realization that his good qualities are "G-dly gifts which were magnanimously bestowed upon him."

THE HEIGHT OF HUMILITY

At a Pesach gathering, Rabbi Yosef Yitzchak, the sixth Rebbe, vividly described how Rabbi Schneur Zalman, the Alter Rebbe, prepared his grandson Menachem Mendel (who later became the third Lubavitcher Rebbe, the Tzemach Tzedek) for the commencement of his Torah studies.

One incident: the Alter Rebbe instructed his grandson's teacher to study the first *parshah* (section) of the Book of Leviticus with the child. When they concluded, the young Menachem Mendel asked the Alter Rebbe why the letter *alef* in the word "*Vayikra*" is written in reduced size.

The Alter Rebbe concentrated intensely for quite a while and then declared: The verse states, "*Vayikra* (and He called) to

193

Moses." However, in Chronicles[1] we find that the name of Adam, the first Man, is written with a large *alef.* Why this discrepancy?

Adam recognized his singular uniqueness, that he had been "created by the Hands of G-d." Indeed, we are told that G-d attested that "the wisdom of Adam surpassed that of the ministering heavenly angels."[2] This awareness of his own importance so influenced Adam that he succumbed to the sin of eating from the Tree of Knowledge.

Moses, too, was fully aware of his unique qualities, but this knowledge affected him in a totally different manner. It induced a broken and contrite heart and a sense of humility rather than superiority. In the words of G-d's Torah: "And the man Moses was exceedingly humble, more than all other men on the face of the earth."[3] This means that no matter how simple and minor in rank another Jew was in relation to Moses, Moses nevertheless held him in high esteem. He did so because he believed that if this Jew had been endowed, not by virtue of his own effort, but through G-d's will, with a lofty, sublime soul such as his own, and with the merit of spiritually great ancestors such as his father Amram, then that Jew would most certainly have surpassed Moses in accomplishment.

Based on his knowledge of his own greatness, Adam, the first man, erred by eating of the Tree of Knowledge. This self-perception of greatness is conveyed by the large *alef* in his name in the Torah. Moses constantly aware of his own limitations, achieved the highest level of humility, as expressed by the small *alef* in *"Vayikra."*

WHY CITE ADAM?

The Alter Rebbe's explanation presents us with a number of problems: The Tzemach Tzedek's question focused on the small *alef* of Leviticus, which symbolized Moses' humility. Why

---

1. 1.1.
2. *Bereishit Rabbah* 17:4.
3. Numbers 12:3.

did the Alter Rebbe dwell in addition on the rationale for the
large *alef* in Adam's name? Moreover, many commentaries,
when explaining the small *alef* as implying the humility of
Moses, do not mention the large *alef* of Adam at all.

The Tzemach Tzedek had just commenced his Torah
studies; he had not yet learned about the large *alef* of Adam,
which is written much further in the books of the Torah. Why
did the Alter Rebbe introduce this later text at this time?

Furthermore, we are aware that the Torah is highly
sensitive concerning the dignity of all created beings. We are
told that "the Torah will not speak disparagingly even of an
impure animal."[4] Doesn't this apply all the more to the first
man, created by the Hands of G-d, who should not be
mentioned negatively without good reason?[5]

In addition, why did the Alter Rebbe dwell at length on the
humility of Moses, rather than allude to it succinctly, as the
Torah does? Why give the details; that Moses was aware of his
greatness, but attributed it to the superior qualities and
ancestors that G-d had bestowed on him, and who believed
other Jews would have surpassed his achievements, given such
gifts?

THE SIGNIFICANCE OF LARGE LETTERS

The letters of the Torah given at Sinai appear in three sizes:
large, intermediate, and small. The Torah was primarily written
with intermediate letters, to teach us to pursue the mid-path
and to avoid extremes in the quest for piety.[6]

Superficially, it would seem that the Alter Rebbe's
explanation of the large *alef* implies that this letter expresses a
negative quality, which causes Adam to act inappropriately,
whereas the small *alef* exemplifies Moses' unique humility.

---

4.   *Baba Batra* 123a.

5.   See *Likkutei Sichot*, vol. 5, p. 281; vol. 10, pp. 26, 264 and ff.

6.   See Maimonides, *Hilchot Dei'ot*.

However, it is a self-evident principle that the large letters in the Torah are of a *higher* level than the intermediate letters, and most assuredly than the small letters.[7] This is apparent even to a small child: if the Torah uses a large letter, it is because, according to the "Torah of truth," there inheres within the letter greater significance and importance. This is the reason that many commentaries state that the large *alef* in Adam's name hints "that no one was comparable to him in greatness...or in his surpassing wisdom, which enabled him to identify every animal by its (appropriate) name.[8]

THE GREATNESS OF ADAM

In *Likkutei Torah*[9] the Alter Rebbe elaborates on the manner in which Adam is higher than Moses. The large *alef,* he declares, refers to Adam who, prior to his sin, was on a lofty and highly exalted level. He was able to receive divine influence from the high spiritual level of the "large *alef,*" which is "*Keter* as it exists in the very being and essence of G-d" (an esoteric concept in *Kabbalah*). In contrast, the Torah states, "And Moses could *not* enter the tent...for the (divine) cloud rested thereon."[10] According to the classic Chasidic interpretation, the 'cloud' refers to a divine flow from "a lofty and highly awesome realm,"[11] the sphere of *Keter* (the Crown), a realm Moses did not attain. This is why the word "*Vayikra*" was written with a small *alef,* because the divine flow and bestowal to Moses (from the cloud) was only "by means of *tzimtzum*," the contraction and condensation of higher levels of G-dliness.

Actually, the Alter Rebbe's reference to the large *alef* of Adam seems puzzlingly to contradict the sense that the small *alef* indicates Moses' greatness. Nor does it refer to Adam *after*

7. See *Or HaTorah,* vol. 11, p. 624 and ff.; *Sefer Hama'amarim 5678,* p. 234; *Sefer Hama'amarim 5699,* "*Vayadabeir Elokim*" (II); and elsewhere.

8. See *Paaneach Raza* and *Toldot Yitzchak* on this verse.

9. Leviticus 1a.

10. Exodus 40:35.

11. *Likkutei Torah,* ibid. See also sources in note 7.

he had lapsed in the sin of the Tree of Knowledge but, on the contrary, it alludes to the dimension of Adam as he was prior to the sin.

The Alter Rebbe, perhaps was not merely clarifying a textual problem; he was primarily concerned about imparting an important principle in the service of G-d, and how it is derived from the small *alef* of Leviticus.

This narrative must also be viewed within the context of my father-in-law's relating, at an earlier gathering, how and why the Alter Rebbe personally assumed the task of educating his grandson.[12] Indeed, this was the reason that he was so intimately involved in the ceremonies related to the Tzemach Tzedek's commencement of Torah study.

A SPARK OF ADAM

By elaborating upon the exalted level of Adam, who fully recognized "his own superior qualities," the Alter Rebbe wished to emphasize that this kind of recognition is necessary for every Jew, for it derives from the "spark" of Adam within his soul. As the well-known adage states, "Just as one must know one's shortcomings, so must there be awareness of one's superior qualities."[13] Indeed this knowledge of one's own greatness is a manner of serving G-d which is decreed by the Torah; it is the form of G-dly service unique to those on the level of *tzaddikim*—the great in piety.

Since Adam was "created by G-d's hands," then it is self-evident that he was totally separate from evil, since G-d his Creator is pure virtue, as the verse states: "from Him Who is Above there shall not emerge evil."[14] It is known that prior to Adam's sin there was no mingling of good with evil in the world. This was so because the *kelipot* ("shells," a Chasidic terminology for evil) were separate and distinct. Sin caused a

---

12. *Sefer Hasichot 5700* p. 40.

13. *Likkutei Dibburim*, vol. 4, 581a.

14. Lamentations 3:38.

decline in Adam and the entire world. However, since G-d's
deeds are eternal, the superior qualities instilled in Adam at the
time of creation endure within him and his descendants
forever, even after the sin—if only in concealed form.

In the precise phrasing of the Alter Rebbe: "Adam, who,
through his awareness of his superior qualities, erred with the
Tree of Knowledge, is described as 'Adam with a large *alef.*'"
These words convey to us that also after the sin he possessed
the lofty spiritual level of the large *alef.* It is well known that
Jews are called Adam: "You are called Adam."[15] This is because
in every Jewish soul there is a part, a "spark" of the soul of
Adam. His eternal, superior qualities are transmitted, to a
greater or lesser degree, to all Jews for all times.

One example of this is in the giving of names. Adam's
wisdom "surpassed even the wisdom of the heavenly
ministering angels,"[16] and he was therefore capable of giving
names to all created beings in accordance with the "living soul"
of every creature. Each Jew possesses some measure of this
quality, and as we find in the writings of the Arizal, the naming
of children by parents involves. "minor prophecy." Parents are
inspired from Above to bestow a name corresponding to the
"living soul" of their child.

Inherent in every Jew, whatever his spiritual level, is a
spiritual quality of Adam prior to the sin. The distinction,
however, is that Adam also possessed a superior physical body,
since even this physical aspect was "the creation of G-d's
Hands."[17] The holiness manifest in all Jews is only from the
soul, which is an "actual part of G-d above."[18] The soul,
therefore, has no relation to sin. As the *Zohar* comments on the
verse "If a soul should sin:"[19] "The Torah and G-d are

---

15. See *Yevamot* 61a.

16. *Bereishit Rabbah*, ibid.

17. *Bereishit Rabbah* 24:5; *Kohelet Rabbah* 3:11 .

18. See *Tanya*, ch. 1.

19. Leviticus 5a.

astonished and cry out in amazement 'if a soul should sin!'"[20]
And if a Jew should stumble in sin, even at such a time the *soul*
is still faithful to G-d.

This is the inner meaning of the verse, "Your nation are all
tzaddikim" (righteous).[21] In every Jew there exists a level of the
spirituality of *tzaddikim,* derived from the level of Adam prior to
the sin. Though a Jew may have lapsed at some time, becoming
immersed in matters contrary to virtue, yet, when he later
involves himself in Torah and *mitzvot,* such actions are derived
from the level of Adam (before the sin) that is within his soul.
This is not due to the special quality of *teshuvah*—of one who
was distant from Torah and good and has returned—but rather
the spiritual service of a *tzaddik,* one who from the very
beginning has had no link with sin or evil.

The *tzaddik* is totally removed from evil and sin from the
very start; his total existence and identity is holiness. This
exaltation of holiness in every Jew can cause an awareness of
superior qualities. Indeed, there is a necessity for such self-
knowledge, for it can serve as a basis for higher levels of service
to G-d. This inspirational pride aids him to rise above the
world's obstructions to holiness, helping the Jew serve G-d
with vigor and assertiveness, similar to the spiritual service of
tzaddikim.

STRIVING FOR HUMILITY

The Torah delineates for us the safeguards necessary for
one who recognizes his "own superior qualities." Even if one
truthfully has these traits, one must nevertheless take extreme
precaution to avoid negative consequences, as can be seen from
the example of Adam. Knowledge of his superior qualities
caused Adam to err in the matter of the Tree of Knowledge, the
sin that is the source for all subsequent evil.

---

20. *Zohar, Parshat Vayikra* 16a; see also 13b.
21. Isaiah 60:21.

Combined with this positive self-awareness, a person must also have an insight into "one's lowliness," because reliance on a sense of self-worth can cause, Heaven forbid, decline and fall. For a Jew who lacks the perfection of a *tzaddik*, "awareness of his superior qualities" must be safeguarded by his "knowledge of his own lowliness," lest the vanity engendered by self-worth make him vulnerable to evil.

This was the reason why the Alter Rebbe addressed these words to the Tzemach Tzedek at the very beginning of his Torah studies: As a child who was destined to mature not only into a *tzaddik*, but also a *Nasi*—a leader of the Jewish people, the Alter Rebbe wanted to emphasize to him the great caution necessary to avoid sin. If even Adam could err, how much more is it necessary that every *tzaddik* protect himself from the pride that can ensue from "awareness of one's worth."

We can thus understand why the Alter Rebbe dwelled at length on the nature of Moses' humility. It did not suffice to explain that Moses perceived his unique qualities as gifts magnanimously bestowed upon him; the Tzemach Tzedek (and all Jews) need to know that Moses was even more humble because of his feeling that had another individual received these qualities, then that person would have certainly surpassed him.

This implies that a Jew must strive for total humility—to be humble, and in a state of total self-nullification.[22] One indication of true nullification is not merely negation of one's self, but a conscious seeking of the superior qualities in others. This can be observed in everyday life. There are those who can be passive and tolerant when another individual humbles them. At the same time, however, he may think to himself: "True, I am of no consequence or worth, but this person who is harassing me is even more inconsequential and of even greater insignificance!"

To effect within oneself a sense of personal humility, while at the same time perceiving the worth and merit of another

---

22. See Maimonides, *Hilchot Dei'ot* 2:2.

individual entails a high level of self-nullification and spiritual service. Indeed, at the time of the giving of the Torah, there was a cleansing from the impurity caused by Adam's sin.[23] Moses, who was capable of such humility, reached so high a level that he rectified the sin of the Tree of Knowledge.

MOSES' HERITAGE

These two traits must co-exist within the person. There must be an awareness of one's superior traits *together* with personal humility. Humility, in fact, does not negate nor exclude knowledge of superior qualities. Even though a person is conscious of his superior capabilities, he cannot permit himself to succumb to a sense of personal superiority because he knows that they are G-d-given gifts and not the result of his own efforts. This humility is not unique to Moses but inheres in all Jews, because they all possess a "spark" of Moses.[24] Moreover, this awareness of personal superiority creates the *necessity* of the trait of humility, which should extend to the extreme opposite of being "extremely humble more than every man," etc.

The implication for us is that every Jew, by virtue of his spiritual heritage, has many surpassing qualities, which he must recognize. When confronted with the need to fulfill a mitzvah or a formidable spiritual task, he should not try to evade his responsibilities behind a facade of humility. The proper Torah response is that at any given moment he possesses lofty qualities which derive from Adam and his exalted level prior to the sin. No matter what the Jew's level of accomplishment up to this point, this realization must impel him to henceforth conduct himself as if, rooted in the early spirituality of Adam, he totally transcends sin.

On the other hand, he must also be mindful that these qualities are G-dly gifts which were magnanimously bestowed

---

23. *Shabbat* 146a.
24. See *Tanya*, ch. 42.

upon him. He must think that if another person would possess his qualities, then that person's accomplishments would be on a far higher level. The realization of one's spiritual uniqueness should not evoke haughtiness, but rather the quality of being "humble in one's own eyes."

Through this self-nullification he will achieve authentic greatness, as in the statement of the *Zohar:* "He who is small is great."[25] This person will merit the level of "and G-d called to Moses. *Vayikra,* "called," alludes to G-d's affection for the quality of Moses inhering to each Jewish soul. And this G-dly call, which introduces the section of the Torah dealing with sacrifices, endows a Jew with the capability of fulfilling the divine service of sacrifices, which will culminate in the fulfillment of the higher G-dly service of sacrifices as they will occur in the Third Temple: "And there we will fulfill, before You, our obligatory sacrifices...in accordance with the command of Your will"[26] speedily in our time.

                                        (*Likkutei Sichot,* vol. 17, pp. 1-8)

---

25. *Zohar Chadash* I:122b.
26. Text of *Musaf* Prayer, *Siddur Tehillat Hashem,* p. 195.

PURIM

MEGILLAT ESTHER

Why is the name for the holiday of Purim derived from the Persian language, and why does the name refer to the casting of lots that led to the initial peril of the Jewish people rather than the miraculous rescue of the Jewish people that occurred on the holiday of Purim? Why, moreover, is G-d's name not mentioned at all in the *Megillah*?

Further questions arise from Mordecai and Esther's response to the harsh decree. Logically, Mordecai, instead of donning sackcloth and ashes, should have tried to use the political influence he had among his prestigious colleagues, and particularly those who sat at the "gate of the king." Esther, too first instructed to fast three days, and that only then would she go to the king. This is surprising, for this would dim and pale the natural beauty, the very reason she found favor with him in the first place! The answers involve the themes of concealment and revelation and the spiritual reality that underlies the world of appearances.

THE NAME "PURIM"

The Talmud[1] states that if someone reads the *Megillah* in reverse order, then he has not fulfilled the mitzvah of reading the *Megillah* on Purim. Rabbi Israel Baal Shem Tov explains[2] this to mean that if someone views the *Megillah retrospectively*, as just the record of an event of the past, believing that the Purim miracle is not linked to present times, he has not fulfilled his *Megillah* obligation. The purpose of the *Megillah* reading is to use it as a guide from which we derive and learn proper Jewish conduct in *our* own times. This is true of the *Megillah* narrative in general, and particularly in relation to the verse which explains the term "Purim."

---

1. *Megillah* 17a.
2. *Divrei Shalom, Bo.*

The name of a thing indicates its uniqueness.[3] This verse, therefore, reveals the inner meaning of "Purim," for the word itself conveys a primary concept in the *Megillah*, a concept which serves as an eternal lesson for the whole Jewish people as well as for each individual Jew.

The verse states, "Therefore these days are called 'Purim'— based on the *pur*."[4]

A number of questions can be raised when we study this passage. The *Megillah* is written in Hebrew, yet the word *pur* is not a Hebrew word, but a Persian one.[5] The verse itself, after stating[6] "Cast a *pur*" adds the translation in Hebrew—"this is the *goral*, the lot (as in casting lots)." The first question that arises is why this holiday is called "Purim—according to the name of the *pur*," the Hebrew word *goralot* (lots) would seem to be more appropriate? For all other Jewish holidays, including Chanukah (which like Purim is Rabbinic), are designated by Hebrew names. Moreover, shouldn't the name of this holiday express, as is the case with all other holidays, the miracle and rescue and cause for thanksgiving? The name *pur* refers to the very reverse, for this casting lots was the means that the wicked Haman intended to use to destroy and annihilate the Jewish people.

Additionally, G-d's name is not cited anywhere in the entire *Megillah*. This is in singular variance with other works of the Holy Scriptures, for in each and every one of them G-d's name is mentioned at least several times. This omission connotes an unusually great concealment of G-dliness.[7] In general, invoking G-d's name is a matter of common practice. Thus, when Jews engage in casual social conversation, "the

---

3. See *Or Torah* by the Maggid of Mezeritch 4b and ff. *Tanya Sh'ar Hayichud Veha'emunah*, ch. 1 and ff.

4. Esther 9:26.

5. Ibn Ezra, ibid. 3:7.

6. Esther 9:24.

7. See introduction of Ibn Ezra to Esther.

name of G-d is frequent upon their lips,"[8] and the custom of writing "*Baruch Hashem*" (by the grace of G-d) at the beginning of a letter is a matter of formal practice common to Jews all over the world, even in purely social correspondence. The reason for this is that since "the world is filled with G-d's glory"[9] and "there is no realm void of Him,"[10] it is self-evident to each Jew that all matters within the total scope of existence are related to G-d's divine providence.

Yet surprisingly, in the entire *Megillah*, which is one of the twenty-four sacred books of the Bible, we do not find G-d's name cited even once.

CONCEALMENT AND REVELATION

As mentioned, the Hebrew name of an entity conveys its unique nature. The quality of hiding and concealment within the *Megillah* is indicated by its very name. The *Megillah* is called "*Megillat Esther*" and the word *Ester* is related by the Talmud to *seiter* (concealment).[11] Beyond this, the Talmud relates the name to G-d's declaration "*haster astir*" ("I shall surely conceal [My face]),"[12] with a repetition of the verb *conceal,* an extreme form of concealment.

Yet in total contrast to this, the book of Esther is often simply called the "*Megillah*." The word *Megillah* is etymologically linked to the word *gilui,*[13] which means openness and revelation, the very opposite of concealment.

The two opposing motifs of concealment and revelation are apparent not only in the *Megillah*, but in the very holiday of Purim itself. On the one hand, this festival is called "Purim," a Persian term for the means used to devise the evil decree against the Jews, which reflects the concealment of G-dliness.

---

8. See *Torah Or* 14b; *Ma'amarei Admor Hazakein 5565* vol. 1, p. 12; etc.

9. Isaiah 6:3.

10. *Tikkunei Zohar, Tikkun* 57.

11. *Chulin* 139b.

12. Deuteronomy 31:18.

13. *Pri Eitz Chaim, Sha'ar HaPurim*, ch. 5. *Torah Or* 119a.

In contrast to this, Purim is observed with feasting and rejoicing in far greater measure than other holidays, a joy so boundless *"ad delo yada"*—till we can no longer distinguish between self-evident opposites.[14]

RESPONDING TO THE DECREE

We must preface our discussion and clarification of these questions with a primary concept which is derived from the *Megillah* and the observance of Purim.[15]

At the time of Haman's decree, the Jewish people possessed eminent representatives in the Persian government. Mordecai had gained the distinction of being among those who "sat at the gate of the king;"[16] in addition he had saved the king's life.[17] Esther was the queen, with the added uniqueness of having been chosen by the king because she found "grace and favor before him."

At first glance, the logical immediate response to the evil decree would have been to have prominent personalities of that time exert their influence upon the king to have him nullify the decree.

The *Megillah*, however, relates that Mordecai's very first response was "to don sackcloth and ashes and go out into the center of the city."[18] He was occupied with repentance, and he called on all other Jews to repent.[19] Only afterward did he ask Esther "to go before the king and entreat and beseech him for her nation."[20] Esther conducted herself similarly. Before going to the king she sent a message to Mordecai, "Go gather all the Jews and fast for me, neither eat nor drink three days both day

---

14. See *Megillah* 7b.
15. See next chapter.
16. Esther 2:19. And see *Megilah* 13a.
17. Esther 2:21 and ff.
18. Esther 4:2.
19. *Targum Sheini* Esther 2:1.
20. Esther 4:8.

and night," and this did not suffice, for she also stated, "And I...will fast as well."[21]

Was this appropriate conduct for Esther? At that perilous moment, her primary concern should have been to once again evoke favor in the king's eyes, especially since her entrance into the king's court was "not in accordance with the law"[21] and actually quite dangerous. A higher measure of "favor" in the king's eyes was necessary at this point, for as Esther stated, "I have not been called to the king for thirty days,"[22] and anyone entering the court without having been summoned, was put to death unless the king intervened. How could she justify an uninterrupted three-day fast, which in normal circumstances would only dim and sap her natural beauty at a time when she needed it most?

CONFRONTING THE UNDERLYING CAUSES

The simple explanation of this conduct is that Mordecai and Esther were certain that the decree against the Jewish people was not a result of natural worldly circumstances, a matter of chance occurrence, but that "because of their evil deed, G-d had brought suffering upon them."[23] It was apparent to them that the *result* (Haman's evil decree) could not be nullified without the removal of the *cause*—the improper conduct of the Jewish people. Therefore, their immediate response was to call Jews to repentance, decree a fast, etc.

The call to repentance did not suffice: they also explicitly delineated the nature of the Jewish people's transgressions. As the *Midrash* explains,[24] "Fast for me, neither eating nor drinking"[21] was decreed because "you are obligated to fast because you ate and drank at the banquet of Ahasuerus." Only after removing the cause for the decree through repentance did

---

21. Esther 4:16.

22. Esther 4:11.

23. See Maimonides *Hilchot Ta'aniot*, 1: 2, 3.

24. *Yalkut Shimoni* on Esther, *remez* 1056.

they concern themselves with natural means, normal channels of action, to cope with the situation. G-d also desires human action, which assures that "G-d will bless you in all that you will *do*"[25]—we must "do," using ordinary human action. But only *after* inspiring the entire Jewish nation to repentance was the effort exerted to intercede with King Ahasuerus for the nullification of the decree.

The audience with Ahasuerus was merely the human means of eliciting the G-dly deliverance in the context of natural turn of events. However, the actual cause of the rescue of the Jewish people was their repentance and fasting. Consequently, the primary effort was not directed to the external reality, to the political events, rather, the essential stress was directed towards the spiritual factors which were the "cause" for the decree.

THE LESSON FOR ALL TIMES

The spiritual implications of this event are manifestly clear: When a time of adversity occurs, there are those who think that the first and primary endeavor should be to seek a natural remedy. The *Megillah*, however, tells us that this must come *later*, after having first strengthened the link of the Jewish people with G-d by learning Torah and fulfilling His *mitzvot*. Only then should a natural means and external "garb" be sought to cope with the difficulty. If there is true realization of the primacy of repentance, then any external vestment or natural efforts expended later will be adequate for bringing the miraculous rescue from a realm far beyond nature.

This applies not only to the Jewish people in general, but to each individual Jew. Each Jew must know[26] that he is united with G-d, Who is not limited in any way by the laws of nature. True, actions must be taken, as indicated by the Biblical words in "All that you *do*," but this is so that the Biblical assurance that

---

25. Deuteronomy 15:18.
26. See *Derech Mitzvotecha* 107a and ff.

G-d "will bless you" should have some outer "garb" or natural expression. Since Man's action is only an external "vestment," it is self-evident that the primary effort should not be on this external "garb," but on the efforts to be worthy of receiving G-d's blessings. This is accomplished through studying Torah and performing *mitzvot*.

However, if a Jew neglects the basic response and is overly concerned with the outer means, this is comparable to one who goes to a bank to withdraw money and yet has no check, or to a person who uses a check from someone without an account. A Jew's first concern should be with obtaining a "check," not a check from the "wells with shattered walls that cannot contain the waters,"[27] but rather one from He Who has said "Mine is the silver, and Mine is the gold."[28] Only after he possesses the "check"—true spiritual merit—only then can he exchange it using the "garb" of natural means for G-d's blessing in "all that you do."

One would think that this applies only at a time when G-dliness is manifest in the world, and not when the Jewish people are in exile, particularly in the pre-Messianic era when great spiritual darkness prevails.

But here we see that at the time of Purim, when Jews were in exile, "scattered and dispersed among the nations"[29] (and this state of exile still persisted even *after the miracle*, as the Talmud declares "we are still the servants of Ahasuerus"[30]), the Purim miracle came not through natural means, but as a result of "Fast for me...for three days," which resulted in the return of the Jewish people to G-d.

THE TRUE PURPOSE OF CONCEALMENT

This, therefore, is the rational for the name "Purim," a Persian word which refers to the evil decree. It is also the reason

---

27. Jeremiah 2:13.
28. *Haggai* 2:8.
29. Esther 3:8.
30. *Megillah* 14a.

why G-d's name is not mentioned explicitly but only by allusion. This is the special concept of Purim and *Megillat Esther*.

In fact, Jews are not subordinate to the laws of nature, neither in the spiritual dimension of their lives (as, for example, divine aid in gaining true insight and understanding in one's Torah study, a reward for sincere piety), nor in material and worldly matters. This transcendence of nature's laws applies when it is necessary to be involved with the Persian "Purim" and "*Esther*," meaning concealment. It is explained in many Chasidic sources[31] that the Persian "*pur*"—the Hebrew "*goral*" (lots)—refers to a lofty level above and beyond the development and creation of the spiritual and material worlds. Also the Biblical phrase "*haster astir*" with its double use of the word "conceal," is preceded by the pronoun "*Anochi*," which is the very first word of the Ten Commandments[32] and higher than all the names of G-d, even the four lettered name *Havayeh*. It refers to a lofty level of G-dly selfhood that cannot even be alluded to by either a "letter of the Hebrew alphabet or even a point of the letter."[33]

Thus, when a Jew reads *Megillat Esther* and internalizes the realization that even those matters which appear as "*Esther*," as in the Biblical phrase of two-fold G-dly concealment, are actually linked to *Megillah*—meaning revelation—then he possesses the knowledge that even the *pur* cast by the evil Haman was really the Hebrew "*goral*"—and all of this is not just an event of the past, but something eternally contemporary and relevant.

Then the Jew advances to the highest level of revelation: *Megillah*—manifest G-dliness—which evokes a progressively greater joy *ad delo yada*—a boundless unlimited joy.

The Talmud states that in a leap year, when there is an added month of *Adar*, Purim is observed in the second *Adar* in

---

31. See *Torah Or* 120d, 123c.

32. Exodus 20:2.

33. *Zohar* III 257b; *Likkutei Torah*, Numbers 80b.

order to "link liberation with liberation,"[34] to link the miracle of Purim with the holiday of Pesach, which takes place in the following month of *Nissan*. If the Jewish people observe Purim with proper joyousness and understanding, then they will move forward from "liberation to liberation," from the rescue of Purim to the Messianic redemption, which is Biblically compared to the exodus from Egypt commemorated on Pesach.[35] At that time "the night shall shine as day,"[36] the darkness of night will be transformed into a source of spiritual radiance. From the "*Ester*" of concealment there shall occur the "*Megillah*" of revelations—with the coming of our righteous *Mashiach*, may he come and redeem us speedily and in our days.

(Likkutei Sichot, vol. 6, pp. 189-195*)*

---

34. See *Megillah* 6b.
35. Micah 7:15.
36. *Psalms* 139:12.

PURIM

THE MIRACULOUS
AND THE NATURAL

This *sicha* begins by examining the puzzling fact that the harshest decree in Jewish history (mandating total annihilation of the Jewish people) occurred in what was apparently one of the times of greatest physical prosperity. The explanation focuses on the fact that, as the Rebbe puts it, "Jews and the natural course of events are two distinct realms." As explored in the both the previous *sicha* and this one, the response of Esther and Mordecai was to address the spiritual causes for the decree and this led to the miraculous rescue and survival of the Jewish people. The lesson, both for those involved in mundane endeavors and those involved in Torah study, is that success depends on a Jew's realization that "all of his concerns are dependent upon and derived from G-d Himself, Who is not limited by natural laws."

THE HARSHEST DECREE

We observe the holiday of Purim to commemorate G-d's miraculous deliverance of the Jewish people from the decree of extermination.

The period in which these events occurred, perceived in a natural context, was one of the happiest eras in the history of the entire Diaspora. The Jewish people had achieved a significant role in the government. Mordecai, the head of the *Sanhedrin*,[1] was also a high government official who sat amongst those assembled at the "gate of the King."[2] Esther was the wife of King Ahasuerus, and as the Talmud states, "One's wife is

---

1. *Pirkei DeRebbi Eliezer*, ch. 50.
2. Esther 2:19.

comparable to one's own body."[3] In all of Jewish history, there is no instance other than that of Queen Esther, when a Jewish woman was the wife of a monarch, and one who reigned over the entire civilized world.[4] It is therefore self-evident that there was no other period in the span of our long exile when Jews could be as confident of their safety as in the time of Ahasuerus.

In actuality, however, the opposite turn of events came to pass. Precisely during this period, when the Jewish people were ostensibly so secure, there occurred the decree "to destroy, slay and annihilate,"[5] all the Jews from "the youth to the aged, infants and children all in one day."[5] This was the harshest decree ever proclaimed against Jews; never in the course of history was there promulgated so absolute an edict of destruction against all Jews as during the time of Ahasuerus.

During other times of exile, Jews were scattered throughout in various lands. Our Sages state, "G-d had done us an act of kindness by dispersing us among the nations."[6] If one nation would proclaim an edict of destruction against the Jews in its domain, then the Jews in other lands would remain unharmed, and other countries could provide refuge.

Even during the era of Pharaoh, when all Jews were subject to his sovereignty and it was utterly impossible to escape from Egypt, as our Sages relate, "Even a single slave was unable to flee from there,"[7] the decree did not apply to all the Jews, but only to the males.[8] However, at the time of Ahasuerus, all the Jews were subject to his rule and there was no possibility of flight for the following reasons: a) he ruled with firm authority over the *entire* populated world, thus no place of refuge existed; b) he desired to destroy all the Jews in *one day*, thus there was

---

3. *Berachot* 24a.
4. *Megilah* 11a.
5. Esther 3:13.
6. *Pesachim* 87b.
7. *Mechilta* and Rashi, Exodus 18:9.
8. Exodus 1:16, *Sotah* 12a.

no time to flee; c) the decree was for the annihilation of *all the Jews without exception*.

BEHIND THE VEIL OF EXILE

How, one must ask, in the normal course of events, in an era when Jews were ostensibly so secure, could such a frightening edict be decreed?

The Talmud gives us the reason for these events: "Because they (the Jews) derived pleasure from the banquet of that evil individual"[9]—from the feast of Ahasuerus.

This is a clear indication that Jews and the *natural* course of events are two distinct realms. Divine Providence in relation to Jews is not subject to the laws of nature.[10] Their fate is wholly dependent upon the fulfillment of the Torah and its commandments. Thus, although it would have been utterly illogical to predict the evil decree in the normal order of things, the pleasure the Jews derived from the forbidden repast resulted—as a consequence of their special fate—in an edict of annihilation.

The same principle can also be seen in the manner in which G-d saved them and caused their triumph. The nullification of the harsh decree did not come about due to a normal sequence of events, but rather by means of their repentance and total commitment to G-d.

When Mordecai and Esther were informed of the edict, it seems plausible that their first endeavor should have been to proceed with a diplomatic mission in an effort to sway Ahasuerus. The *Megillah* relates, however, that the first words of Esther to Mordecai were, "Go and gather all the Jews that are present in Shushan, and fast for me, and neither eat nor drink three days, night and day."[11] This was the initial attempt to nullify the decree.

---

9. *Megillah* 12a.

10. See previous chapter, p. 210.

11. Esther 4:16.

In addition, Esther declared to Mordecai, "I and my maidens shall also fast as well."[11] Esther's queenly role was based upon "And she found favor and grace before him more than all the other young women."[12] It is quite apparent that by fasting for three consecutive days her beauty would, according to normal expectation, hardly be enhanced; in fact, it would be diminished.[13] How then was the decision to fast justified?

The answer to this question is as follows: just as the decree itself was an unnatural occurrence, so too, the redemption would not be by normal means. The rescue of the Jews was accomplished through repentance, and one of the acts of penitence is fasting. Since all Jews in Shushan were fasting, it is prohibited for an individual to deviate from the practice of the community,[14] consequently it is obvious that "I any my maidens shall likewise fast." As for the lessening of Esther's beauty, it is of course true that "One does not rely upon anticipating miracles,"[15] and one must function within the external forms and appearances of nature, i.e., natural cause and effect.

All of this, however, is still only the external *form* and appearance, and not the real cause for the rescue of the Jewish people. The external appearance of things is not of primary importance. If the real cause—the strengthening of one's self in Torah and its commandments—is adequate, then a minimal superficial conformity with natural reality will suffice.

It is only because of the veil of exile that the decree and subsequent redemption were cloaked in the guise of normal events. The true reasons were the neglect and subsequent rededication to Torah and its commandments. The pleasure the Jews derived from the feast of the evil tyrant caused the edict,

---

12. Esther 2:17.

13. See Ibn Ezra on Esther 4:16.

14. Maimonides, *Hilchot Teshuvah* 3:11.

15. Pesachim 64b.

and their fasting and repentance nullified the king's harsh commands.

BEYOND THE LAWS OF NATURE

The teachings to be derived form this narrative and its implications for our times are as follows: There are those who contend that the means for sustaining the existence of the Jewish people in exile are only diplomacy and other worldly efforts and they attempt to substantiate their claims from the manner used to sway Ahasuerus. It must be stated that not only do such individuals interpret the Torah not in accordance with its authentic meaning, but also their explanation reveals a faithlessness concerning the entire existence of the Jewish people.

The Torah states, "You are all standing this day."[16] Our Sages interpret this verse to mean that "even when the entire world wavers, you stand in a firm and secure manner."[17] That is, the existence of other nations is in accord with the laws of nature.[18] Jews, however, are not bound by nature; our bond is solely with the Torah and its commandments.

At a time of adversity or of an evil proclamation, we should not rely merely upon diplomacy and efforts by the nations of the world. Such efforts do not assure our survival. Instead, it is necessary for us to scrutinize our deeds,[19] correct that which is lacking, and strengthen ourselves in the fulfillment of the Torah and its commandments. *Then* our normal efforts will succeed. Even though others in a similar situation, using these same means, would be wholly unsuccessful, we shall be worthy of "you stand," in a firm and enduring manner.

Moreover, we need not be apprehensive about the situation of the Jewish people as it is perceived with mortal eyes, in accordance with the laws of nature. Our task is to evoke

16. Deuteronomy 29:9 and *Sifri* there. And see *Derech Mitzvotecha* 106a and ff.

17. See *Sanhedrin* 4b; *Midrash Hagadol* Deuteronomy 29:9.

18. *Shabbat* 156a, b.

19. *Berachot* 5a.

strength in the fulfillment of Torah and its commands, for then any external actions that we undertake will be endowed with miraculous success, derived from the divine realm beyond the laws of nature.

PRIMARY REALITY—G-D'S BLESSING

The principle that Jews are not subject to nature is not only descriptive of the Jewish nation collectively, but also of each Jew individually. A Jew must be mindful that all of his concerns are dependent upon and derived from G-d Himself, Who is not limited by natural laws.

True, there does exist the need for action, "in all that you *do*,"[20] which will consequently be endowed with "and the Lord thy G-d will bless you."[21] This, however, is only a function of external appearance. The primary reality is G-d's blessing, which occurs because of the bond with G-d resulting from the study of Torah and the fulfillment of its commandments. When an individual possesses this primary aspect, then he will assuredly succeed with the external means he utilizes.

With this insight, we can understand a text in the Jerusalem Talmud[22] which states that the planter "has faith in He Who lives eternally and [therefore he] plants." That is, he plants because he believes in and depends upon G-d to make the crop grow. At first glance, though, it is difficult to comprehend how this attitude is a manifestation of faith. Even those who are heretical and lack faith in G-d sow their crops, for it is a natural sequence of events that after sowing the harvest emerges?

The meaning of this passage, however, is its special definition of the faith of a Jew. The growth of crops is not a phenomenon manifestly dependent upon faith and trust in G-d, since persons wholly remote from G-d also benefit from the growth of their planted crops. Nevertheless, the Jew possesses the awareness that he is unique and distinct in

---

20. Deuteronomy 15:18.

21. Ibid.

22. Cited by *Tosafot*, *Shabbat* 31a.

comparison to the entire world, for the individual Jew's destiny is not dependent upon nature. Therefore, he knows that although crops grow for the entire world as a function of the laws of nature, they flourish for him only as a result of his belief and trust in G-d.

This is true not only for persons involved in commercial endeavors, but, also, for those whose lives are wholly dedicated to Torah study. True success in Torah is not a function of superior talents or other qualities, but is dependent upon Heavenly aid which comes because of spiritual reverence. This emotion causes a person to study devotedly and with intense effort—with the result that he *"find"*[23] in far greater measure than would normally be commensurate with his efforts, for "finding" implies a great discovery, far surpassing the degree of one's efforts. If there is an absence of the essential factor, then talent and endeavor are of no avail, for Torah is G-d's wisdom. However, when reverence and love of G-d are present, then G-d causes great success, success far beyond the norm.

(Likkutei Sichot, vol. 1, pp. 213-214*)*

---

23. *Megillah* 6b.

PESACH

EXILE AND REDEMPTION: THEN AND NOW

Pharaoh, in his evil plans to harm the Jewish people, speaks about slaying the male children, but regarding the female children there is a subtle distinction. When speaking to the Jewish midwives he says, *"vechaya"* ("and they shall live") whereas in speaking to the Egyptians, he uses the word *"techayun,"* meaning "to vivify, animate, be their life source." Thus, the Rebbe states that Pharaoh, who exemplifies all forms of exile, uses as a stratagem either the physical annihilation of the Jewish people or attempting to vivify and adrenalize them with the vibrancy of alien cultures and thus alienate them from Judaism.

In this *sicha* the Rebbe dwells upon the heroism of the Jewish women, who chose to have children, and who inspired their husbands from despondency and despair to faith in the future of the Jewish people. Similarly, parents providing their children with a Torah education with teachers who inspire them to the fulfillment of Torah and *mitzvot* will bring about the realization of G-d's promise "I will show him wonders" in the future Messianic redemption.

PHYSICAL AND SPIRITUAL DESTRUCTION

"Every son that is born you shall cast into the Nile and every daughter you shall cause to live,"[1] such was Pharaoh's stern decree to the Egyptians. Concerning this verse, the question is asked:[2] What need was there for Pharaoh to conclude "and every daughter shall you cause to live"? Since his primary concern was that the newly born Jewish male children should be cast

---

1. Exodus 1:22.
2. See *Shemot Rabbah* 1:18.

221

into the Nile, one would think that the fate of the female children would not interest to him. Yet the very fact that he concluded with the statement "and every daughter you shall cause to live" implies that this, too, was a decree.

The explanation of this decree, "you shall cause to live," to the Egyptians (in Hebrew, "*yechayun*") is that *you*, the Egyptians, should not merely let them live, *you* should be the dominating influence of their lives. The very same Egyptians whom Pharaoh had commanded to cast Jewish baby boys in the Nile in order to destroy their bodies were also instructed about the survivors, the girls. Those children who remained physically alive should be "caused to live" by the Egyptians; the Egyptians were to educate them in their culture, in the life-styles of Egypt, in order to destroy their souls.

Consequently we can understand the reason why Pharaoh expressed himself differently concerning the decree to the Jewish midwives. On that occasion, he spoke only of not harming the daughters, in order to more easily sway the midwives to obey his command to harm the sons—but he did not say "*techayun*" to them, rather "*vechaya*" ("she will remain alive").[3]

The fact that the Torah includes the two commands about the males and females in the very same verse indicates that "You shall cause to live" is as severe a decree as "Every male child shall be cast into the sea." The destruction of the soul is as significant as the destruction of the body; spiritual annihilation is, in fact even more severe than physical destruction.[4]

The aforementioned decree of "Every daughter you shall cause to live"—of educating Jewish children in the life-styles of Egypt—is also included in the prior command of casting the male children into the Nile. The river Nile was the pagan deity of the Egyptians. On a simple level, the Nile was the source of their economic well-being, since rain does not fall in Egypt and

---

3. Exodus 1:16.
4. *Derech Chaim*, ch. 1; and see Rashi, Deuteronomy 23:9.

the fields are watered by the river.[5] Thus, the command to cast the children into the river has two implications: first, their physical destruction; and second, their spiritual destruction. By casting them into the Nile, the pagan object of worship and the source of Egyptian corporeal pleasure, the Egyptians would destroy their souls. The Nile embodied the concept of pleasure because it was comprised of water which "causes all manner of pleasurable objects to grow."[6] Pleasure pursued for its own sake without service to G-d leads to self-indulgence, and constant self-indulgence in turn culminates in yielding to matters that are completely forbidden, and finally to the destruction of the soul.

THE MODERN PHARAOH

The exile of Egypt is the prototype for all subsequent exiles.[7] It is thus self-evident that decrees similar to those enacted in Egypt existed in all exiles, including the present one, even in this very generation.

Today, too, Pharaoh the king of Egypt still exists in the guise of modes and norms of alien cultures, in the demand that Jewish children should be cast into the mold of assimilation. Our little children, says the modern Pharaoh, should be submerged in the river, in whatever will ostensibly provide them with economic sustenance. Jewish children should be placed into the walls of Pithom and Ramses,[8] the treasure cities of Egypt; they should be wholly involved in those matters which symbolize the economic power and most intensive preoccupation of the land.

It is therefore necessary to know that all the contentions of "Come let us deal wisely with Him,"[9] i.e. "with their G-d,"[10] is

---

5. Rashi, Exodus 7:17.

6. See *Tanya* chapter 1.

7. *Bereishit Rabbah* 16:4.

8. See *Sanhedrin* 111a; *Pirkei DeRebbi Eliezer*, ch. 48.

9. Exodus 1:10.

10. *Shemot Rabbah* 1:9.

still derived from Pharaoh, king of Egypt. He desires that no remnant of Judaism survive, no remnant of Jewish souls nor of Jewish bodies. Consequently, we must stand with the greatest fortitude against his decrees and educate our children in the spirit of eternal Israel.

Practically, this means that when we are involved with the education of Jewish children, it is not only unnecessary, but actually forbidden to immerse them in the rituals of the land. It is prohibited to overwhelm children with concern about the pursuit of adult economic and occupational goals. The soul's way of life is a complete and thorough Torah education with the "Torah of life."

There is no need to concern ourselves with other parents who push their children to high degrees of occupational proficiency and economic achievement. Nor should there be apprehension that one's son in a *yeshivah* will not be capable of mastering simple tasks or elementary skills.

We must never forget that G-d provides and sustains all living creatures, and if we act in accordance with His will— "And you shall teach them to your sons and speak of them when sitting in your house, when walking on a path, when you lie down, and when you rise"[11]—then He shall do as we beseech Him, for ourselves and for our children.

As part of this thorough Torah education, the child should be under the tutelage of a teacher who is himself devoted to our Torah, the "Torah of life," one who lives "in them"[12]—that is, within the commandments of the Torah. The teacher will then educate his students in his own way on the life-path of Torah and its commands. By this means we will save our children and thereby also the entire Jewish nation.

---

11. Deuteronomy 6:7.
12. Leviticus 18:5.

"I WILL SHOW HIM WONDERS"

Just as the exile of Egypt is the root of all exiles, and therefore the decrees of that era exist in our own times as mentioned above, the exodus from Egypt is the prototype for the future redemption.

The prophet states, "As in the day of your departure from Egypt, I shall show him wonders"[13]—the ultimate redemption will be similar to the exodus from Egypt. This implies that the preparations and the means for the final redemption must likewise be similar to those that brought about the departure from Egypt.

Regarding the exodus from Egypt it is written, "Due to the merit of righteous women in that generation our forefathers were redeemed from Egypt."[14] What was the meritorious action of the righteous women? They were not afraid to establish a generation of Jews.

When Pharaoh proclaimed his harsh decree, the women asserted: "We must not concern ourselves with Pharaoh's edict that every male child must be cast into the sea. Since G-d has so commanded us, we must continue to bear children despite Pharaoh's decree. The future and ultimate purpose are His concern, not ours."[15] Due to the merit of these righteous women, our ancestors were freed from Pharaoh and liberated from Egypt.

In our age also, in every land and particularly in America, we must not concern ourselves with the material goals that are pursued so intensively by others, nor be preoccupied with economic goals. We must educate our children as G-d has commanded us, and the Almighty will provide for the children and their parents.

---

13. *Micah* 7:15.

14. *Sotah* 11:2.

15. Ibid. 12a.

By ignoring the decree of Pharaoh we shall merit the rescue of our own children, and this will cause the general redemption of the entire Jewish nation through our righteous *Mashiach*, may he come speedily.

(*Likkutei Sichot,* vol. 1, pp. 111-113)

PESACH

SLAVERY AND FREEDOM— MODERN PARALLELS

The Torah states that a Jewish slave may not be subjected to overly oppressive labor. Maimonides defines this as work which is "without purpose" or without limit." The *Hagahot Maimonit* derives this from the Biblical description of the Egyptian servitude of the Jewish people, "'and they embittered their lives.' In what manner? With work devoid of limit or purpose." This has modern parallels both physically and spiritually. An individual can be "self-enslaved," obsessed with business success, expending all his energies on this goal. Thus, his efforts are "without limit," dreaming even at night of stratagems to increase his income. They are also "without purpose," for it is G-d who is the actual source of material success. Spiritually, a Torah scholar may be similarly "enslaved," with concern for his "dignity and other vain fancies."

The remedy is service of G-d, "without limit" or "without purpose"—without concern for physical gratification—as exemplified by the heroism of the Jewish people at the time of their liberation from Egypt.

SPIRITUAL EMBITTERMENT

One of the basic tenets of Judaism is that the true life of a Jew is not the physical aspect of his existence but its spiritual dimension.[1] Taking this into consideration, the phrase "And they embittered their lives,"[2] the Torah's description of Pharaoh's oppression of the Jewish people, requires further explanation. True, our Sages voiced the principle that "the text

---

1. See *Igeret Hakodesh*, ch. 27.
2. Exodus 1:14.

of a Torah verse does not depart from its plain meaning,"[3] but if the essence of life is its spiritual dimension, then this verse also implies that the Egyptians embittered the *spiritual* lives of the Jews through the arduous labor of working with "mortar and bricks," etc.

This requires clarification: Intense labor can embitter one's physical life, but how could the demanding labor with "mortar and bricks" affect their *spiritual* lives? True, exacting work can distract and impede the desire to study Torah and do *mitzvot*. The precise wording used by the Torah, however, is that these tasks *embittered* their lives, not merely hindered, causing bitterness in their very spiritual lives. How is this possible, and in what manner is this to be understood?

Torah law states that a Jewish slave may not be subjected to "overly oppressive labor." Maimonides explains that this refers to any task which is "without purpose" or "without limit."[4] *Hagahot Maimonit*, a commentary on Maimonides, states that this law is derived from the Scriptural description of the harshness of the Egyptian exile, and that the oppressive labor in Egypt was "purposeless" and "limitless." We thus gain insight into the spiritual embitterment of Jewish life in Egypt.

When a Jew applies himself to material matters in accordance with Torah principles, then his material and vocational tasks have a "limit" and a "purpose." Indeed, the Torah explicitly states the degree to which a Jew may be preoccupied with his livelihood: He should involve himself only to the extent necessary for making a "vessel" and means to receive G-d's blessing. There is thus a "limit" imposed upon his efforts to make a living. The word "hands" from the verse in Psalms[5] "When you eat (from) the labor of your hands" refers to an external and lower aspect of one's selfhood, not one's higher, innate talent and soul powers.[6] The amount of time one

---

3.   *Shabbat* 63a.

4.   *Mishneh Torah; Hilchot Avadim* 1:6.

5.   Psalms 128:1.

6.   *Likkutei Torah* Numbers 42d; 66c.

may devote to material pursuits is also limited by Torah. When allocating this time it is necessary to provide for adequate time, every day, to pray with a *minyan* and maintain set times for Torah study. This assures that his labors will be with purpose; since his work conforms to Torah's guidelines, his "doing" and labor will be a vessel and means by which "G-d your G-d will bless you."[7]

However, when one expends all his energies for material gain, his mind constantly preoccupied with various stratagems to increase his profits, this is a labor which is "limitless" and "purposeless." His striving is "without purpose," for as the verse declares: "Nor is there bread for the wise,"[8] for G-d is the sole source of Man's material sustenance and Man cannot create his own material wealth. On the contrary, his effort may well be counterproductive.[9]

This striving for material gain can also be described as "without limit," for there may be no limitations to an individual's preoccupation and efforts. To illustrate: It is already night, the personnel have all left for home, and it is time to close the shop. But the shop owner is still preoccupied with his business. Even when the shop is closed and the proprietor is home, his mind is still fixed on the pursuit of profits instead of on setting aside a regular time for Torah study, whether Talmud or *Chasidut*, or any other area of Torah study. He is obsessed with his business; even when he is not physically involved, his mind is preoccupied with his monetary pursuits. When he goes to sleep, "his thoughts come to him in bed."[10] His mind pulsates with original ways to advance his business, and his dreams abound with the ideas with which he has been obsessed all day.[11]

---

7. Deuteronomy 15:18; and see *Derech Mitzvotecha* 106a and ff.

8. Ecclesiastes 9:11.

9. See *Derech Mitzvotecha* 107b.

10. See Daniel 2:29.

11. See *Berachot* 55b.

THE ENSLAVEMENT OF THE TORAH SCHOLAR

This relentless pursuit can also obsess a Torah scholar. Although not concerned with financial pursuits, he can be enslaved by concern for his dignity and other vain fantasies. Perhaps he believes that someone has offended him, and since he is a Torah scholar, he must be zealous in the defense of *kavod haTorah*—the dignity of Torah. And since the "righteous are similar to their Creator,"[12] then he must proceed in the ways of his Maker. Just as G-d, as it were, repays, "measure for measure,"[13] he, too, is obligated to exact retribution for the perceived slight. If he values *kavod haTorah*—"the honor of the Torah"—then he must inflict "double" and "quadruple" retribution on the perpetrator. This idea can possess him to the exclusion of other thoughts; even upon going to sleep, the *cheshbon hanefesh*—spiritual accounting—required prior to sleep is his preoccupation with this one concern. And of course it will inevitably affect his dreams.

"YOU SHALL INDEED HELP WITH HIM"

Concern with one's physical well-being is justifiable for, as Maimonides states, guarding "the health and well-being of the body"[14] is one of the ways of serving G-d, since a healthy body is necessary for serving G-d. This can be understood even more profoundly by means of the Chasidic explanation of the verse "You shall indeed help with him,"[15] which instructs us to help a fellow Jew by lightening the load of an overburdened animal. Rabbi Israel Baal Shem Tov explained[16] that, in addition to the plain meaning, this verse teaches that one should not *withdraw* into a life of spiritual *isolation*; the soul must "help" and strive to edify and refine the physical body in which it abides. This is

---

12. *Rut Rabbah* 4:3.

13. See *Sanhedrin* 90a , etc.

14. Maimonides, *Hilchot Dei'ot* 1:1.

15. Exodus 23:5.

16. Quoted in *Hayom Yom*, 28 *Shevat*.

particularly underscored by Rabbi Schneur Zalman, the Alter Rebbe, in *Tanya*,[17] in which he explains that G-d's choice of the Jewish people refers specifically to the body. G-d's will is fulfilled specifically through *mitzvot* performed physically by a Jew. Since the body of a Jew is so esteemed in G-d's view, it is especially important to take care of it.

But to be completely immersed in all-pervasive thoughts of material profits or illusory honor based upon one's grandiose self-concept is utterly worthless, and is in effect, labor that is both "limitless" and "purposeless."

THE TWO SOULS OF A JEW

This explains why the oppressive labor of the Jews in Egypt, also "embittered their lives" spiritually.

Everything created by G-d in the world is finite, with a set limit and purpose. Man's capacity for the infinite, that which is above material purpose and gain, is derived from his *nefesh ha'elokit*.

What is the *nefesh ha'elokit*? *Chasidut*[18] tells us that there are two dimensions to a Jew's selfhood, eternally in conflict in their attempts to gain complete mastery over him. These are the *nefesh ha'elokit* and the *nefesh habahamit,* the two souls within Man. The *nefesh ha'elokit*, the G-dly soul, strives to elevate Man by the study of Torah and the performances of *mitzvot*. On the other hand, the *nefesh habahamit*, the animal soul, strives to corrupt and debase Man by urging him to succumb to his evil desires.

The G-dly soul is linked with G-d, who is Infinite, without limitation or constraint. Thus, there exist within the soul unlimited powers beyond reckoning and limitation, as for example, the capacity for altruistic self-sacrifice which exists within each Jew, a quality transcending reason and understanding. Utilizing such traits, one can reach a level of

---

17. Ch. 49.
18. See *Tanya*, ch. 9, and elsewhere.

spiritual service truly devoid of any hint or thought of personal gain or self-service, serving G-d only with the profound commitment of selfless altruism.[19]

However, when these G-dly powers are misused for the very reverse of the spiritual, "making darkness into light and light into darkness, the bitter, sweet and the sweet, bitter,"[20] this constitutes an oppressive labor "without limit and purpose." The vitality of the G-dly soul is embittered, as in the Biblical words, "and they embittered their lives."

THE SUBTLETY OF THE EVIL IMPULSE

The embittering of one's spiritual life can also occur on a more subtle level. An individual may, indeed, utilize his spiritual energy for sacred matters and not for material pursuits. However, he might not use it for the task which is his unique responsibility.

Every Jew has a particular responsibility for which his soul was sent down to the material world. The *Yeitzer Hara*—the Evil Inclination—desires to block him from fulfilling *his* task. He knows full well that the attempt to persuade a Jew to totally neglect the service of G-d will fail. Hence, the evil impulse works more subtly, urging a Jew to work in G-d's service, but at a task which really is designated for another.

The Jewish people can be categorized into two general categories, the first being those who study Torah—"tent-dwellers." *Yeshivah* students would most particularly fit this category, since their primary occupation is Torah study. It is self-evident that they must also perform acts of kindness, giving charity both in the material and spiritual sense, because "anyone who declares that he only possesses Torah does not even have Torah."[21] But his primary responsibility remains the assiduous study of Torah.[22]

---

19. See Maimonides, end *Hilchot Teshuvah*.

20. Isaiah 5:20.

21. *Yevamot* 109b.

22. See also *Likkutei Sichot*, vol. 3, p. 830.

The second general category is business people, whose primary spiritual task is doing *mitzvot*, with charity being their foremost obligation[23]—material charity and also spiritual charity, promulgating the wellsprings of Judaism, Torah and *Chasidut*. However, since all matters of sanctity are interrelated, they *must* set aside a fixed specific time for learning Torah in addition to their essential involvement with the mitzvah of charity.

There are, however, "erring souls"[24] who, instead of fulfilling their own tasks, seek pursuits which are others' responsibility. There are laymen who, when asked to give charity or get involved in mitzvah activism, respond that they are unable to do so because they require the time themselves, to pray at length, to study assiduously, etc., and after they apply themselves to these efforts, no time remains, because they must then hasten off to business.

Similarly, there are Torah scholars and *Yeshivah* students who get involved with charity in the time which should normally be set aside for Torah study.

Often, these "erring souls" dedicate more zeal and effort to the matters that are intrinsically not their primary concern, although these are indeed holy matters. However, since this is not their primary responsibility, this is an instance of "they embittered their lives" because the vitality of the G-dly soul is not used for its *particular* goal, and hence it is obstructed and thwarted from its G-dly task.

TRUE LIBERATION

G-d has endowed every Jew with the great talent and capacity to live a life spiritually radiant with Torah and *mitzvot*. If a Jew lives up to his potential, then his life has profound meaning and significance and reflects, even if in a small degree, the infinite light of G-d. He thus enters, in either a major or

---

23. See *Tanya*, ch. 37.
24. See *Sefer Hasichot 5704*, p. 154.

minor manner, the eternal mainstream of Jewish history. But if these spiritual qualities are thwarted or stifled, no greater anguish can be imagined, for Man has then relinquished his chance to live a life of true meaning and worth. Too late he discovers that he has expended G-d-given abilities to pursue illusory mirages, devoid of value. No greater tragic "embitterment" and remorse can be imagined.

It is for this reason that the liberation from Egypt commenced with the divine command to "draw and take to yourselves"[25] the Pesach sacrifice. Because the Egyptians worshipped these animals, this act of slaughtering them in full view of the Egyptians entailed a heroism and courage derived from a source and soul power beyond human limit, self-sacrifice above reason and understanding and in total defiance of Egyptian beliefs.

The Jewish people thus actualized the highest spiritual potential of their souls, completely fulfilling G-d's commandment. This resulted in the freedom described in the *Tikkunei Zohar*, "freedom from folly"[26] and in complete release from the embitterment of Egyptian bondage. They achieved the understanding which enabled them to differentiate between that which is derived from the *nefesh ha'elokit* and that which is derived from the *nefesh habahamit* and lower.

It was necessary for the Jewish people to first free their enslaved spiritual strength, which every Jew possesses in potential, and use it in the service of G-d, in order for them to be liberated from the embitterment of Egyptian slavery.

This is the spiritual significance of the liberation and freedom from Egypt. The liberation and utilization of the powers of the *nefesh ha'elokit* from the embitterment of spiritual bondage resulted in the complete redemption of the Jewish nation, including the actual physical departure of the Jewish

---

25. Exodus 12:21.
26. *Tikkun* 56.

people from Egyptian servitude and their journey to Sinai for the giving of the Torah.

(*Likkutei Sichot*, vol. 3, pp. 848 - 852)

PESACH

AHAVAT YISRAEL—
SELF INTEREST
OR COLLECTIVE CONCERN

> This *sicha* of the Rebbe discusses the issue of the responsibility of
> each Jew for the physical and spiritual welfare of others, individually
> and collectively. The paradigm, the supreme example of such active,
> even aggressive assumption of responsibility and true leadership, is
> our great leader Moses, as he obeyed G-d's directives in leading the
> Jewish people from slavery to freedom and service to G-d.

"GO TO YOUR TASKS"

The Torah tells us that when, at G-d's behest, Moses and
Aaron came to tell Pharaoh to release the Jewish people, "the
King of Egypt said to them, 'Moses and Aaron, why do you
disturb the nation? Go to your tasks!'"[1] By the terms "your
tasks" Pharaoh meant their *personal* endeavors, not the difficult
toil, the slavery of the Jewish people in general. This indicates
that the entire tribe of Levi—the tribe of Moses and Aaron—
was exempt from the harsh labor that was the burden of the rest
of the Jewish people.

Nachmonides explains that "It is the custom of each nation
to have Sages to instruct others in their [indigenous]
teachings."[2] The tribe of Levi was given this singular status and
freed from work because they served as the "Sages and the
elders" of the Jewish People. When Pharaoh told Moses and

---

1. Exodus 5:4.
2. Ad loc.

Aaron to "go to their tasks," he meant to their role as teachers of the Jewish people.

Implicit within Pharaoh's words was the argument that Moses and Aaron should be content with their own personal liberty from labor and not encourage their people to disobey the law of the land and cease their work. The mere fact that Moses and Aaron were free at times to teach the Torah tradition to the Jewish people should have been enough to satisfy them.

The *Zohar* declares that the wisdom of Egypt "surpassed that of all other nations (of that period)." Moreover, Pharaoh himself was a great sage.[3] There is, thus, significant meaning to Pharaoh's words. Indeed, our Sages tell us that the slavery of Egypt was so harsh that it was "impossible for a slave to flee Egypt."[4] Since according to Heavenly decree the span of exile in Egypt was to be for a period of four hundred years,[5] seemingly the harsh conditions in Egypt were to serve as the means to fulfill this decree. In effect, Pharaoh was arguing that there should not be any attempt to change the divine declaration concerning the length of time the Jews had to be slaves. The servitude was meant to, and should, continue; Moses and Aaron were to preoccupy themselves with their private Torah studies and teachings.

THE ARGUMENT OF AN ENEMY

Though this would seem to be a valid contention, we must nevertheless be aware that this is the *argument of Pharaoh*, our enemy. Had his words been accepted, the possibility of freedom and liberation from Egypt could have been totally lost. For, as the great mystic teacher the Arizal states, it was necessary that the liberation of the Jewish people take place in great haste. Had they remained longer, for even the briefest

---

3. *Zohar Chadash* II 52b.

4. *Mechilta*, Exodus 18:11.

5. Genesis 15:13.

instant, they would have been so totally immersed in the evil of Egypt that they would have lost the opportunity for freedom.

Though Pharaoh's argument seems logical, it does not consider the Jewish people's transcendence of the limitations of human intellect and the natural order of things. Notwithstanding the initial decree of slavery for four hundred years, G-d decided to accelerate the pace of those historical events and to cause an overleaping to the end of the exile. The bitter slavery experience ended more speedily than Pharaoh assumed to be divinely decreed.

This part of our history has profound implications for every individual. No Jew should succumb to the premise that one should be concerned only with his own welfare and safety and think "I have saved my own soul." Nor should he yield to the rationalization that giving Torah classes from time to time is adequate involvement with others' spiritual needs. Why should he care about the extent of another Jew's mitzvah observance? Why try to ascertain whether that Jew is dedicated to serving G-d or subservient to the authority of an evil Pharaoh? This, indeed, was the argument of the Egyptian Pharaoh, which was sweepingly rejected by Moses and Aaron.

THE OUTBREAK OF FIRE

We must view such a situation as comparable to the outbreak of a fire in a Jewish home. No one in his right mind would delay and deliberate whether to be involved. Any normal person would take speedy action and thrust himself into the rescue effort and try to save those in danger. If this applies to physical safety, how much more is it relevant when both physical *and* spiritual safety are involved! Speed is of the essence—lives must be saved.

There is a profound link uniting all Jews. Regarding the nature of this relationship, the sixth Lubavitcher Rebbe, Rabbi Yosef Yitzchak, relayed in the name of the Baal Shem Tov: The obligation of love for a fellow Jew is not merely related to someone who is familiar, an acquaintance. It extends even to a

Jew who is somewhere in a remote region in the world. And it must be in the manner of loving your fellow Jew "as your very own self." Just as self-love has no limitations, so must a Jew be concerned for a fellow Jew in a boundless, unlimited fashion.

Rabbi Yosef Yitzchak once said that it was the fervent wish of the Mezritcher Maggid that he would kiss a *Sefer Torah* with the same intense feeling and love that his teacher, Rabbi Israel Baal Shem Tov, had for a fellow-Jew.

Though this mitzvah of *Ahavat Yisrael*—love of fellow Jews—seems to impose an enormous obligation upon every Jew, we are nevertheless told that "G-d does not come to overburden His creations."[6] Thus, we can be certain that G-d has endowed us with the spiritual capabilities to execute this responsibility. But it is imperative that we act speedily, without even a moment's delay. Just as in the case of Egypt, at stake is whether the Jewish people remain in exile or merit redemption.

The obligation of love and responsibility for every Jew has profound implications even for someone whose primary endeavor is Torah study, which includes *yeshivah* students or dedicated teachers and scholars. One cannot be smugly complacent about personal Torah achievement and accomplishment, concerned only with one's personal advancement, at the cost of neglecting others. Indeed, since all Jews are a *komah sheleimah*—one collective soul—a defect in another Jew is also a glaring stain on the identity of the Torah scholar.

Even a distinguished individual is affected by the shortcomings of individuals who may be on a lesser level. The Torah declares, "You stand *all* of you today before G-d your L-rd, your heads of tribes...from he who chops wood to he who draws water."[7] When a parade passes in procession before the king, than an obligation exists for perfect discipline and order. If the buttons of the lowest ranking soldier are dull and

---

6. *Avodah Zara* 3a.

7. Deuteronomy 19:9-10.

unpolished, then the highest ranking military officer is held responsible for this breach of discipline in the king's presence.

We must be profoundly conscious of the fact that we are constantly standing arrayed together in the presence of G-d. The "wood choppers and drawers of water" are not held solely responsible for their possible shortcomings. On the contrary, the primary responsibility is borne by the "heads of the tribes." Their argument that their own self-improvement is their primary concern will be totally unacceptable in the eyes of Heaven.

When we are completely permeated with the consciousness of our *"komah sheleimah,"* one unified spiritual identity, it will motivate us to act accordingly, and make of all "one [perfect] union." We will then merit the actualization of "to do Your (G-d's) Will with a complete heart." At that time there shall be the fulfillment of the Messianic revelation of G-dliness: that "G-d is One and His Name is One."[8]

(Likkutei Sichot, Vol. 16, pp. 29-32)

---

8. Zechariah 14:9.

PESACH

THE PATH TO SINAI—
VARIETIES OF JEWISH
RELIGIOUS EXPERIENCE

The present *sicha* examines the four responses of the Jewish people
when pursued by the Egyptians at the time of the Exodus. One
group advocated leaping into the sea, another waging war against the
Egyptians, another returning submissively to Egypt, and a fourth
crying out in prayer. The Rebbe analyzes each response as
exemplifying a particular approach to the service of G-d, each one
with its own drawbacks. The Rebbe goes on to explain the
significance of G-d's command "speak to the children of Israel that
they go forward," the path in spiritual service that leads an
individual Jew and the entire creation ever closer to Torah, and the
revelation of the G-dly power animating all existence.

FOUR CAMPS

The Torah relates that when the Jews, pursued by the
armies of Egypt, arrived at the Red Sea, Moses declared:[1] "Fear
not, stand still and see the deliverance of G-d that He will do
for you this day; for as you have seen Egypt today, you shall
never see them again, forever. G-d will do battle for you and
you shall remain silent." The *Mechilta*[2] comments on this verse
that because of their fear of Egypt, the Jewish people divided
into four camps, each with a different opinion about how they
should respond to the crisis. One group declared: "Let us leap
into the sea" and not submit to the cruelty of the Egyptians
again. A second group stated: "Let us return to Egypt" and

---

1. Exodus 14:13-14.
2. Ibid 14:13.

subject ourselves once again to slavery. The third group said: "Let us wage war against them," let us battle against Pharaoh and his massive army. And the fourth group was of the opinion that the only appropriate reaction to this perilous threat was to "Cry out against them"—to pray to G-d for His aid.

Moses' two statements are a reply all of these factions. To those who would "leap into the sea" the answer was, "stand still and see G-d's salvation." To the despairing who said, "Let us return to Egypt," the reply was: "For as you have seen Egypt today you shall never see them again, forever." To those daring to wage war with the Egyptians, the response was: "G-d will wage war for you." And to the fourth group, who sought to cope with the crisis by "crying out to G-d," Moses declared: "And you shall remain silent."

What, then, was to be done in the face of this fearful threat? "Speak to the children of Israel that they go forward."[3] The Jews were to advance on the way that lead to Sinai, hastening forward to receive the Torah, which was G-d's purpose in liberating them from Egypt.[4]

Torah may be interpreted on many levels. Explaining this incident in a Chasidic manner, we may assert that none of the aforementioned opinions actually conflicts with the fulfillment of Torah and its *mitzvot*. For if a Jew adheres to an opinion which does not conform to Jewish law, this indicates that he is still enslaved and has not been liberated from the "land of Egypt." The four opinions cited were those of individuals who, although they had left both the physical and "spiritual" Egypt, had not yet advanced to the spiritual and physical stage of the "splitting of the Red Sea."

Complete spiritual liberation from Egypt entails the splitting of the Red Sea, "turning the sea into dry land."[5] This means that the G-dly power which is *concealed* in creation—in

---

3.   Ibid. 14:15.

4.   Ibid. 3:12 and Rashi there.

5.   Psalms 66:6.

the "sea" that conceals all that is below—is set aside, and the "dry land," i.e., G-dly power, emerges. When the spiritual service of a Jew results in his ability to see the G-dliness inherent in all existence, then he has totally departed from Egypt. Not only does the world no longer obstruct the G-dly light, he actually perceives G-dliness in the world itself.

LEAPING INTO THE SEA

The four groups, as hinted at in the Biblical verses and explained in the light of *Chasidut*, may be seen as four different levels of serving G-d, enumerated in ascending order. The first opinion was "to leap into the sea." Existing in a world where it was possible that Pharaoh and his army, which represent the forces of evil, could achieve victory, they chose to have nothing to do with the world. A person adhering to such an opinion chooses to enclose himself, seclude himself from the world and his fellowmen, and cast himself into the sea, a "sea" of repentance, and to link himself in this manner with G-d. If such an individual is confronted with the question of what will then happen to the world or to a fellow Jew, or if he is urged to strive to shatter the might of Pharaoh, his response to this challenge is to disclaim personal responsibility. Firstly, let another Jew cope with the problem, and even more, what need is there to interpret the concealed thoughts of G-d?![6] This is a matter related to G-d, he thinks, and he does not feel obligated to save the entire world; his primary concern is his own survival. He will therefore cast himself into the "sea" and isolate himself from the world.

This mode of conduct has been referred to in the past by the phrase "a *tzaddik* in *peltz*," the supposed righteous man who is warmly insulated in his own fur coat. As for the bitter cold that torments others—what can he possibly do? He defends himself by arguing, "Is it possible for me to warm up the entire world?" Attempting to provide warmth for another Jew, for

---

6. *Berachot* 10a.

another two Jews, or for a small area in the world—this is not a task appropriate for him. His question "is it possible" etc. indicates that according to his self-perceived grandeur, he must preoccupy himself with matters of far greater significance, such as providing warmth for the entire world. Since, however, this is beyond his power, he garbs himself in a "fur coat" and is complacent and content.

RETURNING TO EGYPT

A higher manner of serving G-d is "to return to Egypt." Aware of G-d's intention, that "He formed [the world] to be inhabited,"[7] man must, perforce, be involved with worldly matters, he submissively complies, for "Against your will do you live."[8] G-d has willed upon him existence in the physical world, the divine soul has been vested in a physical body and animalistic soul. Therefore, if he receives a clear directive that he must perform a virtuous action in the world, he does so, but he regards it as a burdensome task. His action is devoid of enthusiasm or feeling, and he will not seek or expend great effort on his own to spiritually refine himself with the radiance of G-dliness. In this area he lacks initiative, zeal, and vitality; he acts only in response to a specific command.

This stance is one of despair and futility. He believes that he can accomplish nothing, neither with the world nor with his own self. He can in no way escape the inevitable path of "returning to Egypt" and subservience to "Egypt"—the material world—and this is his fate and destiny. Obligated to comply with Jewish law, he does so with a sense of "burdensome labor."[9] The sun rises and he recites the *Shema* as the most pious do, at those very moments that are most praiseworthy; he recites the afternoon prayer of *Minchah* at the right time; at mealtime he recites the appropriate prayers, both before and after eating; if he should meet someone who requests an act of

---

7.   Isaiah 45:18.

8.   *Avot* 4:22.

9.   Exodus 1:13.

kindness, he responds sympathetically, and when told of one who is in need of material or spiritual compassion, this he also fulfills, because of the Biblical command "And You shall love thy neighbor as thyself."[10] However, all his actions are without will and gratification, without vitality and energy. Everything is done in the manner of "burdensome labor," for he has given up and he assumes that despite his many efforts, he shall remain enslaved in the "Egypt" of the physical world.

Submission to the heavenly yoke in the manner of a loyal servant is indeed the way one must begin to serve G-d. However, this is only the *beginning* of the path in the service of G-d.[11] When one studies Torah and is aware that through Torah he is united with G-d, this knowledge must awaken within him such intense feelings that an observer can actually perceive that he is not just obedient, but rejoices in being able to perform G-d's Divine Will. This should also be true of his performance of other *mitzvot*. For example, the knowledge that taking the skin of an animal and writing upon it the four Biblical sections actually transforms this parchment into a medium for G-dliness, and that by then placing the *tefillin* on his left hand and on his head he fully accomplishes G-d's will,[12] should awaken great joy in him.

One should feel that every word of Torah that he learns and every mitzvah that he performs affects the destiny of all existence[13] and lessens the "Egypt" that is found in the entire world. As long as one is gripped by a sense of futility and despair, perceiving Torah and its commands as a heavy burden which must be constantly borne with neither joy nor enthusiasm, then one is in the spiritual state of enslavement to the "Land of Egypt."

---

10. Leviticus 19:18.

11. *Tanya*, ch. 41; *Kuntreis Ha'avodah*, ch. 3 and ff.

12. See *Sha'arei Orah*, "Yavi'u levush malchut," sec. 7; sec. 73.

13. See Maimonides, *Hilchot Teshuvah* 3:4.

WAGING WAR

An even higher level is "to wage war against them." Despite the great darkness and cloud that Pharaoh and his army cast upon the world, this Jew does not submit—he struggles and wages war against Egypt. This response is far superior to returning to "Egypt." His is not a posture of despair. On the contrary, he senses the enormous might of the powers of holiness, which can conquer and prevail over all the forces of darkness, and as a result he acts with great zeal and initiative.

But each manner of conduct must have its proper time. If the Almighty has commanded that Israel must journey towards the goal of "You shall serve G-d on this mountain,"[4] to the receiving of the Torah, then there should be no delay or distraction, no seeking to serve G-d in other ways. If his task at this specific time is to illuminate the world with the light of Torah, then it is wholly inappropriate to evade his responsibility—even by waging war against Egypt. Now is the time for "And they shall go forward," the time to advance a step closer to the giving of the Torah and its *mitzvot*, and not the time to start a war against Egypt.

It is apparent that since the divine command was to proceed toward Sinai, it would have been an unnecessary diversion of time and energy to engage in war, when these very same qualities were needed to hasten the journey toward the giving of the Torah. In addition, in warfare even the victor suffers casualty and loss. One must be cautious when striving to serve G-d by "waging war" against the forces of evil. Since he has not inquired of either G-d or Moses "His servant," and is formulating his own military tactics, acting on the basis of his own intellect and judgment, he may actually delude himself. It may be that his efforts and initiative are not derived from the realm of sanctity, but rooted in a desire to assert his own ego.[14] *Chasidut*[15] frequently emphasizes that if one has the choice of

---

14. See *Derech Mitzvotecha* 89b.

15. See *Tanya*, chapter 32.

influencing a fellow Jew either by affection or by means of "war and animosity," then the choice of friendship is more desirable, for even if one is unsuccessful in his efforts, he will still be rewarded for the mitzvah of "Love they neighbor as thyself."

CRYING OUT IN PRAYER

The fourth and highest level is, "Let us cry out against them" to invoke the quality of prayer. Here the Jew is united and linked with G-d and desires to fulfill His Will. He therefore does not choose to "leap into the sea," to protect himself by isolation from the world, because it is G-d's Will that the world itself be made an abode for G-dliness. He will not "return to Egypt," submitting to despair, because he possesses absolute trust that G-d's Will shall certainly be accomplished. He does not involve himself in waging wars against the foe, using his own strategies, because he is united with and totally submissive to G-d, wholly given over to obeying His will. Therefore, he does not actually attempt to change matters of the world, but leaves everything to G-d. His self-perceived task is simply to pray and beseech G-d to provide the necessary help in worldly matters, and he sincerely hopes that G-d will respond to his prayers, setting right that which is wrong and aiding those in need.

Though this is a posture of nullification and submission to G-d—of being almost wholly dependent upon G-d with the unshakable faith that he need do nothing but pray—this is not always desired by G-d. Man must labor and endeavor to spread the light of G-dliness within the world. A Jew must not see himself as self-reliant; he should constantly be aware that all he does is not due to his own power and might, but that it is G-d "who gives me strength to acquire wealth."[16] Yet, at the same time, he must make use of *all* of his G-d-given talents, in his divine service.

---

16. Deuteronomy 8:18.

The Jew is united with G-d Who is not bound by the laws of nature and who can sustain opposites within Himself.[17] Similarly, two diametrically opposed kinds of spiritual service are expected of each Jew. On the one hand, total submission to G-d, based on the awareness that G-d causes all things, yet simultaneously striving to serve G-d to the utmost of his ability.

Regarding one's material needs, two diametrically contrasting attitudes are expected: Man must possess the simple faith that all is derived from G-d, who is absolute in His goodness, and that all that occurs is therefore good. Moreover, even if things seem to be the *very opposite* of good, they are still rooted in the exalted goodness of G-d's incomprehensible Wisdom in the "world of concealment," which cannot descend to be revealed in this world.[18]

At the same time, man must also have perfect trust that, without the slightest doubt, all things will eventually be good also in a visible and obvious way.[19] The meaning of trust and reliance upon G-d is not that one trusts that G-d will act in a way whose goodness is known only to G-d Himself, but rather the certainty that G-d will better the situation in such an open and clear manner that *Man* will see that all is good. Man must trust in G-d even at a time when the course of natural events is highly distressing and oppressive, and there seems to be no basis for optimism. The Jew believes and trusts in G-d's certain help; that G-d can assuredly help him since He is not bound by any power and is capable of changing even the laws of nature itself.

Absolute trust in G-d[20] occurs when the slightest hope of aid does not exist, when even the proverbial "straw" clutched by a drowning man, or the hope based on the "red thread" is absent. In the Biblical book of Joshua,[21] Rahab was assured that

---

17. See Responsa of the Rashba, ch. 218; *Sefer Hachakirah* of the *Tzemach Tzedek* 34b.

18. See *Tanya* chapter 26.

19. See *Likkutei Sichot*, vol. 26, p. 95 and ff.

20. *Igrot Kodesh* of the Previous Rebbe, vol. 6, p. 398 and ff.

21. 2:18.

she and members of her household would be spared by the armies of Israel if they displayed a red thread hanging from their roof. Though this was something that could be seen by all, it was nevertheless a fragile and weak hope. Many things might happen: the thread could snap, the wind blow it away, etc. Hope is based on the anticipation that nothing will disturb the thin thread. However, absolute trust in G-d exists when there is no visible sign of rescue; in the absence of any avenue of hope, the individual relies only on G-d. This is absolute trust.

Even in such a case, if the person is embittered, and expresses melancholy and sadness, he falls short of absolute trust in G-d. For he who has such trust will not permit his difficult situation to oppress or embitter him. He must do all that is within his power, in harmony with Torah and human logic, and at that same time not yield to the slightest doubt that G-d shall aid him. For His encompassing and compassionate Providence extends to every created being and endows life and power to all living things in Heaven and earth.

If suffering has already befallen an individual, Heaven forbid, then "he must accept it with joy."[22] He must have the perfect and complete faith that G-d only causes that which is good, though the human mind cannot at times fathom the ways of G-d. Both *faith* and *trust* are expected of a Jew: *faith* in G-d's hidden goodness even while enduring pain, and *trust* in the face of seemingly unavoidable impending suffering that G-d will bestow goodness in an open and visible manner. These qualities are required of a Jew because a Jew is united with G-d. And just as G-d can contain opposites within Himself, so too can a Jew experience the submissive quality of faith with the optimistic outlook of trust at the very same time. Trust in G-d does not contradict faith in G-d. On the contrary, trust and reliance upon G-d is one of the basic components of this faith.

---

22. See *Berachot* 60b.

The same is true of spiritual service to G-d: a Jew must be aware that "All things are in the hands of Heaven,"[23] and at the very same time he must endeavor to serve G-d with his own strength, talent and ability. And though the adage "All things are in the hand of Heaven" concludes with the phrase "except the fear of Heaven," meaning that fear of G-d is a responsibility specifically given over to Man—even here Man cannot be wholly self-reliant, and must depend upon G-d's help.

Total dependence upon G-d and personal intense effort and initiative to fulfill the Will of G-d come from the *Nefesh Ha'elokit* (G-dly soul), a part of Man which is joined with G-dliness. Since G-d can contain opposites within Himself and is not subject to the laws of nature, a Jew similarly can have faith and serve G-d at the same time; and under such circumstances these qualities are not contradictory, but actually complementary.

GOING FORWARD

The G-dly command given then through Moses was, "Speak to the children of Israel that they go forward."[24] The spiritual endeavor must be to constantly proceed ever closer to the mountain of Sinai—not isolation from the world nor service devoid of all zeal and initiative; not to ignore one's mission and task and engage in conflict with the world; and finally not to stand with idle hands and to leave everything to G-d. These were the beliefs of the four groups at the edge of the Red Sea. Man must serve G-d and strive within the world itself to illuminate it, and to bring himself and the entire creation ever closer to Torah in the path of "They shall go forward." The world remains an existent entity, but the concealment of the "ocean" is removed, revealing the G-dly power within the world, the animating power of G-dliness sustaining all existence.

---

23. *Berachot* 33b.

24. Exodus 14:15

This results in the revelation of the giving of the Torah, which is a prelude to the future revelations of *Mashiach*, when the goal of all creation shall be fulfilled and the world transformed into a visible "abode for Him."[25]

(Likkutei Sichot, vol. 3, pp. 876-887*)*

---

25. See *Tanchuma Nasso* 17; *Tanya,* ch. 36.

PESACH SHEINI

THE NEVER-ENDING QUEST
FOR SELF-BETTERMENT

The Torah describes the plea of those who were subject to ritual impurity and thus unable to bring the Pesach sacrifice in the desert. They cry out to Moses, "*Lamah nigarah*"—"Why should we be found wanting and lacking" in the service of G-d? The result of their plea was the introduction of a new mitzvah, the "second Pesach sacrifice," which could be brought on the 14th of Iyar in certain cases when a person was unable to do so on the 14th of Nissan. From this narrative the Rebbe derives an important lesson concerning the power of every Jew: to refuse to be complacent and to reach new unprecedented heights in his spiritual service, even to the extent of adding a new mitzvah to the Torah. On the deepest level, we learn also that it is proper for us to demand and clamor for the complete redemption through Mashiach.

"WHY SHOULD WE BE FOUND WANTING?"

The observance of Pesach *Sheini*—the obligation to bring a Pesach sacrifice on the fourteenth day of *Iyar* if a Jew was unable to do so a month before on Pesach itself—is unique among the other commands in the Torah. This mitzvah did not begin with a command from G-d, but was the result of the plea of a small group of Jews who were in a state of ritual impurity at the time when the Pesach sacrifice was brought. They said to Moses: "*Lamah nigarah*"[1]—"Why should we be deficient and found wanting [in the service of G-d]?"

G-d has created the world in such a way that Man is not solely a "recipient"—one who takes; Man also has the spiritual

---

1. Numbers 9:7.

privilege and ability to be a *mashpia*,[2] one who "bestows" and elicits spirituality from Above to the world below. In matters of Torah and *mitzvot*, generally, the task of a Jew is to be a "receiver," so much so that at Sinai the Jewish people faithfully affirmed their acceptance of the Torah by proclaiming "We will do and we will hear,"[3] "receiving" and accepting the Torah with such profound faith that they committed themselves to fulfilling its precepts even before they had any knowledge of G-d's specific positive or negative commands.

However, in what way is the Jew also a "bestower" and "giver" in the process of the revelation of Torah to the Jewish people? This concept is illustrated in the laws of Pesach *Sheini*, which were *only* the result of the zealous efforts of those who declared *"Lamah nigarah"*—"Why should we be found wanting?"—in the fulfillment of this precept. It was only in response to their profound involvement that the new law of offering the Pesach *Sheini* was given to the Jewish people.

Indeed, this concept of Jews being "bestowers" can also apply to Torah knowledge in general. Though the Torah and all of its *mitzvot* were given to Moses at Sinai, there still exist "newness" and creative insight into its hidden dimension. The Talmud states explicitly that any "new" original concept formulated by a dedicated Torah student subsequent to the revelation at Sinai was actually given to Moses implicitly at Sinai.[4]

The declaration "And give us *our* share in Your Torah"[5] (in our prayers) can be understood similarly. Each Jew has his *own* share in the Torah, which only he is capable of discovering and revealing.[6]

Still, this concept of Jews as initiators and "bestowers" is most clearly expressed in Pesach *Sheini*, for this mitzvah came

---

2. *Shemot Rabbah* 31, 5.

3. Exodus 24:7; *Shabbat* 88a.

4. See *Megillah* 19b; Jerusalem Talmud, *Peah* 2:4; etc.

5. *Pirkei Avot* 5:7.

6. See *Likkutei Sichot*, vol. 19, p. 253.

into existence solely through the pleas of the Jews who proclaimed "Why should we be found wanting?" When Moses brought their contention before G-d, the "Giver of the Torah," Who commanded us to do *mitzvot,* He imparted to us the *new* mitzvah of Pesach *Sheini.*

From this we can derive a profound insight into the way that a Jew should serve G-d. At first this incident seems difficult to understand. The entire claim of "Why should we be found wanting" is quite puzzling, for if indeed G-d desired that there be an observance of Pesach *Sheini,* then He could have revealed it initially at Sinai when Jews were commanded to observe all the *mitzvot.* If Moses did not instruct them at all regarding this mitzvah, then this obviously implies the absence of any obligation. Why, then, did these individuals come with the clamorous demand of *"Lamah nigarah,"* while simultaneously displaying their profound loyalty and faith in Moses, along with their awareness that he had not commanded this *mitzvah* either at Sinai or subsequently.

From this we can derive a new and significant concept. When a Jew senses within himself a shortcoming or glaring defect, then he should rely on no one, but plead to Moses and to G-d Himself, "Why should I be lacking, and imperfect in my service to G-d?!"

When someone is concerned about his bond with G-d and his inadequate awe and fear of G-d, then he must be conscious of the fact that "All is in the hands of Heaven except for the fear of Heaven."[7] It is therefore G-d's Will, as revealed to us through the narrative of Pesach *Sheini,* that a Jew should entreat and demand on his own initiative, express his inner sense of shortcoming, and exclaim *"Lamah nigarah."* As we see in the case of Pesach *Sheini,* G-d is compassionately responsive and reveals to us a new mitzvah of the Torah which was heretofore concealed.

---

7. *Berachot* 33b.

THE POWER OF THE INDIVIDUAL

This has meaningful implication for even a "simple" Jew. When reflecting on his status and his limited capabilities, he may sense that he has no right to plead. Indeed, what can he gain by such efforts? Pesach *Sheini* is G-d's response to this self-doubt. G-d is infinitely greater than Man; nevertheless, these individuals came and successfully entreated Him and benefited the entire Jewish people. There is an obvious lesson here about the great significance and spiritual strength of every single Jew. Despite the incredible distance between him and His Creator, when something affects him deeply in his yearning to be united with G-d through His *mitzvot*, and he senses his alienation and remoteness from G-d, then he is empowered to cry out, "Why should I be found wanting and lacking?" As a result, G-d deems him as one who declared "I have labored and (as a result) found,"[8] and G-d responds accordingly.

This concept is also found in relation to Jewish women. The daughters of Zelophehad argued vigorously for their father's inheritance, "Why should our father's name be diminished or found lacking?"[9] As a result they merited G-d's revealing a new law not only for them, but for the entire Jewish people. G-d declared through Moses: "And to *the Jewish people* you shall speak, saying: If a man die and have no son, then you shall transfer his inheritance to his daughter."[10]

This idea is also related to the individual Jew, for it is incumbent upon him to be aware of his own capabilities. A Jew must be aware of his constant dependence upon G-d, and never yield to the vain thought that "My mind and the strength of my hand have produced for me all this power (and accomplishment)."[11] Nevertheless, together with the realization

---

8. *Megillah* 6b.

9. Numbers 27:4.

10. Ibid. 27:8.

11. Deuteronomy 8:17.

that it is "G-d your L-rd Who has given you the strength to do"[12] and accomplish powerfully and successfully, there must be cognizance of the fact that concerning the awe and fear of Heaven, G-d waits for a Jew to perceive that his shortcomings affect him in every aspect—not solely in the depths of his innermost soul and his thoughts, but also in external aspects of his life, his speech and his deeds. When a Jew acts on the basis of this realization and prays and pleads to G-d to aid him towards self-betterment, then G-d compassionately responds to his longing, even to the very significant extent of giving a Jew a hitherto unrevealed mitzvah of the Torah which results in a "wholeness" in the observance of the complete Torah by the entire Jewish nation.

Nor is this mitzvah of Pesach *Sheini* solely for those who, because of their state of ritual "impurity," could not fulfill the original observance. "Heads of the Tribes,"[13] Jews distinguished by their piety, erudition and leadership, Jews whose entire life is "dedicated to repentance"[14] in the profound sense of intense effort to ascend to higher levels of spirituality, are also part of this underlying concept. Individuals who are involved in the constant study of Torah, Torah being their "vocation," or those involved in virtuous deeds, as "a master of good deeds"[15] can deceive themselves by thinking that the statement "Why should we be lacking" does not apply to them. But we are told that the true indication of a Torah scholar is that he has no rest or tranquillity, as our Sages tell us, "Torah scholars have no rest, but advance from *chayil*—strength (a high level) to *chayil*—strength" (an even higher degree).[16] This text depicts a Torah scholar who, by definition, is unceasingly involved in the study of Torah without wasting a single moment, whose observance of the *mitzvot* is in the most meticulous manner possible. Why

---

12. Ibid. 8:18.

13. Ibid. 29:9.

14. *Shabbat* 153a.

15. See *Igeret Hakodesh*, ch. 5 (109a).

16. *Berachot* 64a, Psalms 84:8.

does he lack an inner sense of tranquility and peace? The answer is that even on his lofty level of piety he is impelled by the inner sense of "*Lamah nigarah*" (why should we be lacking). With his awareness that spiritual advance is an infinite journey "from strength to strength," he can never be passively placid in his efforts.

Any absence of this inner impelling force means not only that he is lacking in "wholeness," but that actually he does not merit the name *Talmid Chacham*—a Torah Scholar. Indeed, the authentic indication of a Torah Scholar is the sense of "*Lamah nigarah*," of personal inadequacy and constant striving for higher achievement and perfection.

DEMANDING THE REDEMPTION

There is an even profounder dimension to the plea of "*Lamah nigarah*." There are those who question the constant emphasis on the topic of the coming of *Mashiach*. Maimonides in his Thirteen Principles of Faith states, "I believe...in the coming of *Mashiach*...and I await his coming *every day*." Superficially understood, this would seem to imply that we should rely on G-d's decision to redeem the Jewish people whenever He deems it is the proper time.

G-d Himself sent the Jewish people into exile and it is a part of His plan when He shall redeem them. As expressed by the sixth Lubavitcher Rebbe, Rabbi Yosef Yitzchak, "We were not exiled from the Holy Land of our own free will nor is it within our grasp to return to the Holy Land. G-d our Father and King caused us to go into exile and He, May He Be Blessed, will redeem us and gather our dispersed from the four corners of the earth through *Mashiach* our righteous Redeemer."[17] Then why the clamor and demand for redemption? We should be wholly reliant on G-d's will!

The mitzvah of Pesach *Sheini* comes to teach and clarify this matter for us regarding the need for personal Jewish

---

17. *Sefer Hasichot 5687*, p. 168.

initiative. Superficially, this law should have been given to us with all the other *mitzvot*. However, we acquired it through the plea and demand of the Jewish people, which resulted in the perfection of Torah in terms of our receiving 613 *mitzvot* in their entirety. Thus, the clamor and outcry for the coming of *Mashiach* is not contrary to the Torah, the Torah itself tells us that we must act this way. The authoritative historic Rabbinic group, "The Members of the Great Assembly," in their compilation of the texts of our *daily* prayers, enacted that each Jew is obligated to recite during the most solemn *Amidah* prayer: "May You cause the sprout of Your servant David [*Mashiach*, who is a descendant of King David] to grow speedily...for we hope for Your deliverance the *entire day*" and "May our eyes see Your return to Zion." This prayer is recited three times daily. When a Jew stands reciting the *Amidah* prayer, his stance must be with the humbleness of "A servant before his master,"[18] with forethought and profound *kavanah*—devotion and intent in each word. In the words of the Torah itself, "Your words should be few,"[19] characterized by deliberation and forethought. Nevertheless, there is not a single prayer service that does not include this plea for the redemption of the entire Jewish people.

Maimonides delineates the essence of prayer: "Beseeching the needs which a Jew requires."[20] Thus, if he only possesses meager economic sustenance, it is permissible and obligatory, according to the Torah, to beseech G-d to provide generously for his needs. Indeed, the Talmud states that since Jews are the descendants of Abraham, Isaac and Jacob, even the bountiful banquet of King Solomon at the height of his reign is still not adequate in providing for the needs of a Jew in terms of his personal merit.[21] How much more is this true in relation to the

---

18. *Shabbat* 10a.

19. Ecclesiastes 5:1; and see *Berachot* 61a.

20. *Hilchot Tefilah* 1:2.

21. See *Bava Metzia* 83a.

redemption of the Jewish people. Notwithstanding his profound faith and certainty in the Messianic redemption, a Jew cannot be serenely complacent. His own sense of anguish and his knowledge of the suffering of the entire Jewish people in the dispersion of exile compels a Jew to cry out and implore to G-d for deliverance and "the Coming of *Mashiach Now.*"

ES IS NIT DA KEIN FARFALEN

Rabbi Yosef Yitzchak of Lubavitch stated that the essence of Pesach *Sheini* is that "*Es is nit da kein farfalen*"[22] ("There is nothing irretrievably lost"). It is never too late. Repentance can correct all things and also transform events of the past, even for those who were "impure" and "distant" from the Holy Temple, even including those who consciously excluded themselves from the first Pesach observance. For such individuals G-d provides the spiritual concept of Pesach *Sheini,* the awareness that one can always rectify and set aright events of the past through repentance.

Maimonides states[23] that one should perceive his deeds as having cosmic significance. A Jew should always view both himself and the world in its entirety as in a state of delicate balance, both [his and the world's] merits and defects equal to each other.

Merely one deed can cause the scales to incline to the side of virtue and thus bring rescue and deliverance both for himself and the entire world.

How much more is thus true if this deed is motivated by the repentance concept of Pesach *Sheini:* that one should never despair of past defects or shortcomings.

Inherent to one's plea is the realization of one's of a Jew's remoteness from the Temple's sanctity and purity and also the profound faith that just as G-d responded mercifully in the past, so, too, will He answer our pleas for "*Mashiach* Now" and

---

22. *Hayom Yom* 14 *Iyar; Sefer Hasichot* 5701, p. 115.
23. *Hilchot Teshuvah* 3:4.

we will go forth to greet our righteous Redeemer—never again to endure the suffering of exile, but to experience the Messianic revelation and knowledge of G-dliness as described by the Prophet: "And the earth shall be filled with the knowledge of G-d as the waters cover the sea."[24]

(Based on *Hitvadiot* 5744, pp. 1674-1688)

---

24. Isaiah 11:9.

LAG B'OMER

RABBI SHIMON BAR YOCHAI

The following *sicha* examines the stature and spiritual significance of the Talmudic sage, Rabbi Shimon Bar Yochai, the anniversary of whose passing we celebrate on Lag B'Omer, and whose teachings comprise the primary work of Jewish mysticism, the *Zohar*. As the Rebbe observes, "Although his personal mode of learning Torah transcended the norms or general behavior, for 'Torah was his sole vocation,'[1] Rabbi Shimon Bar Yochai still related to the world compassionately." In addition to deriving inspiration from his life and an important teaching in spiritual service, every Jew can also be assured that the Rabbi Shimon's merit will evoke divine mercy for the Jewish people in the complete redemption through Mashiach.

"IN ONE BOND AM I BOUND WITH G-D"

One of the reasons for the joyous observance of *Lag B'Omer* is that it is the *yahrzeit* of Rabbi Shimon Bar Yochai.[2]

When the soul departs from the body, all the spiritual service, study of Torah, and fulfillment of commandments performed by that individual during his lifetime merge together and are elevated.[3] For this reason, Rabbi Shimon Bar Yochai declared, in the last moments of his mortal life, at the time that he ascended to a lofty spiritual level: "In one bond am I bound with G-d; with Him am I united."[4] He had linked himself with G-d—the source of all life—in an eternal bond. The spiritual ascent that occurs at the time of demise is "remembered and

---

1. *Shabbat* 11a.
2. See *Zohar* III 296b; *Pri Eitz Chaim, Sha'ar Sefirat Ha'omer,* ch. 7; *Mishnat Chasidm Masechet Iyar* 1, 46.
3. See *Igeret Hakodesh,* ch. 27.
4. *Zohar* III 288a.

again effected"[5] every subsequent year on that very same day, and this is the rationale for the joyous observance of *Lag B'Omer*.

The Jerusalem Talmud[6] states that when Rabbi Akiva ordained his students Rabbi Meir and Rabbi Shimon Bar Yochai, he said: "Let Rabbi Meir be seated first," and the face of Rabbi Shimon Bar Yochai paled. Whereupon Rabbi Akiva said, "It is enough that I and your Creator are aware of your power." Rabbi Shimon Bar Yochai's greatness was of so transcendent a nature that even his peers, who were great scholars and students of Rabbi Akiva, did not discern its full extent. Regarding Rabbi Meir's greatness, the Talmud says "His fellow scholars could not fathom to the depths of his intellect";[7] they were not capable of fathoming the full depths of his teachings. Nevertheless, they did understand that his greatness made him worthy of being "the first to be seated." But in the case of Rabbi Shimon Bar Yochai, they were totally unaware of his true stature. Only Rabbi Akiva, whose spiritual service was so lofty, could say "it suffices that G-d and I discern your power."

If during the course of his mortal life Rabbi Shimon Bar Yochai completely surpassed and transcended his contemporaries, how much greater was his ascent on the day of his demise! Consequently, it would appear that the ascent and joy of *Lag B'Omer* can in no way relate to other Jews because it is the *yahrzeit* of so rare and exalted a soul.

It is related[8] that one of the students of the famed mystic Rabbi Yitzchak Luria would customarily recite the prayer *Nachem* in his daily recitation of grace after meals. This prayer, a plea that G-d console His people, is normally recited only on *Tisha B'Av*—the ninth of the month of *Av*, the day of mourning for the destruction of the Temple—in the *Minchah* prayer,

---

5. *Esther* 9:28.

6. *Sanhedrin* 1:2.

7. *Eiruvin* 13b, 53a.

8. *Shulchan Aruch Ha'arizal, Hilchot Kavanot Omer.*

while it seems that it was this student's custom to recite *Nachem*
even on Shabbat and holidays. One *Lag B'Omer* he
accompanied his teacher, Rabbi Yitzchak Luria, to the gravesite
of Rabbi Shimon Bar Yochai to pray there. The soul of Rabbi
Shimon Bar Yochai looked upon his recitation of *Nachem* with
disfavor. There are souls so exalted that they are beyond being
affected by the destruction of the Temple. Rabbi Shimon Bar
Yochai was such a soul,[9] and mourning was completely
inappropriate to his *yahrzeit* observance. He therefore declared
to Rabbi Yitzchak Luria that this student would himself require
solace and comfort to alleviate the anguish resulting from the
penalty for inappropriate conduct.

We thus derive two concepts: a) that *Lag B'Omer* possesses a
unique quality not found in any other day of religious
observance, even Shabbat and Holidays. This is evident in the
fact that the student was punished only for reciting *Nachem* on
Lag B'Omer and not for any other day of the year; b) that the joy
of *Lag B'Omer* is related to all Jews, even to those lesser souls
who are not above being affected by the Temple's destruction,
like the student who recited *Nachem* daily. It is only that, he
should not have recited the anguish inducing prayer of *Nachem*,
on the day that we commemorate the piety of Rabbi Shimon
Bar Yochai, for this is a day that requires spiritual joyousness.

BRINGING THE INFINITE TO EARTH

Simply stated, Rabbi Shimon Bar Yochai exemplifies the
linking of two extremes: drawing down the highest level of
spirituality from the realm of "with one bond am I bound," etc.
and bringing it down to the nethermost realm of human
existence.

The joining of these two extremes may be discerned within
the framework of Rabbi Shimon Bar Yochai's views on the
study of Torah and in his explicit *halachic* opinions relating to
the Torah.

---

9. Quoted in *Pelach Harimon*, Exodus, p. 7.

The Talmud gives varying opinions about the meaning of the verse in the Bible: "The book of the Torah should not cease from your mouth."[10] Rabbi Yishmael does not interpret this verse to mean that one is literally required to study the Torah unceasingly, but explains that study should be combined with a worldly vocation for self-support—planting, plowing, etc. Rabbi Shimon Bar Yochai, however, understood this verse literally and taught that a Jew is obliged to study Torah constantly and uninterruptedly the entire day. As to providing for material existence, if "Israel will fulfill the will of G-d, then their work will be performed for them by others."[11]

The Talmud concludes: "Many acted in accord with Rabbi Yishmael's opinion and succeeded. Many did as Rabbi Shimon Bar Yochai, but did not succeed." Thus, we see that Rabbi Shimon Bar Yochai's manner of studying was far beyond the pattern of normal conduct, and "the many" emulating his example did not succeed.

Although his personal mode of learning Torah transcended the norms of general behavior, for "Torah was his sole vocation,"[12] Rabbi Shimon Bar Yochai still related to the world compassionately.

When Rabbi Shimon Bar Yochai and his son Rabbi Elazar emerged for the second time from the cave in which they were hiding for thirteen years to escape the death decree of the Roman oppressors, Rabbi Shimon Bar Yochai had reached an exceedingly high level in the learning of Torah, particularly during the last year. Rabbi Elazar was disturbed to see people engaged in ordinary labor rather than being totally preoccupied with the study of Torah. He could not tolerate their forsaking the spiritual pursuit of eternal life, which comes from Torah study, for preoccupation with worldly matters. But Rabbi Shimon Bar Yochai reacted differently, and "wherever Rabbi

---

10. Joshua 1:8.

11. *Berachot* 35b.

12. *Shabbos* 11a.

Elazar wounded, Rabbi Shimon Bar Yochai healed."[13] He explained to his son, "You and I suffice for the world"; his and his son's Torah study were enough to sustain the world.

In addition, Rabbi Shimon Bar Yochai said that if a person has "merely read the morning and evening *Shema,* he has fulfilled the Biblical command that 'the word of Torah should not depart from your mouth.'"[14] This would apply even according to the opinion that the mitzvah of *Shema* can be observed by merely reading that one Biblical verse.[15] This means that if one is unable to study Torah the entire day because he is involved in tasks which, according to the Torah itself, free him from the obligation of Torah study, or if one is unlearned and incapable of Torah study, not only is he released from the obligation of Torah study (since an individual is not held responsible for negligence of Torah obligations due to impossible circumstances[16]), but by reading these brief selections he actually fulfills the command that the word of Torah should not "depart from your mouth."[17]

This is the unique ability and power of Rabbi Shimon Bar Yochai: to elicit, from the highest level of literally unceasing study, from the level of his own personal Torah study, the spiritually infinite and limitless aspect of Torah and link it even to a person whose studying consists of one verse in the mornings and one verse in the evenings. Rabbi Shimon Bar Yochai linked that individual and his limited study of Torah with the infinite eternal dimension of Torah.

---

13. Ibid. 33b.

14. *Menachot* 99b.

15. See *Shulchan Aruch Harav* ch. 58, sec. 1.

16. *Bava Kama* 28b.

17. See *Hilchot Talmud Torah* of the Alter Rebbe (In *Kuntreis Acharon,* ch. 3) which explains the apparent contradiction between these two statements of R. Shimon Bar Yochai.

EXEMPTING THE WORLD FROM JUDGMENT

Moreover, after his isolation in the cave, Rabbi Shimon Bar Yochai sought ways to "rectify the world" in aspects of ritual defect and impurity. He did not wait until others came to inform him of what required correction, but he took the initiative and inquired: "Is there something that must be set aright?" When he was told about a field which was in a state of doubtful ritual cleanliness because of the possibility of graves or human remains concealed there, thus, preventing *Kohanim* (persons of priestly descent) from passing through that area, Rabbi Shimon Bar Yochai located the human remains and purified the field.

This incident has a deeper meaning. Only after reaching the highest degree of spirituality, resulting from his thirteen years of Torah study while concealed in the cave, could Rabbi Shimon Bar Yochai relate to the world of the mundane as well as descend and set aright that which required cleansing from the most intense form of impurity.

In addition, Rabbi Shimon Bar Yochai declared: "I can evoke divine Mercy so the entire world can be exempted and forgiven from G-d's judgment."[18] He was willing to evoke G-d's mercy and compassion for the Jewish people and to cleanse them from any punishment for transgression. Being such a spokesman for his fellow Jews entails awesome descent from Shimon Bar Yochai's lofty spirituality and necessitated involvement with individuals on a far lower plane. After the sin of the Tree of Knowledge, mankind so declined that death and its related ritual impurity are an intrinsic part of human existence and not subject to the control and free will of Man. Sin and transgression are on an even lower level, for they result from Man's free choice and bring about G-d's judgment and punishment. Rabbi Shimon Bar Yochai willingly descended even to this nethermost level.

---

18. *Sukkah* 45b.

In order to defend and find redeeming merit in another, it is necessary to "go down," identify and empathize with that person's life situation,[19] searching out some measure of saving worth to evoke G-d's mercies and forgiveness.

His descent was unlike that of Moses who, after the incident of the golden calf, was commanded: "Go and descend,"[20] for Moses was compelled by the divine edict to go down, whereas Rabbi Shimon Bar Yochai chose of his own accord and initiative to completely "exempt the world from judgment." This capacity and willingness of Rabbi Shimon to descend to such a depth resulted specifically from the high spiritual degree which he had attained, the singular level of *b'nei aliyah*—"lofty distinguished spiritual personalities who are few in number."[21]

When discussing a certain *halachic* case, the Talmud states, "One may rely upon Rabbi Shimon Bar Yochai at a time of difficulty."[22] *Chasidut*[23] interprets this as meaning that when Jews are in difficulty and distress during their exile, the merit of Rabbi Shimon Bar Yochai is enough to evoke protective divine mercies until the Messianic era. As it is stated in the *Zohar*, "With your Torah work (the *Zohar* and his mystical teachings) the Jewish people shall depart from exile by means of G-d's divine mercies."[24] The unique quality of Rabbi Shimon Bar Yochai, which transcends exile and the destruction of the Temple, will extend and influence the entire world, even the realm of imperfection and impurity. His teachings will bring G-d to cause "the unclean spirit to pass from the earth."[25] Thus, the entire world will be purified and made worthy of being an

---

19. See *Tanya*, ch. 30.

20. Exodus 32:7; and see *Berachot* 9a.

21. *Sukkah* 45b

22. *Berachot* 9a.

23. Cited also in *Sha'ar Yisachar*, end of *Ma'amor* for *Lag Ba'omer*.

24. *Zohar* III 124b, cited in *Igeret Hakodesh*, ch. 26.

25. Zechariah 13:2.

abode for G-d, may He be blessed, and even within the realm of the mundane there shall be the revelation of G-dliness.

(*Likkutei Sichot,* vol. 3, pp. 1002-1007)

SHAVUOT

TWO VIEWS OF
SINAITIC REVELATION

There are two related controversies between Rabbi Akiva and Rabbi Yishmael concerning the giving of the Torah on Mt. Sinai. One controversy concerns whether the Jewish people answered "yes" to the positive commandments and "no" to the prohibitions. The second concerns the sensory effect of the great revelation. According to Rabbi Akiva, and in opposition to Rabbi Yishmael's view, the Jewish people experienced sound as something visible and visual perception as if it were sound. The elaborate interplay among the various issues of these two controversies ultimately leads to profound insight into two contrasting modes of spiritual service, that of the *tzaddik* and that of the *baal teshuvah*.

THE RESPONSE AT SINAI

The Ten Commandments are preceded in the Bible by the verse "And G-d said all of these things *leimor*."[1] The word *leimor* is usually translated as "to say;" "and G-d spoke to Moses *leimor*" is a frequently recurring Biblical verse, meaning G-d told Moses to say and repeat all He had told him to the Jewish people.[2] This specific verse, however, cannot be explained this way, because when giving the Torah G-d *Himself* spoke to the entire Jewish nation.[3] Midrashic sources state G-d spoke to *all* Jewish souls, including those of future generations, for they were all present at the receiving of the Torah and heard the Ten

---

1. Exdodus 2:1.
2. See Rashi, Exodus 19:12; Leviticus 1:1, etc.
3. See *Sotah* 27b and Rashi there.

Commandments from G-d Himself.[4] To whom, then, should the Ten Commandments be "said?"[5]

The *Mechilta*[6] states that this *leimor* was the response of the Jewish people to each individual commandment, indicating their acceptance and commitment to observe all of the commandments. The *Mechilta* cites two opinions concerning Israel's verbal affirmation of the Ten Commandments. Rabbi Yishmael states: "They responded to the positive commands '*Hein*' ('Yes') and to the negative commands '*Lav*' ('No')." Rabbi Akiva is of the opinion that to both the positive and negative commands, the Jewish people answered "*Hein*," committing themselves to observe both positive and negative commands.

Superficially, there seems to be no practical distinction since the result seems identical—an expression of willingness to fulfill the will of G-d. What is the difference?

SEEING THE AUDIBLE AND HEARING THE VISIBLE

Rabbi Akiva and Rabbi Yishmael also disagree about another aspect of the giving of the Torah. Scripture states, "And all the people saw the sound and the flame," etc.[7] Rabbi Yishmael explains this Biblical verse as meaning the Jewish People "saw that which is to be seen and heard that which is to be heard." Thus, the verb "saw" does not relate to the word "sounds" but to "flame," which appears later in the verse. However, Rabbi Akiva states that they "*saw* that which is to be *heard* and they *heard* that which *is* to be *seen*."

It is an established principle that "G-d does not perform a miracle in vain."[8] Thus, the miracle of "seeing that which is to be heard"—the opinion of Rabbi Akiva—can not to be viewed as an extraneous aspect of the receiving of the Torah (for this

---

4. *Pirkei DeRebbi Eliezer*, ch. 41; *Shemot Rabbah* 28:6.

5. See *Torah Or* 67b.

6. Exodus 2:1.

7. Exodus 20:15.

8. See *Derashot HaRan, Drush 8 Hakdamah*.

would be a "miracle in vain"), but rather as a miracle intrinsic to the giving of the Torah. The giving of the Torah elevated the Jews to the loftiest level, and as an aspect and result of this ultimate exaltation "they saw that which is to be heard and they heard that which is to be seen."

Rabbi Yishmael concurs that when the Torah was given the Jewish people achieved their highest level of spiritual ascent, his viewpoint is problematic. How can he maintain that the surpassing spiritual merit of the Jewish people at that time resulted in ordinary human experience—seeing that which is to be seen and hearing that which is to be heard?

THE SIMPLE MEANING OF THE TEXT

Since both disputes are between the very same Rabbis and related to the same topic—the giving of the Torah—it is logical to assume that they are interdependent and that there is a consistent conceptual rationale that applies in both cases. Thus, according to Rabbi Akiva, the opinion that the Jewish people "saw that which is to be heard" is consistent with the position that they answered the positive commands with "*Hein*"—Yes— and the negative commands with "*Lav*"—"No." Similarly, Rabbi Yishmael's position that they "saw that which is to be seen and heard that which is to be heard" is consistent with the position that they answered "*Hein*"—Yes—to the positive commands, *and* "*Hein*"—Yes —to the negative ones.

Rashi, however, draws on both positions in his commentary. Explaining the "*leimor*," Rashi, relying on Rabbi Yishmael, comments, "This teaches us that they responded to the positive commands with '*Hein*' and to the negative commands with '*Lav*.'" As for the phrase "they saw the sounds," he interprets it according to Rabbi Akiva: "They saw that which is to be heard." Rashi explains the verses in this manner, seemingly based on two ultimately incompatible opinions, because his concern in his commentary on the Torah is to provide an explanation which is most consonant with the *peshat*—the literal meaning of the text. "For I have only come to explain the simple meaning of the text"[9] is Rashi's primary guiding principle in his commentary, and apparently Rabbi Yishmael's opinion fits the plain sense of "*Leimor*" better, while Rabbi Akiva's opinion on the phrase "they saw the sounds" is closer to the *peshat*.

SEEING AND HEARING

The theoretical distinction between the opinions of Rabbi Yishmael and Rabbi Akiva can be understood by first discussing the general distinction between "seeing" and "hearing."

a) Visual experience is more profound, penetrating far more deeply into the soul of the perceiver and consequently causing profounder awareness than that of aural experience. If a person actually sees an event, then no degree of persuasion can possibly convince him that the event was otherwise. Visual perception is clearer and more certain than an opinion based wholly upon intellect. This is reflected in the legal principle that a witness cannot act as a judge in the trial related to events he has personally witnessed.[10]

In contrast, the experience of hearing does not penetrate so deeply within the soul; this is certainly the case when "hearing" means intellectual comprehension. The process of understanding is neither as firm nor as assured as the awareness resulting from actual vision.

b) There is also a difference between "hearing" and "seeing" in relation to the experienced object: Sight is vivid. The material object is "grasped," so to speak, when seen. "Hearing," however, does not possess the clarity of sight, and is by nature less concrete and subtler. This awareness is even more vague and less certain in the "hearing" that refers to intellectual comprehension of an abstract idea.

The above distinctions in the person experiencing and the object perceived are interdependent.[11] A person is a physical

---

9. Rashi, Genesis 3:8.

10. See *Rosh Hashanah*, 26a.

11. See *Or HaTorah, Va'etchanan*, p. 63.

entity. It is his nature to assimilate and grasp a physical object—
by visual perception—with a greater affinity than something
spiritual. Mortal man is not "proximal" to the spiritual and he
therefore can only apprehend it by "hearing," by the faculty of
intellect which can grasp something distant from his physical
existence.

SEEING THE SPIRITUAL

This is the unique accomplishment of the giving of the
Torah: "They saw that which is to be heard and they heard that
which is to be seen." That which is "heard," which can only be
comprehended by the mind, i.e., spirituality and G-dliness,
were experienced at Sinai with the vivid certainty of "seeing," as
with *visual* perception. The Jewish people, as it were, *perceived*
G-dliness. As for the physical world, it receded from their
awareness to the extent that they related to its existence in a
manner of "hearing," as something known merely by "hearing"
about it.[12]

The miracle of "seeing that which is to be heard" was not
extrinsic to the G-dly revelation at the time of giving of the
Torah, but was an integral part of that event. At that time the
world's manifest material existence receded from their
consciousness and they merely "heard" and understood the fact
of worldly existence. (This is similar to the concept in
Chasidut:[13] that since G-d is uniquely One and aside from Him
there can be no existence, it is possible that worldly existence
may only be a figment of the imagination. *Chasidut* answers that
the very fact that the Torah itself declares that "In the
beginning G-d created [the world]"[14] indicates the reality of
worldly existence.)

---

12. See *Sefer Hama'amarim 5672*, vol. 1, p. 31.

13. *Sefer Hama'amarim 5629*, p. 161.

14. Genesis 1:1.

TWO INDIVIDUALS HOLDING A GARMENT

In everyday life we also see how differing frames of reference can significantly affect our perception. One example is the classic Talmudic case of two contesting individuals holding a garment, each claiming ownership. This situation is viewed from three perspectives: the view of the judge, that of the court officer, and that of the disputants. In the eyes of the disputants, their entire "reality" is the oath each must take corroborating his contention and the dividing of the garment. Indeed, upon inquiry they can be told of the judge's Torah thought process and the verdict rendered, but this is abstractly distant to them. The "reality" and certainty of a court officer is solely the verdict rendered by the judge. In the mind of the judge, primary "reality" is the complex interplay of various arguments based upon Torah legal sources, with the verdict merely a derivative consequence.

THE OPINION OF RABBI YISHMAEL

The position of Rabbi Yishmael seems to require further clarification. At the time of the giving of the Torah the Jewish people had reached a peak of religious fulfillment, the ultimate level of spiritual self-actualization. How was this reflected in Rabbi Yishmael's position that they merely "saw that which is to be seen and heard that which is to be heard?"

The accomplishment of the giving of the Torah was that "G-d descended upon Mount Sinai,"[15] causing the manifestation of G-dliness on earth, specifically within a world which retains its natural finite existence. The Jewish people, in that finite world, through the dedicated study of Torah, apprehend the Giver of Torah and G-dliness.

Rabbi Yishmael assures us that at Sinai the Jewish people functioned within the finite dimensions of worldly existence. Yet, it was specifically in this state that the ultimate revelation occurred. "They saw that which is to be seen and heard that

---

15. Exodus 19:20; *Shemot Rabbah* 12, 3.

which is to be heard"–this very, natural, "hearing" and "seeing," was thoroughly permeated with the illumination of the "Truth of G-d" deriving from transcendental G-dliness. This influenced them so profoundly that it evoked in them a deep sense of self-nullification, to the extent that "they saw and trembled and stood from afar."[16]

TZADDIKIM AND BAALEI TESHUVAH

The views of Rabbi Yishmael may be attributed to the fact that he was a *Kohein,*[17] who by virtue of his spiritual heritage and nature is "holy and dedicated to his G-d;"[18] his service of G-d task is in the manner of *tzaddikim.* In accord with his inner spiritual nature, Rabbi Yishmael assumed that the ultimate ascent was to elicit and to bring about the manifestation of G-dliness in the world from "above to below,"[19] in a manner conforming to nature.

The spiritual service of Rabbi Akiva, on the other hand, was in the impelling stance of *teshuvah*—spiritual return to G-d. Rabbi Akiva was a descendant of converts to Judaism,[20] and he himself commenced his Torah studies at the age of forty.[21] His G-dly service was in the spiritual striving of *teshuvah*—return— to depart from worldliness and ascend to the realm of spirituality—service from "below to above."

[As he declared, "All my days I have looked for the fulfillment of actual self-sacrifice for G-dliness"[22] (and in accordance with the teaching of Rabbi Israel Baal Shem Tov, "the realm in which Man's will is found, therein lies his total existential being."[23] Rabbi Akiva's *entire* life was characterized by

---

16. Exodus 20:15.
17. *Chulin* 49a.
18. Leviticus 21:7.
19. See *Sefer Hama'amarim 5661*, p. 163.
20. See the article on him in *Seder Hadorot.*
21. *Avot DeRav Natan* 6, 2.
22. *Berachot* 61b.
23. *Keter Shem Tov* , Additions, ch. 38 and sources cited there.

self-sacrifice)]. It is this determining factor of his spiritual life-outlook that resulted in Rabbi Akiva's view that the highest level of spirituality consisted of "seeing that which is to be heard and hearing that which is to be seen."

BEYOND POSITIVE AND NEGATIVE

There are two aspects to all *mitzvot*:[24]

a) The common denominator inhering to *mitzvot* is that they are all commands from G-d himself.

b) These commands are also differentiated into various general categories and finally subdivided into individual imperatives with particular details. These individual details of the *mitzvot* purify Man, causing specific spiritual refinement within the various aspects of his soul as well as refining the material objects involved in fulfilling the G-dly command.

The above distinction provides us with insights into the contrasting opinions of Rabbi Yishmael and Rabbi Akiva.

Rabbi Yishmael's position that the Jewish people "saw that which is to be seen and heard that which is to be heard" is derived from his view that the highest level of spiritual ascent is actualized when G-dliness is elicited *within* the framework of the numerous details of *worldly existence*. It is for this reason that Rabbi Yishmael states that the Jewish people answered to the affirmative commands, "*Hein*" (Yes) and to the negative commands "*Lav*" (No) for they apprehended the quality unique to each command: the positive goodness and ascent of "*Hein*" and the very reverse of good that characterize the prohibitions of the "*Lav*."

Rabbi Akiva's position, on the other hand, is that ultimate ascent consists of transcendence over worldly existence. The emphasis in the fulfillment of the *mitzvot* is above specific detail and limitation, and therefore the Jews did not differentiate in their response between positive and negative commands. They declared "*Hein*"—they would obey *all* G-d's decrees.

---

24. See *Tanya*, ch. 41 (56b).

PERCEIVING THE POSITIVE IN EVERYTHING

Another rationale for the position of Rabbi Akiva, is that answering "*Hein*" to both positive and negative commands was not only motivated by the perception of their common element—the fulfillment of G-d's will—but in addition there was also the awareness of the "*Hein*" quality inhering in the "*Lav*" commands. Even within the very "*Lav*" prohibitions, they only sensed the "*Hein*" dimension, the goodness and sanctity which become manifest as a result of Man obeying G-d's negative commands. This is in harmony with his opinion that Sinaitic revelation was experienced by the Jewish people as ascending to the level of "hearing that which is to be seen," perceiving the material world only with the distant, conceptual awareness of "hearing," of intellectual comprehension. Because of the vivid awareness of spirituality, the material world is refuted in the mind of the individual on this level, and the existence of the physical world is comprehended only because of the proofs the Torah itself provides. At that time, the only aspect perceivable in the material world is the inner content related to the fulfillment of Torah and its *mitzvot*.

Consequently, when one encounters a "*Lav*," a matter which is opposed to sanctity, even in the "*Lav*" of idolatry, the most extreme form of defiance to the "Oneness of G-d," he does not sense the "*Lav*," the evil aspect, but rather, he senses the "*Hein*"–the virtuous aspect contained therein. By opposing the falsehood, one can observe the Biblical command, "You shall have no other gods" etc.[25] Thus, even in the case of "*Lav*," there is essentially the observance of "*Hein*," the awareness of G-d's Unity.

Rabbi Akiva's seeing the "*Hein*" even in the "*Lav*" is reflected in a Talmudic narrative. Rabbi Akiva and his Rabbinic colleagues saw a fox roaming on the site where the Holy Temple formerly stood. The others reacted with intense grief, while Rabbi Akiva looked on with a beaming countenance. He

---

25. Exodus 20:3.

explained that if the dire prophecy of Uriah regarding the destruction of the Temple was fulfilled, then Zechariah's optimistic prophecy about the redemption of Jerusalem would, surely, also inevitably occur.[26]

FOR BEGINNERS

The position of Rabbi Yishmael as to the spiritual service of the righteous, and Rabbi Akiva's view emphasizing the spiritual task of serving G-d through repentance are, both related to individuals who are already far advanced in their spiritual striving.

Rashi in his commentary is concerned with the "five year old child commencing Biblical study,"[27] or even an older person who is still in the early stages of his spiritual development. Thus, he draws on the position of both Rabbi Yishmael and Rabbi Akiva because they aid him in explaining the literal text. In addition, this also depicts a composite portrait of a personality on an initial level of spiritual growth.

Rashi cites Rabbi Akiva's position that the Jewish people "saw that which is to be heard." The individual commencing his spiritual services must in a certain sense "see that which is to be heard," accustoming himself to act in accordance with the Torah teaching at the very beginning of the Code of Jewish Law, "I have set G-d before me constantly."[28]

The awareness of G-d should be unquestionable certainty, "seeing" with simple faith. Yet, this world in its palpable multiplicity is a reality, not receding or fading from one consciousness, thus Rashi also cites Rabbi Yishmael's opinion, "to 'Hein' they answered 'Hein' and to 'Lav' they responded 'Lav.' But the concluding phrase of Rabbi Akiva cannot be asked of *such an individual*, and so Rashi omits the phrase "they heard that which is to be seen"—which indicates that

---

26. *Makkot*, end.

27. *Pirkei Avot* 5:22.

28. Psalms 16:8.

worldliness should merely be comprehended in an abstract manner.

Also, Rabbi Yishmael's concluding phrase of "hearing that which is to be heard" cannot be required of such a person, because this would imply that even amid the many "shadows" of evil and doubt in the world, the individual has the capacity to "hear" and comprehend the G-dliness and spirituality in worldly existence.

The literal or figurative "five year old" beginning Torah student whom Rashi addresses accepts as axiomatic that he must learn Torah and perform *mitzvot*, and this certainty is so natural to him that no element of self-coercion is entailed in the performance of his actions.

At the same time, however, the physical aspects of his life are *to him* also a matter of self-evident reality. He has not grown spiritually to the degree that his material needs are of no consequence to him, nor is he on the lofty level of being motivated solely by the thought that "All of your actions should be for the sake of Heaven."[29]

We cannot expect of him either surpassing spiritual sensitivity or profound intellectual comprehension. He is indeed capable of the faithful certainty of G-d's all-pervasive Presence, but at the same time there is also the intrusive awareness of worldly reality. The levels of spirituality described and exemplified by Rabbi Yishmael and Rabbi Akiva are far beyond his limited spiritual capability.

In summation, Rashi's description of spiritual certainty expressed in the phrase "They saw that which is to be heard" coexists with the awareness of a material world to the extent of "*Lav, lav.*" Negating and struggling against seemingly substantive evil is necessary only at the beginning of Man's spiritual ascent; subsequently, a person must advance to one of the two manners of G-dly spiritual service.

---

29. *Pirkei Avot* 2:12.

One approach is the spiritual effort of eliciting G-dliness from "above to below" through profound contemplation upon G-dliness in order to overcome the encroaching evil which conflicts with spirituality. Or conversely, there is the spiritual service of uplifting from "below to above," elevating the world from its natural boundaries and limitations so that they do not conceal G-dliness, and moreover "that which is to be heard is seen"—one experiences the vivid experiences of spiritual reality. Even beyond this, the world is seen not as an independent entity, but that material existence is subordinate to the dimension of spirituality; one "hears"—remotely comprehends—the physical world which normally is "seen" and vividly experienced because of its physical nature. Consequently, G-dliness is apprehended even in the most negative aspects of human existence, and in response to the negative "*Lav*," the reply is "*Hein*"—an affirmation of G-d as ultimate reality.

Since the two positions are both part of the Oral Torah, and since Torah is derived from the word *hora'ah* meaning instruction and guidance,[30] both modes of G-dly service are expected of every Jew. One should endeavor to elicit G-dliness from "above to below," and elevate and uplift the G-dliness within the world to reunite it with its source Above.

May these two forms of service be the preparation to the fulfillment of the prophecy "And I shall make your windows from the *kadkod*."[31] "*Kadkod*" is a precious gem; but there is a dispute in the Talmud as to its exact identity. One opinion is that it is the *shoham* (onyx) and the other, the *yashfeh* (jasper).[32]

The Talmud states that from the word "*kadkod*" we can derive the phrase "*kedain* and *kedain*" ("It is as this one and as this one"), hinting that both opinions are correct. In *Likkutei Torah*[33] it is explained that these two gems correspond to the

---

30. See Redak, Psalms 19:8; *Zohar* III 53b.

31. Isaiah 54:12.

32. *Bava Batra* 75a.

33. Deuteronomy 25d, 27d.

mystical descent of light from "above to below" and also the ascent of light from "below to above." In relation to the above discussion this is respectively relevant to the service of *tzaddikim* and of *Baalei teshuvah*.

The full revelation of the radiance of these spiritual lights shall be accomplished at the time of the true and complete redemption through our righteous *Mashiach* speedily in our times.

(*Likkutei Sichot,* vol. 6, pp. 119-129)

SHAVUOT

THE NOCTURNAL SLUMBER
OF *ATZERET*

The present *sicha* discusses the fact that the Jewish people slept
through the night before the giving of the Torah and had to be
awakened by the Almighty. This is the reason for our custom of
staying up the night of Shavuot. This "sleeping in" is difficult to
understand given the eagerness of the Jewish people to receive the
Torah and their lofty spiritual state at the time. Although, as the
Rebbe explains, the sleep of the Jewish people actually reflects a
desire for spiritual achievement through transcending the physical
realm, the ultimate focus of our spiritual task is *in* the physical
world.

OVERSLEEPING AT SINAI

The *Midrash* relates[1] that the Jewish people slept the entire
night prior to the receiving of the Torah, "for the slumber of
Atzeret is pleasant and the night is short," and even a *purtana* (a
biting insect) did not disturb them. When the Almighty was
ready in the early morning to give the Torah and found Israel
asleep, it was necessary for Him to wake them, and He
declared: "Why, when I came was there no man? When I called,
was there none to answer?"[2] For this reason we now observe
the custom of staying awake the entire first night of Shavuot,
occupied with the study of Torah—to rectify the slumber of the
Jewish nation on the night prior to the giving of the Torah.[3]

---

1. *Shir Hashirim Rabbah* 1, 12 (Ibid. 1, 2).
2. Isaiah 50:2.
3. *Magen Avraham, Orach Chaim,* beg. ch. 494.

Every narrative of the Torah provides guidance for us in our own spiritual endeavors. A story such as this—for the Torah goes to great lengths to avoid that which is disparaging or derogatory[4]—must certainly include a most significant moral precept, one which justifies the story's inclusion in the Torah.

PREPARATION FOR RECEIVING THE TORAH

Some questions immediately arise. It is known that a great longing was evoked within the Jewish people when they heard that after their departure from Egypt they would be given the Torah, and they commenced counting the days until the anticipated time. In response to their longing, G-d decreed the mitzvah of counting the days of the *Omer*.[5] Now, if at the onset of the seven weeks they were impatient to receive the Torah, it is obvious how great their yearning must have been immediately before the event itself. How, then, was it possible for them to sleep the very night before the giving of the Torah?

Moreover, their counting of the days was also a preparation for receiving the Torah. During these forty nine days, they underwent progressive spiritual purification till they were worthy of receiving the Torah. Every day, they evoked within themselves the revelation of another gate of the *Sha'arei Binah*— Gates of Understanding. When they had concluded the evocation of all the forty nine gates, (the maximum degree achievable by human effort) then the Almighty, at the time of the giving of the Torah, endowed them with the "Fiftieth gate."[6]

Thus, if immediately after their departure from Egypt, just rescued from the "forty nine Gates of Impurity,"[7] they longed to receive the Torah, how immeasurably greater was their yearning for the Torah after they had achieved the sublime degree of the "Forty-ninth Gate of Understanding." After the

---

4. See *Bava Batra* 123a.

5. Ran, end Pesach*im*.

6. See *Likkutei Torah*, Leviticus 35a, Deuteronomy 10a and ff., etc.

7. See *Zohar Chadash*, beg. *Parshat Yitro*.

great spiritual ascent of the forty-nine days and after becoming progressively worthier of receiving the Torah, how could they permit themselves to recline in slumber?

We must conclude that their sleep is not be seen at face value, but was rather in itself a preparation for receiving the Torah. Further proof that their sleep was actually a form of preparation is the fact that the insects did not bite them. If their sleep had been but a lapse of consciousness and a distraction from their preoccupation with receiving the Torah, then the Almighty would not have caused a *miracle*—that they should not be disturbed.

THE ASCENT OF THE SOUL DURING SLEEP

Rabbi Schneur Zalman, the Alter Rebbe[8] states that the loftiest degree of comprehension and cleaving to G-dliness achieved during human existence, when the soul is vested in human form, is still incomparable to the exalted level of cleaving achieved by the soul prior to its descent into the human body. This is so because the physical body cannot apprehend such a high degree of union.

At the time of sleep, however, the soul divests itself of the body and ascends to its source;[9] there remains within the body "but a small measure of life"[10] from the soul. Therefore, at the time of slumber, the soul can sometimes achieve more sublime apprehension than during the time of wakefulness, when it is vested in the physical garb of its body.

It is known, for example, that those who engage in Torah study with great dedication and zeal during their waking hours, may achieve in the course of their sleep even further revelation in Torah matters. This is sometimes true to such a degree that problems these persons strove to clarify while awake, and which remained unanswered, are resolved upon their awaken-

8. *Tanya*, ch. 37.

9. *Bereishit Rabbah* 14, 9.

10. See *Zohar* I 83a.

ing from a period of sleep. This is due to the soul's ascension Above.[11]

Therefore, after the Jewish people had achieved all that is possible for the soul in bodily garb, i.e. the forty nine Gates of Understanding—they wished to slumber prior to receiving the Torah, for they desired that the soul divest itself of its bodily garb and ascend Above to attain even more sublime heights. They thought that the exalted state thus achieved would be the most appropriate, the very culminating point of their preparation for the revelation from Above when the Torah would be given.

And this is what the *Midrash* states, "The slumber of *Atzeret* is pleasant and the night is short"—the more a person strives and refines himself while awake, when the soul is in its bodily garb, the higher the soul ascends to achieve loftier conceptions during the period of sleep. At the conclusion of the spiritual labor of counting the *Omer* for forty-nine days, the Jews had already achieved the spiritual preparation for "*Atzeret.*" And "the night (the spiritual darkness and "concealment" of the world) is short," that is, there remained but a small degree of concealment, for the entire labor had been completed, and in a very short while the revelation of the Torah would take place. At such a time, the slumber is "pleasant," for by means of sleep one can achieve the most sublime spirituality.

This great ascent of the Jewish People at the time of their sleep affected even the surrounding world and nature—to the extent that not even an insect disturbed them.

"THE TORAH IS NOT IN HEAVEN"

Nevertheless, the Almighty was not content with Israel's slumber prior to receiving the Torah, for this was not, in truth, the appropriate preparation; the preparation for receiving the Torah should have been in an entirely different manner.

---

11. See *Sefer Hama'amarim 5700*, p. 5; *Hayom Yom 4 Tevet.*

The purpose of Torah and *mitzvot* is essentially to serve G-d using the physical human body.[12] By this means, the relationship with the essence of G-dliness can be truly achieved. So significant is the importance of laboring *with* the physical body, that the Heavenly court above recognizes the judicial decisions rendered by the Torah scholars on *earth*. Though their opinion may be at variance with the Heavenly decision, the Almighty declares, "My children have prevailed over Me!"[13] for the Torah is "*not* in Heaven."[14]

Since the singular importance of the giving of the Torah was the endowment of exalted significance to the soul's labor *within* the body, the preparation for the giving of the Torah had to be in a similar manner—not slumber, not the soul's separation from the physical body, but labor and service *with* the body.

DESCENDING TO THE PHYSICAL REALM

How does this concept apply to our own spiritual endeavors? There are those who argue: Why should I be concerned with the spiritual darkness of the world; why get involved with mundane matters? Far better to remove myself from the world, to labor in Torah and prayer in seclusion. I have expended great effort and already achieved the level of "*Atzeret*" and "the night is short," the darkness within me is greatly diminished; by isolating myself from the world I will achieve even loftier spirituality.

We are therefore told that even prior to receiving the Torah (but on the very same day that it was given), such conduct was not in accordance with the will of G-d, and there now remains the continual need to rectify the slumber of the past. Most assuredly, after the giving of the Torah, our spiritual labor must be in a manner of "descent below"[15]—the spiritual descending

12. See *Tanya*, ch. 35 and ff.

13. *Bava Metzia* 59b.

14. Deuteronomy 30:12.

15. *Shemot Rabbah* 12, 3.

and concern with the physical, preoccupying ourselves with helping a fellow Jew of lesser spiritual degree. Precisely by such means will the scholar succeed in achieving ascent—"and from my students have I derived more than from the others."[16]

This is the reason for our custom of not sleeping during the night of Shavuot. The preparation for receiving the Torah is not "slumber," not the soul's ascent and departure from the physical to attain sublime apprehension. Each Jew must labor with the human body, with his baser nature and his share in the material world, and thus prepare for the receiving of the Torah joyfully and inwardly—for the entire year.

(*Likkutei Sichot*, vol. 4, pp. 1024-1027)

---

16. *Ta'anit* 7a.

SHAVUOT

THE UNIQUENESS OF SINAI—
THE TERRESTRIAL
AND THE CELESTIAL

> The following *sicha* discusses a primary concept in *Chasidut*, the
> fusion of the spiritual and the physical which is accomplished
> through a mitzvah, reflecting the change in the fabric of creation
> which came about at the giving of the Torah on Mt. Sinai. This
> change is reflected in the wording of the Ten commandments, as
> well as in the first three words of the commandment, "I am the
> L-rd, your G-d."[1] Thus, through understanding the transformation
> which took place at Sinai, a Jew gains insight into the primary goal
> of his spiritual service here on Earth.

UNITING "ABOVE" AND "BELOW"

We have frequently discussed[2] the basic Chasidic concept
that the purpose of receiving the Torah was to unite the realms
"above" with the realms "below," and those "below" with those
"above." Prior to the receiving of the Torah the spiritual and
material were two separate realms incapable of merging—"The
Heavens are the Heavens of the L-rd, but the earth He has
given to the children of men"[3]. But when the Torah was given,
G-d nullified this decree, declaring: "I shall commence,"[4] this
empowered the Jewish people with the ability to unite "earth"
with "heaven," by performing *mitzvot*.

---

1. Exodus 20:2.
2. See also *Likkutei Sichot*, vol. 4, p. 757 and ff., 776 and ff. and sources cited there.
3. Psalms 115:16.
4. I.e., "I shall be the first One to descend." *Shemot Rabbah* 12, 3.

Hence, though the Patriarchs, who lived prior to the revelation at Sinai, fulfilled many *mitzvot* with material objects, they did not have the ability to instill sanctity into those objects so that the materials themselves became holy. The possibility did not yet exist at that time, before the Torah was received, of creating a bond between spirituality and material objects.

The primary purpose of the *mitzvot* performed by the Patriarchs was to cause the *spiritual* revelation of G-dliness. The Patriarchs had the status of a *merkavah* (chariot)[5] a vehicle and bearer of G-dliness even with their physical limbs.[6] They achieved such a lofty degree of self-nullification to G-dliness that they did not perceive themselves as separate beings and entities—just as every movement of a chariot is wholly subject to the will of its rider. Thus, their spiritual service permeated the entirety of their existence until it found expression even in the *mitzvot* which they performed with material objects. The goal, however, was not to change the material object; the object was merely a means for eliciting in the realm of the spiritual. For this reason there was less meticulous concern about the way a mitzvah was performed. As is well-known, Jacob caused, by means of the peeled "staffs,"[7] the spiritual revelations that we now achieve after receiving the Torah by the mitzvah of *tefillin*.[8] The same is true of other *mitzvot*.

In contrast to the limitations which existed before the Torah was given, the *mitzvot* we now perform have the power to cause the revelation of sanctity even within the material object; the substance itself acquires holiness. Thus, precise details and exact requirements are necessary for the overwhelming majority of *mitzvot* to ensure the achievement of this purpose.

This power of *mitzvot* to elicit and instill sanctity in material objects is in fact derived from G-dliness which transcends both

---

5. *Bereishit Rabbah* 47:6.

6. See *Tanya*, ch. 23.

7. Genesis 30:37 and ff.

8. *Zohar* 1:162a.

the realms "above" and "below." For since G-d is truly not subject to limitation, not bound by the finitude of either the celestial or terrestrial realms, He can therefore bestow the ability to unite the two.

THE TEN COMMANDMENTS

The unity of earthly and heavenly realms is also implied in the text of the Ten Commandments, which were given publicly at the time of the giving of the entire Torah. At first glance, the commandments consist of highly contrasting categories of *mitzvot*. The first commandments, "I am the L-rd your G-d,"[9] and "You shall not have any other gods before me,"[10] express the most profound matters related to G-d's unity. The other commandments, however, consist of such simple decrees as "You shall not murder," and "You shall not kidnap;"[11] these are obvious truths, even for persons of ordinary intellect.

The fact, however, that G-d placed these two categories of commands together in the Ten Commandments is a subtle reference to the union of "above" and "below:"

"Above"—the commands of "I am the L-rd" and "You shall not"—should descend "below"—i.e., penetrate and be understood in the commands of "You shall not kill," and "You shall not kidnap." Even these commandments, which are clear and obvious to human intellect, must be permeated with the G-dly basis and quality of "I am the L-rd."

Why is human understanding not sufficient? It is a fact that self-love can so distort a person's judgment that a transgression can be rationalized as a *mitzvah*, as stated in Proverbs: "All transgressions are concealed by love"[12]—the love for one's own self. A small finger placed before the eyes will conceal the entire world. This is true of subtle forms of transgressions. In the

---

9. Exodus 20:2.

10. Ibid. 20:3.

11. Ibid. 20:13.

12. Proverbs 10:10.

same way, since "Man is related unto himself,"[13] emotionally enmeshed with himself, self-love can so distort matters that he may be brought to serious "transgressions," rebellious acts performed intentionally.[14] Furthermore, even if it were possible to fulfill the *mitzvot* on the basis of human intellect alone, it is the task of a Jew to unite all his deeds, even the simplest, with "I am the L-rd your G-d." Consequently, in every one of his actions, including the virtuous deeds dictated by human intellect, there must be manifest "I am the L-rd." They should all be permeated with G-dliness.

This is also derived from the adage of our Sages of blessed memory: "If the Torah *were not given* we would learn modesty from a cat, and the prohibition against forceful theft from an ant."[15] If, Heaven forbid, the Torah had not been given to us, we would follow moral laws because of a lesser motive, because of our human understanding of animal behavior. That is, if not for the giving of the Torah, there could be no joining of grossly mundane matters with G-dliness. Once the Torah was given, and the ability was granted to unite "above" with "below" then even those virtuous qualities also possessed by simple animals must be permeated with the sanctity of the Torah. They should be performed as acts of submission to the "yoke of Heavenly majesty" because G-d has so decreed.

"And the realms below shall ascend above": this statement also refers to persons on so low a moral plane that they are capable of terrible moral transgressions. For them, therefore, the shattering sounds and the great flames, the entire tumult associated with the giving of the Torah were necessary—G-d Himself, as it were, standing and proclaiming to such individuals: "You shall not murder," "You shall not kidnap." But even such a person should ascend "above." He, too, must

---

13. *Yevamot* 25b.

14. *Yoma* 36b; *Shevuot* 12b.

15. *Eiruvin* 100b.

acquire a contemplative outlook and knowledge of G-dliness, which is the loftiest degree of wisdom.

"I AM THE L-RD, YOUR G-D"

This ability to achieve the unity of "above" and "below," is also implied in the first three words of the Ten Commandments: *"Anochi Havaya Elokecha"*—"I am the L-rd your G-d." These three terms delineate three general levels of revelation of G-dliness. These three separate Hebrew terms— *Anochi, Havaya, Elokim*—are revelations on an ascending scale:

Elokim indicates G-dliness as it is vested in creation. G-dly power vests itself in every created being and manifests itself according to the conditions of that object. The term *Elokim* therefore is plural,[16] because there are varying degrees of G-dliness; each object possesses a unique measure of divine spirituality specifically appropriate for that object.[17] Hence the word *Elokim* is numerically equivalent to *hateva*[18] (nature) because this aspect of G-dliness is vested in a creation upon which G-d has imposed the so-called "laws of nature."

This, too, is the meaning of *"Elokecha"* ("your G-d") the only name of G-d which can be expressed in a relational manner to created beings. Since this name indicates the category of G-dliness which condenses and vests itself according to the needs of created beings, this aspect of G-dliness can be comprehended with the human mind. This quality is expressed in the term *"Elokecha,"* the relational *"your* G-d," He Whom it is possible for you to comprehend.[19]

The name *Havaya*, on the other hand, the next category of revelation, denotes G-dliness which transcends the constricting finitude of nature and its laws. *Havaya* is defined as the simultaneous unity of past, present and future.[20] Although past,

---

16. See Joshua 24:19; *Derech Mitzvotecha* 5b.

17. See *Tanya, Sha'ar Hayichud Veha'emunah*, ch. 1.

18. *Pardeis, Sha'ar* 12, ch. 2.

19. *Likkutei Torah*, Numbers 73b, Deuteronomy 53c.

20. *Zohar* III 257b, *Tanya, Sha'ar Hayichud Veha'emunah*, ch. 7.

present and future are three separate categories of time which cannot coincide, *Havaya* is beyond time and nature, and in this realm all three categories are as one.

Anochi—"I"—the third category and the highest revelation, is the essence of G-d, which no letter or symbol can denote, as expressed in the saying, "*Anochi*—I Who am *Anochi*, neither alluded to in a letter, nor even in a point of a letter."[21] This means not only that *Anochi* is beyond the revelation of *Elokim*, which is the numerical equivalent of *hateva*, but that it also transcends the revelation of *Havaya*—G-dliness above nature. It is not bound by any limitations whatsoever, not even the limitations of that which is beyond nature. *Anochi*" is therefore capable of causing these two realms to merge and be united.

The revelation of this level of G-dliness—*Anochi*—was manifest in the Holy of Holies in the Temple. The ark, according to Biblical law, measured two-and-a-half cubits by one-and-a-half cubits. The wingspread of each of the two cherubim standing adjacent to the ark in the Temple made by King Solomon was two cubits, i.e. each wing extended outward *beyond* the body of the cherubim a distance of five cubits.

The wings of the cherubim were stretched forth so that the wing of the one touched the one wall, and the wing of the other cherub touched the other wall; and their wings touched one another in the midst of the Holy of Holies.[22] Thus the wingspan was twenty cubits; this sum does not include the measurement of their bodies. Our Sages tell us that from each side of the ark to the wall of the Holy of Holies was only ten cubits. Thus, the wingspread of the cherubim was not bound by the physical dimensions of the Holy of Holies, which was twenty cubits by twenty cubits.[23]

This, then, is the meaning of "*Anochi Havaya Elokecha*" ("I am the L-rd your G-d"). At the time of the giving of the Torah,

---

21. *Likkutei Torah*, Numbers 80b.

22. I Kings 6:27.

23. See *Yoma* 21a.

G-d bestowed the power of *Anochi*, which is not bound by any sort of limitation. It is *"Anochi"* that effects the joining of *Havaya*—that which is beyond nature and human intellect— with *Elokecha*, the level of G-dliness of which Man can comprehend to some extent. This union is expressed through the *mitzvot*, as explained above, by the merging of the commands "You shall not murder" and "You shall not kidnap" with the most sublime aspects relating to the unity of G-d, the very first commandments—*Anochi* (I am the L-rd) and the prohibition against idolatry.

This is the Jew's primary task: to cause, through Torah study and performing *mitzvot*, the merging of the "realms above"—spirituality—with the "realms below"—the physical world, thus, the entire world is irradiated with G-dliness.

(Likkutei Sichot, vol. 3, pp. 887-892)

SHAVUOT

SHAVUOT AS A CONSTANT AND A VARIABLE

The problem of the International Date Line, when a day can be either "lost" or "gained" by the traveler, and its implications for the observance of Shabbat, holidays and in particular Shavuot, has challenged the mind of many outstanding Halachists in our own age, and has been the subject of much dispute. The following *sicha* offers a bold and lucid resolution of this problem.

The implications of a Shavuot that is twofold—fixed and variable—should evoke within each Jew the desire to strive and hasten towards his own personal receiving of the Torah. The knowledge that every Jew, whatever his own spiritual level, has been granted the unique divine bestowal of a fixed, inevitable "Time of the giving of the Torah" should serve as a source of humility as well as spiritual strength.

"EACH AND EVERY ONE OF YOU SHALL COUNT"

Sefirat Ha'omer—the Counting of the *Omer*—is a preparation for the holiday of Shavuot, on which we celebrate the giving of the Torah, and which occurs immediately upon the conclusion of the forty-nine days of counting.

The relationship of the *Omer*-counting to the giving of the Torah is manifested specifically to each Jew as an individual. In reference to the counting of the *Omer* the Talmud states" "That each and every one of you shall count."[1] This directive contrasts the method of counting required for the seventh, the *Shemittah* year (in the Sabbatical cycle) and for the fiftieth, the *Yovel* year (the agricultural jubilee), when no agricultural labors could be

---

1. *Menahot* 65b.

done. These were determined solely by the Jewish court of law—one counting that fulfilled the requirement for the collective community.[2] The counting of the *Omer* is, however, a function of each individual's separate activity.

Similarly, the Torah was not only given to the Jewish people as a collective body, but G-d also addresses Himself to each individual Jew, declaring, "I am the L-rd *your* G-d"[3]—in the singular form. G-d gives the Torah to each Jew individually,[4] commanding each Jew to study and fulfill all six-hundred-thirteen *mitzvot* and endows each of them with the spiritual capability to achieve this goal.

"YOU SHALL COUNT FIFTY DAYS"

In this context, Rabbi Schneur Zalman, the Alter Rebbe, in *Likkutei Torah*[5] explains the Biblical verse, "You shall count fifty days,"[6] even though in practice we count only forty nine days. By *means* of our counting forty-nine days, we cause the manifestation of the mystical "forty-nine Gates of Understanding," and on the fiftieth day the manifestation of the "fiftieth gate of understanding" occurs, which is the giving of the Torah.

The manifestation of the "forty-nine Gates" is achieved specifically through the spiritual labors of counting the *Omer*. We therefore enumerate the sum total of past days in cardinal numbers as "two days," "three days" and so forth, including the earlier days rather than simply stating the ordinal number designating the specific day—"second day," "third day," etc.— because with the passage of each day we achieve the evocation of another "gate of understanding;" the first day one gate, the second day two gates, and so on.[7]

---

2. Maimonides, *Hilchot Shemittah Veyovel* 10:1.

3. Exodus 20:2.

4. See Nachmonides Exodus 20:2; *Pesikta Rabtai* 21, 6.

5. *Bamidbar* 10d, *Shir Hashirim* 35c.

6. Leviticus 23:16.

7. See *Torah Or* 44b.

Attaining the exalted "fiftieth gate" is not, however, a result of our spiritual labors alone, because human spiritual labor can not extend to, nor affect, so lofty a realm. After having achieved the manifestation of the forty-nine Gates of Understanding by our counting of the *Omer*, the fiftieth gate is conferred upon us from Above as an *itaruta dile'eila*—"an arousal from Above," that is, an action performed by G-d based upon His own will and not by the evocative action of Man below. This is the meaning of the Biblical verse "You will count fifty days," because the fiftieth level is actually granted to Man, but only after the preceding spiritual labor of counting "seven whole weeks."

"THE TIME OF THE GIVING OF OUR TORAH"

The "fiftieth gate" manifested on the fiftieth day of the *Omer* is linked to the giving of the Torah. Nevertheless, the Alter Rebbe renders the *halachic* decision in his Code of Jewish Law[8] that we recite the phrase "the time of the giving of our Torah" on Shavuot, because *nowadays* our observance of Shavuot *always* coincides with the sixth day of *Sivan*, the date when the original giving of the Torah occurred. This occurs because our present Jewish calendars are fixed. However, in the Talmudic era, when the time of the New Moon was established by the testimony of witnesses, then Shavuot—the fiftieth day of the *Omer*—could have occurred on the fifth day of *Sivan* if both earlier months were established as having thirty days. Or it could have been the seventh day of *Sivan* if the Jewish courts fixed the months of *Nissan* and *Iyar* as having only twenty-nine days each. In such cases, although the holiday of Shavuot is always observed on the fiftieth day of the *Omer*, this date would not coincide with the sixth of *Sivan*, and the phrase "the time of the giving of our Torah" would not be recited. This event could occur because the Biblical command to observe Shavuot is not linked to the specific day of the giving of the Torah, i.e., the

---

8. *Torat Chaim*, ch. 494, sec. 1.

sixth of *Sivan*, but is actually dependent upon the fiftieth day of the *Omer*.

There are, then, two aspects to the giving of the Torah: one is that it occurred on the fiftieth day of the *Omer*, and the other, that this date was originally the sixth day of *Sivan*—and it is specifically for this latter reason that we recite the phrase "the time of the giving of the Torah" only on the sixth day of *Sivan*.

The distinction between the above reasons as they relate to our spiritual efforts is as follows: the aspect of the giving of the Torah related to the fiftieth day of the *Omer* occurs after the preceding spiritual labors of Man, and takes place only in the manner of *itaruta dile'eila*—an arousal and bestowal from Above. After having concluded the efforts of the forty-nine days of *Sefirah*, Man can then be a vessel to this revelation of the Torah. In contrast, the other aspect of the giving of the Torah, the sixth day of *Sivan*, is entirely independent of Man's spiritual labor. This is a bestowal wholly contingent upon Torah; the time is the *specific* day—the sixth of *Sivan*.

CROSSING THE INTERNATIONAL DATE LINE

The fiftieth day of the *Omer* and the sixth day of *Sivan* can occur on two separate days (the fiftieth day being on either the fifth or seventh of *Sivan*). This is true not only in the times when the new month was established by the visual testimony of witnesses who had sighted the New Moon. In our own times, it can also occur that these two events do not coincide, but take place on two separate days.

Individuals traveling across the International Date Line "gain" or "lose" a day. One can lose a day traveling from east to west or gain a day traveling from west to east. Thus, the questions arise; what if someone would travel across the International Date Line in the midst of *Sefirah*? Since the obligation to fulfill the *Sefirah* command is *exclusively* incumbent upon the individual, he must count according to the reckoning of *his* own days, and this has nothing to do with the number being counted by a fellow Jew who resides in the very same place to which the traveler has journeyed.

For example, if the first day of Pesach occurs on Shabbat, and an individual travels from east to west on Monday after having counted the second day of the *Omer*, he will skip a day and find that it is Tuesday in the new locale. The next evening, however, he must sustain his *own* count; having counted the second *Sefirah* the night before, he must now count the *third Sefirah*, even though all the people in his present region are already counting the *fourth Sefirah*. The reverse is also true if one has traveled from west to east: he must now count the *third Sefirah*, though all other individuals dwelling in that place will be reciting the *second Sefirah*.

Thus, the counting of the *Omer* is not a command incumbent upon the Jewish people as a collective body, but is rather an obligation for each person *individually*, and each must count the amount of days, that *he has experienced personally* since the beginning of the *Omer*.

In contrast, with regard to Shabbat and other holidays, the individual must conform with the reckoning of the *local* inhabitants of the area. His journey across the International Date Line cannot establish the need for a personal Shabbat observance, because Shabbat does not depend on each person individually. The same is true of all other holidays since they are wholly dependent upon the calendar decisions of the Jewish court acting as the legal representative body for all Jews, even in our own times. *Sefirah*, however, is uniquely related to each particular person, therefore the counting is not dependent upon the reckoning of another individual, but is wholly contingent upon one's own calculating of the days which he has experienced.

THE INDIVIDUAL AND THE COLLECTIVE

As mentioned, the holiday of Shavuot is not fixed to a specific day of the month, but depends on the reckoning of the *Omer*, the fiftieth day of the *Omer* being Shavuot. Thus, at the time when the new month was established by the sighting of the New Moon, Shavuot could possibly occur on the fifth, sixth, or seventh day of *Sivan*.

This relationship of Shavuot to *Sefirah* does not imply that Shavuot comes by means of *Sefirah*, that the forty-nine days which we are obligated to count bring about and result in the holiday of Shavuot. This is not so, for we know that even individuals who are not obligated to count *Sefirah*, such as children or gentiles who have converted in the midst of *Sefirah*, must nevertheless observe the fiftieth day after Pesach as a holiday. Furthermore, while the counting of *Sefirah* in our own time is not a mitzvah *d'oraita*—a Biblical commandment—the observance of Shavuot is a Biblical command just as in the days of yore (although early *halachic* commentators had various opinions, this is the final ruling[9]). How, then, is it possible for Shavuot to occur in the cases when the counting of forty-nine days have not been fulfilled? We cannot say that the counting of the *collective* Jewish people creates the holiday even for the child who has matured and the Gentile who has converted because they are acting in accord with the *congregation* of Israel; we have explained that in this instance there is no such entity as "the *Sefirah* of the collective Jewish people" since each individual counts the *Omer* for himself.

It is therefore self-evident that Shavuot is not *caused* by means of *Sefirah*. The Torah designates the day of the holiday only as the "fiftieth day" according to the *Omer*. The day after the 49 days is the holiday of Shavuot; the purpose of *Sefirah* is to *clarify* and inform that the next day is Shavuot—even for the maturing child and for the convert accepting Judaism in the midst of *Sefirah*.

Consequently, if someone would conclude counting *Sefirah* earlier or later than the members of the community in which he resides, the days which *he* has counted reveal and designate that he must observe Shavuot according to his own personal

---

9. See *Shulchan Aruch Harav, Orach Chaim*, ch. 489, sec. 2.

counting. (We cannot say that although *Sefirah* applies separately to each individual person, the observance of Shavuot is contingent on the community as a whole. This concept must be rejected because the *only* means for determining and clarifying when Shavuot occurs is that it is the fiftieth day of *Sefirah*, a fact *not* related to the collective Jewish community, and fulfilled *only* as a function of each individual person.)

All of the above only concerns the holiday of Shavuot which was established by the Torah as occurring after the forty-ninth day of the *Omer*, and not on a specific day of the month. "The time of the giving of the Torah" is, however, specifically on the sixth day of *Sivan* as cited above from the Alter Rebbe's *Code of Jewish Law*. Therefore, the individual who has passed the International Date Line and who, as a result, observes Shavuot a day earlier or later than the sixth of *Sivan* must omit the phrase, "the time of the giving of the Torah" from his prayers.

Even if one has passed the International Date Line after the first day of *Sivan*, and when counting chronologically, his personal sixth of *Sivan* will coincide with his fiftieth day of the *Sefirah* order, nevertheless, he cannot recite the phrase "the time of the giving of the Torah" because the counting of the days of the *month* are related to the community as a whole, fixed by the Jewish court in its calculations, and his personal counting in this specific matter is of no significance.

ACHIEVING SPIRITUAL REFINEMENT

In conclusion: When someone crosses the International Date Line from west to east, then the fiftieth day of his *Sefirah* sequence occurs on the fifth day of *Sivan*. He must then observe all of the laws of Shavuot on this day, but omit the phrase "the time of the giving of the Torah" from his prayers. Any person in our time living outside of Israel must also observe the next day in conformity with the law of observing every holiday for two days, "*Yom Tov sheini shel galuyot.*"

Similarly, if someone has journeyed across the International Date Line in the opposite direction, from east the west, the seventh day of *Sivan* is to be observed as Shavuot by him as well as the following day.

The spiritual implication of these concepts is as follows: Counting the *Omer* entails the refinement of one's inner qualities.[10] We therefore count *Sefirah* for forty nine days, "seven complete weeks," to refine the seven emotional attributes of the animalistic soul within Man. Each attribute includes the entire range of all seven attributes, and Man must refine these qualities of the personality and make them "complete," perfect and purged of evil. Upon the successful conclusion of refining these emotional attributes, he is awarded, from Above, that aspect of Torah which occurs subsequent to the forty nine days of *Sefirah*. The status of others in no way affects him. If he has completed and perfected his own emotional traits, then he receives the "fiftieth gate" of Torah revelation, though others have not achieved this sublime level he has not yet fulfilled this profound spiritual responsibility, then he must wait for the completion of his task, though others have surpassed him and have already received the Torah.

This holds true for receiving that dimension of the Torah which is revealed subsequent to the spiritual labor of Man. There is, however, an aspect of Torah wholly independent of Man's labor, far beyond the realm of Man's deeds, and not at all related to his efforts of spiritual self-refinement. This G-dly bestowal takes place and affects the entire Jewish people on the sixth day of *Sivan*, "the time of the giving of the Torah."

(Likkutei Sichot, vol. 3, pp. 995 -1001)

---

10. *Likkutei Torah*, Leviticus 35b and eleswhere.

Twelve-Thirteen of Tammuz— Liberation of Rabbi Yosef Yitzchak Schneersohn of Lubavitch

Spiritual Courage

The 12th and 13th of Tammuz marks the anniversary of the final liberation after release from prison of the sixth Lubavitcher Rebbe, Rabbi Yosef Yitzchak Schneersohn. This event constitutes a crucial confrontation between the forces seeking to preserve Judaism in the U.S.S.R., led by the Rebbe, and the brutal Communist determination to eradicate religion. The Rebbe's miraculous survival of his prison ordeal was a significant event that was a source of courage for religious Jews in Russia to fight on, until they finally emerged triumphant after the recent fall of communism. The following two selections are examples of the Rebbe's many talks which provide details of the arrest and insights into its spiritual significance. The first selection describes an instance of Rabbi Yosef Yitzchak's courage and self-sacrifice to help the Jewish people before becoming Rebbe, the same qualities that he exhibited during the arrest. The second selection deals more directly with the incidents and significance of the arrest.

I. Shabbat in a Tavern

For[1] many years during the Czarist reign Pyotr Stolypin served as Russian premier and minister of the interior. He was notorious for his hatred towards Jews and the harsh decrees he enacted against them. The fifth Lubavitcher Rebbe, Rabbi Shalom DovBer Schneersohn once learned of an impending edict planned by Stolypin, and dispatched his son and future

---

1. See *The Heroic Struggle* Kehot, 1999. See also *Sichat* Simchat Torah 5708.

successor, Rabbi Yosef Yitzchak, in an effort to nullify the decree.

Rabbi Yosef Yitzchak traveled to the capital city, S. Petersburg, to discuss the matter with communal leaders. After many futile efforts, it was decided to attempt to sway Stolypin through Konstantin Pobedonostsev, whom Stolypin esteemed highly and who had exerted great influence upon him. Though this official was also anti-Semitic, he was very pious, and therefore accorded reverence to clergymen of all faiths, including rabbis.

After many efforts, an audience was arranged for a Friday evening. Since Pobedonostsev lived in a remote suburb of S. Petersburg, Rabbi Yosef Yitzchak had to leave S. Petersburg early and spend the entire Shabbat in that area.

The capital and its suburbs were forbidden to Jews at that time. Despite notable exceptions in the city itself, such as affluent merchants, physicians, and others of similar social rank who could circumvent the regulations against Jewish inhabitants, in the suburban area there lived not a single Jew.

Not having access to a single home where he could possibly stay, and knowing it was impossible to walk the streets for any length of time because of the severe cold as well as the physical dangers involved, Rabbi Yosef Yitzchak was compelled to seek refuge in a tavern. He waited there for a few hours till the time of his appointment. After successfully fulfilling his mission, he returned to the tavern and spent the entire Shabbat there.

It is not difficult to imagine how Rabbi Yosef Yitzchak felt in the company of drunken Russian peasants, feigning participation for a complete twenty-four hours of the sacred day of Shabbat. There was, in addition, the ever-present danger of being among people notorious for their hatred of Jews. Yet, Rabbi Yosef Yitzchak was willing to endure this perilous and difficult situation even if there was only a remote *possibility* of revoking an evil decree against the Jewish people.

Such behavior is questionable. If, on the one hand, the heavenly court had rendered a decision that the decree should take effect, then his efforts with the official would be of no avail. If, on the other hand, the heavenly court had decided that the decree would be nullified, then no endeavor was necessary.

It is also true that one must use "normal" actions in order to achieve one's goal, but these actions are merely the external means by which Man receives divine blessings. As the Torah declares, "And G-d will bless you in all that you will *do*."[2] The Torah commands that Man must "do," act in the earthly world, in order to enable the divine blessings to permeate his efforts. This does not, however, apply in a case where one's life is actually endangered, as when it was necessary to spend a Shabbat among drunkards, assume a false identity, and remain unobtrusively in their midst until able to return home.

The above reasoning is valid and has a basis in Jewish Law and, as a result, one may render such a decision to others. However, when Rabbi Yosef Yitzchak was confronted with the possibility that Jews would endure anguish and oppression, it affected him profoundly, to the very core of his soul wherein there is no place for speculation and logic. He acted wholly on the basis of the possibility that *perhaps* he would be successful in nullifying the decree.

When as Rebbe, he recounted this incident, it was not to indulge in nostalgic reminiscences, he did so with the specific intention of indicating spiritual pathways for those who follow in his ways and adhere to his teachings:

When one is informed of the pain and anguish of a fellow Jew, whether physical distress or most surely spiritual suffering—that his fellow is enmeshed in vain and futile worldly endeavors and is remote from G-d and His Torah— out of authentic *Ahavat Yisrael* (love for a fellow Jew) this pain should affect the very essence of one's soul. And it is obvious that this empathy will impel a Jew to do all that he is capable of, without hesitation or reflection, even on the remotest *possibility* that he can help another Jew.

---

2. Deuteronomy 16:18.

II.

IMPRISONMENT AND RELEASE

Among the many incidents that the Rebbe related[3] about his arrest and release are several which describe his time in prison, where he endured terrible, harsh treatment.

Immediately upon being taken to the prison, the Rebbe firmly resolved to maintain a steadfast composure during all interrogations by the G.P.U. (Russian secret police, forerunners of the K.G.B.), never to waver or betray signs of weakness or anxiety. This resolution would not only pertain to religious matters, but also to his general demeanor. He would conduct himself as if these people were insignificant, to the extent that they would be, in his eyes, in the words of the Rebbe, "naught and non-being."[4]

While in his cell, the Rebbe had no way of distinguishing between night and day, since there was only one small window in the ceiling, and it was obstructed by a looming wall which blocked out any light. However, by means of the regular prison schedule, the hours fixed for bringing water and so forth, the Rebbe was able to determine and keep track of the hours and days.

Thursday, *Rosh Chodesh Tammuz*, eleven o'clock in the morning (the Rebbe also related that in general he prayed at great length while in prison), a guard entered his cell and commanded him to stand. The guards spoke Russian, but it was the Rebbe's decision to respond to them in Yiddish, and he replied that he would not stand.

Prison procedure required that the prisoners stand whenever they received any kind of information. This was to demonstrate that the prisoner was subject to the authority of his captors; it was for this very reason that the Rebbe refused to rise.

---

3. *Sefer Hasichot 5701*, p. 138 and ff.
4. See *Sefer Hasichot 5687*, p. 227.

It seems that one of the guards was a Jew who understood the Rebbe's Yiddish reply. To the Rebbe's answer, the guards repeated in Russian, "If you will not obey, we will beat you." The Rebbe responded with a non-committal "*Nu....*" The guards beat him harshly and departed.

Later, another group of guards entered the cell. Among them was Lulav, one of those who had participated in the midnight arrest of the Rebbe, his escort to prison, and the later interrogation.[5] He was a descendant of a Chasidic family, and he addressed the Rebbe with the word "Rebbe."

"Rebbe, why this strange conduct with them? Why are you so obstinate and resistant? They have come to inform you that your sentence has been lightened; therefore, if you are told to stand, then do so!" The Rebbe remained totally unresponsive. Lulav asked, "Should they beat you?" Again the Rebbe did not answer. Once again the guards began to brutalize the Rebbe and then left. One of them struck him under the chin, and the Rebbe suffered pain from the blow for many years later.

A group of guards came to the cell a third time; among them was a Jew name Kavalov. They instructed the Rebbe to stand, and he again refused. Kavalov began to beat him, but to no avail. Kavalov, infuriated, cried out in Russian, "We shall teach you!" The Rebbe replied in Yiddish, "We shall see who will teach whom."

After a while some guards came to the cell and told the Rebbe to proceed to the office. There he was informed that his sentence had been reduced as Lulav had mentioned. He was to be freed from prison, sent for three years to the city of Kastroma.

As the Rebbe approached the table, he observed the documents of his case lying upon it. He noticed that the first line had been crossed out, nullifying the original death sentence. The next line stated that the Rebbe should be sent away to prison for ten years to Solovaki in Siberia; next to it was

---

5.   See *The Heroic Struggle*, p. 29 and ff.

written, *"Nyet"*—"No!" On the last line was written: "Three years Kastroma."

When the Rebbe was told he was being exiled to Kastroma for a three-year term, he was asked at the same time which class train accommodations he desired, and he answered, *"Medzunarodni"* (International) the top class reserved for high government officials and affluent businessmen. He was asked if he was capable of paying the high price; the Rebbe replied that if the money confiscated from his bureau at the time of his arrest was inadequate, he would instruct the members of his household to pay the remainder.

It was Thursday; the Rebbe asked when the train would arrive in Kastroma, and he was told on Shabbat. The Rebbe declared that he would not travel on Shabbat under any circumstances.

When the Rebbe recounted this story, he concluded, "Thank G-d, I did not travel on Shabbat. I remained in the jail until Sunday." The officials refused to allow him to remain in his home for a lengthy period, i.e., from Thursday to Sunday. To avoid traveling on Shabbat the Rebbe chose to stay in jail until Sunday, when he returned home and then started on his journey to Kastroma that very same night.[6]

The Rebbe added to this narrative the fact that the *Chasid* Rabbi Michoel Dworkin had arrived in Kastroma beforehand, and by the time the Rebbe arrived, Rabbi Michoel had gathered many children in anticipation and had established a *cheder*. He had also been involved in preparing the *mikveh* there.

Thus, the Rebbe persisted in the very same actions—providing the essential spiritual needs of Jews, Torah education, *mikva'ot*, etc.—which had caused his imprisonment and the threat of a death sentence, though it had miraculously been modified and reduced to three years in Kastroma. Scripture states: "He sent Judah to guide before him to the land of

---

6. See following discourse on the halachic aspects of this decision.

Goshen;"[7] even as our forefather Jacob sent his son Judah, the Rebbe had sent an emissary to establish a *cheder* and prepare a *mikveh* for the Jews of that area.

(*Likkutei Sichot*, vol. 6, pp. 287-289; vol. 4, pp. 1061-1063)

---

7.   Genesis 46:28; and see Rashi there.

Twelve-Thirteen of Tammuz

Refusal to Travel on Shabbat

The following *sicha* again focuses on the arrest and liberation of Rabbi Yosef Yitzchak, in Soviet Russia, this time offering an extended analysis of the Rebbe's refusal to travel on Shabbat when released from prison, even though considerations of mortal danger might ordinarily make it permissible to do so according to Jewish law. In the course of his analysis, the Rebbe delves into an essential quality of the Rebbe's spiritual identity.

Refusal to Travel on Shabbat

On Thursday, the first day of *Rosh Chodesh Tammuz*, shortly before noon, the Rebbe was informed that he would be released from prison and exiled to the city of Kastroma for three years. He was also told that he would be freed that very day, and he would be able to spend six hours with his family; that night he was to commence his journey to Kastroma.

Since it was Thursday, the Rebbe inquired when he would arrive in Kastroma and was told, on Shabbat. Only through the exertion of great effort in the higher levels of government was permission obtained for the exile journey to be delayed until Sunday, the third of *Tammuz*.

One of the officials who had conducted the actual arrest of the Rebbe stated that if he would not leave at the scheduled time and arrive in Kastroma on Shabbat, then he would not release him from the prison. The Rebbe replied that he was prepared to remain in prison for a protracted period of time, but under no circumstances would he travel on Shabbat.

This requires clarification: in rebuffing the instructions to travel immediately to Kastroma, the Rebbe was placing himself

317

in certain mortal danger. Was such behavior permissible under Torah law?

Initially, the Rebbe had been sentenced to death. Extensive efforts on the part of his devoted *Chasidim* and admirers, who successfully organized international declarations of outrage and protest from countless individuals, including many distinguished world leaders, were successful in having this terrible penalty rescinded. The sentence was first diminished to ten years of hard labor, and then further reduced to an exile of three years in the distant city of Kastroma. The situation was nevertheless fraught with great peril, for those who had initially issued the decree still adhered to their original harsh view. They were compelled by higher governmental sources to change their plans, but still retained their original position and authority. The fact that the Rebbe was still in their jurisdiction obviously entailed great danger for him. Indeed, the Rebbe's rejection of the intended Shabbat journey was a source of great provocation. He had acted contrary to their dictates. His affirmation of Shabbat in their sphere of authority was a challenge to their own prestige.

On the other hand, there were other mitigating factors which would have perhaps *halachically* justified his leaving the prison. Since he would be released that day, he was not facing an immediate possibility of violating Shabbat. Moreover, there was an element of doubt, indeed many factors of uncertainty, whether the journey would actually occur. For once he was freed on Thursday, there would be greater freedom for extended endeavors under the Rebbe's personal guidance to defer his scheduled departure that night. Even presuming he would leave at the set time, there still remained a complete day of travelling, during which those concerned with his welfare could exert themselves to effect the interruption of his journey. Thus, the Rebbe might be enabled to observe the entire Shabbat under *halachically* permissible circumstances.

Superficially, we are faced with a very profound problem. Why did the Rebbe take so tenacious a position when it entailed the possibility of immediate peril? The more pragmatic response would have been to immediately leave the danger of prison confinement and then formulate strategies to avoid the Shabbat journey.

INHERENT SELF-SACRIFICE

Indeed, this stance of heroic self-sacrifice in the face of great peril was an all-pervasive quality that characterized all of the Rebbe's activities, even prior to his arrest for the promulgation of Torah and the strengthening of Judaism in that land.

As is well known, the Rebbe's stance of self-sacrifice during that era encompassed not merely those instances where it was necessary to act in this way; he acted this way even when it was a matter of choice, with other less dangerous possibilities available. Moreover, as discussed at length elsewhere,[1] the Rebbe chose such acts of self-sacrifice in cases where eminent Torah scholars were of the opinion that it was not necessary to endanger one's life.

Viewed from the perspective of general communal responsibilities, this posture is understandable. The Rebbe was fully aware of the precarious situation of those times, conscious of the fact that the very existence of Jews and Judaism was being threatened. Thus, to assure that the "flame of Israel" would not be extinguished, mindful of his role of spiritual leadership and motivated by a sense of responsibility for the survival of the entire Jewish people, he could act in a boldly and display self-sacrifice, undeterred by the reckonings of limitations, of arguments for and against.

In this specific case, however, it would appear that the journey affected only him personally, and not the welfare of the general Jewish community. Why, then, did he choose so dangerous a course? Indeed, this act could have endangered his whole life work.

---

1. *Likkutei Sichot*, Vol. 18, p. 321.

KIDDUSH HASHEM—CHILUL HASHEM

One answer to this problem is to view the entire matter in the context of the twin concepts of *kiddush Hashem* (sanctification of G-d's name) and *chilul Hashem* (profanation of G-d's name). The goal of the Rebbe's tormentors was to nullify his multi-faceted endeavors for the promulgation of Torah Judaism. Had the Rebbe not resisted their directives, this would have been, in effect, a victory for them: The Rebbe had agreed to travel on Shabbat! Most of those learning of his acquiescence would be unaware of the many mitigating factors mentioned previously. Jewish law is explicit that in the area of *Kiddush Hashem* and *chilul Hashem*: the primary concern is the possible misperception of those viewing the act, who may see it as a violation of Jewish law, regardless of the actual severity or laxity of the conduct itself.

This concept of *kiddush Hashem* is the link between the third day of *Tammuz* and the Torah reading of *Chukat*, which is usually read on a Shabbat close to the third of *Tammuz*, the day the Rebbe was released from prison. That Torah reading describes "the waters of conflict," which resulted in the punishment of Moses and Aaron by the divine decree "You will not bring this assemblage (of the Jews) into the land (of Israel)."[2]

At first glance that punishment is problematic. Why was the sin considered so severe that it would prevent Moses from entering the land? We are told of other instances when Moses, as it were, was held to account, yet never was so severe a punishment accorded to him. Only in this case, the difference between *hitting* the stone rather than *speaking to it* resulted in the awesome, harsh decree that he could never enter the land of Israel?!

The rationale for this is indicated in the Torah: "For you did not believe in me to sanctify Me before the eyes of the

---

2. Numbers 20:12.

Jewish people."[3] Rashi explains that when Moses argued in a previous incident, "Shall flocks and herds be slaughtered for them?"[4] implying, as it were, that meat could not be provided for the entire Jewish people, he was not punished for this.

As Rashi comments, "This is because the event occurred privately and he was spared. But in this instance (the striking of the stone), since it occurred in the presence of the entire Jewish people, he was not spared, because of the sanctification of G-d's name."[5]

Thus, when the factor of the sanctification of G-d's Name is present or its reverse, then the primary focus is how the occurrence will be perceived by others.[6]

WRITTEN LETTERS—HEWN LETTERS

The Rebbe's conduct can be explained on an even deeper level. The Rebbe's response to his captors was not only in relation to matters affecting Judaism; he had firmly resolved that he would act firmly and steadfastly in any matter. He endured much physical punishment for this stance, even though his response was not related only to matters of the sanctification of G-d's name or the promulgation of Torah.

What is the explanation for such bold courage? The name of the Torah portion *Chukat* conveys the primary concept. Rabbi Schneur Zalman, the Alter Rebbe, explains that the word *Chok*—usually translated as a law with no apparent rationale—is to be understood here as deriving from the Hebrew *chakok*—'carved and hewn'—in contrast to mere writing.[7] When one writes, the letters are added to the surface of the parchment. Though the letters are absorbed in the parchment, they and the

---

3. Numbers 20:12.

4. Numbers 11:22.

5. Ibid.

6. See Maimonides *Mishneh Torah, Hilchot Yesodei HaTorah* 5:11 for one view in this matter.

7. *Likkutei Torah*, Numbers 56a.

parchment remain two separate entities. Therefore, the letters can be easily changed or totally erased from the parchment.

But hewn letters are not independent; they are intrinsic to the substance into which they are carved, an actual part of the stone. Thus, it is impossible to separate them, and any attempt to modify the letters invariably affects the stone itself.

Similarly, on a spiritual level, if the service of G-d is merely an added dimension to an individual's identity, then changes and variations in that service may occur under various conditions. Extenuating factors or compelling circumstances may cause an individual not to fulfill a particular aspect of the service of G-d, but his essence is not affected.

However, if the service of G-d is hewn into his personality, an actual dimension of his essential selfhood, then no differentiation can be made. To deprive such a person of the fulfillment of his service to G-d would mean to destroy his basic identity. This would be analogous to letters carved on a precious gem; any attempt to change the letters destroys the very gem itself.

When the service of G-d is carved out on the very soul itself, then such a personality will undergo self-sacrifice for any detail of Judaism. No rationalization, however seemingly justified, will ever be given to explain any inactivity, any less-than-perfect service to G-d, because this person's identity is totally merged with any and all action related to such service. He and his actions are indivisible.

This was the life-mode of the Rebbe. Fulfillment of Torah and its commands was in the manner of "hewn letters," intrinsic to the essence of his identity. Therefore, his self-sacrifice was not a function of intellectual deliberation as to whether an action was obligatory or desirable. His response to existential challenge occurred naturally, because his service of G-d was the very core of his existence.

(*Likkutei Torah*, vol. 28, pp. 124-130)

THE THREE WEEKS

G-D'S CONSOLATION
AND MERCIES

Commenting on the custom of referring to the month of Av as
"Menachem Av," the Rebbe notes a Midrashic statement that G-d's
role of "Menachem" ("Consoler") involves two roles: a mother's
consolation and a father's mercy. The distinction between
consolation and mercy is that the former involves solace for a loss,
while the latter completely erases the loss and its accompanying
sorrow. If so, what need will we have of consolation in the future,
when G-d shows His great mercy? The answer provides insight into
the ultimate purpose of Creation—that the physical world should
retain its nature while at the same time revealing G-dliness.

"MENACHEM AV"

The name *"Av"* dates back to the time of *Targum.*[1]
However, according to tradition (which has the authority of
Torah itself[2]), it is the common custom when blessing the
month of *Av,* on Shabbat prior to its occurrence, to call the
month by the name of *"Menachem Av."* This naming also has
relevance in Jewish law, so that in the writing of legal documents and bills of divorcement the phrase *Menachem Av* is also
acceptable. Even writing only *Menachem* is adequate, "since it is
known and widely accepted that the month *Av* is called the
month of *Menachem*; consequently, the divorce would be
regarded as conforming with the legal requirements."[3]

---

1. See *Targum Sheini* to the Book of Esther 3, 7; *Targum Yehonatan ben Uziel,* Numbers
   13, 25; *Mishnah, Ta'anit* 4:5-6.

2. Jerusalem Talmud, Pesachim 1:1.

3. *Pischei Teshuvah Shulchan Aruch: Even Ha'ezer* 126:112; *Kenesset Hagedolah,* ibid., sec.
   141.

Simply interpreted, the word "*Av*" has negative and tragic connotations, as implied by the Talmudic phrase: "When *Av* occurs there is a lessening of joy."[4] It is for this reason that the phrase "*Menachem Av*" is used, for we thus beseech of G-d to be our "*Menachem*" (Consoler) for the painful memories of *Av*. *Av*, however, also has positive connotations and alludes to a level beyond the simple meaning of the word "*Menachem*." Our Sages of blessed memory state on the verse "I (G-d) am your consoler:"[5] "It is the manner of a father to have mercy, as it is written, 'As a father has mercy on his children.'[6] It is the manner of a mother to console, as it is written: 'As a man whose mother consoles him. And G-d declares: 'I shall do as both a father and a mother.'"[7]

Consequently, these three are different aspects to the name of the month: a) *Av*—in the negative sense of sad historical remembrance, b) *Menachem*—a mother's consolation, c) *Av*—a father's mercies.

CONSOLATION AND MERCY

There is a distinction between consolation and mercy. Consolation is related to the loss for which solace is expressed. Even after consolation, the sense of absence and loss is still experienced. Various rationales are expressed to comfort the pained individual, even to the extent of somehow influencing him to accept the ordeal of his experience with joy, to accept it with faithful gladness, submitting to G-d's will. Nevertheless, he is always conscious of the void and the lack.

It is for this reason that the Jewish law stipulates that once the specified time for comforting a mourner has passed, it is forbidden to console.[8] The rationale is that since the painful period has already passed, an expression of consolation would

---

4. *Ta'anit* 99a.

5. Isaiah 51:12.

6. Psalms 103:12.

7. *Pesikta deRav Kahana; Piska "Anochi anochi."*

8. *Shulchan Aruch, Yoreh Deah*, ch. 385, sec. 2.

re-open the wound and cause further pain, because consolation does not banish pain but merely attempts to diminish its effect.

At first glance this would seem to imply that at the time of resurrection, consolation is not relevant, for we are assured that G-d "will wipe away tears from all faces."[9]

G-dly mercy is, however, completely different from consolation. His mercy implies complete resolution and compensation for any lack or loss. Thus, the pain is completely erased. This is an explanation for the prayer which praises G-d "Who resurrects the dead with great mercies."[10] The quality of "great mercies" is mentioned because the tragedy of death and its related suffering is totally erased.

This is illustrated by the narrative regarding Rabbi Zusha of Anapoli. The Maggid of Mezritch, the teacher of Rabbi Zusha, once sent one of his students to Rabbi Zusha—who lived in wretched poverty and who was constantly beset by troubles—for instruction in learning how to accept his troubles with joy. When the student came to Rabbi Zusha and related his mission, Rabbi Zusha replied that he was totally unaware of what he could teach him on the subject, for he—Rabbi Zusha—had never experienced any suffering and lacked nothing. He had achieved so lofty a state of nullification to G-dliness that he was totally oblivious to experiences that the Torah itself describes as suffering. It was precisely to perceive this profound degree of humility, self-nullification and acceptance that the Maggid had sent his student to Rabbi Zusha. He wanted the student to experience empathy with so unique a personality.

This is the meaning of the phrase that G-d declares, "I shall be as both a father and a mother." In the future there shall be not only the revelation of consolation, but also the manifestation of G-dly mercies.

---

9. Isaiah 25:8.
10. Liturgy, *Amidah* prayer.

CONSOLATION IN THE FUTURE

We are, however, confronted by the following problem: since G-d shall reveal Himself in the future with great mercies, thereby removing any conditions of loss and pain, what need is there for consolation? What form will consolation have in the future?

The explanation is that the G-dly intent of created existence is for G-d to have, as it were, an abode in the realm of the mundane. In other words, the world should retain its finite dimensions and in all circumstances provide an abode for G-d, Who is infinite. However, the G-dly revelation entailed in G-d's mercies is derived from so high a source that the world's finitude is wholly nullified in relation to it.

Thus, this manifestation of G-dly mercies could possibly effect a nullification and total dissolution of created existence. But, G-d's ultimate intent is that the finite lower realms *should* exist. And, though within created existence there shall be a longing for reversion and union with the upper source, nevertheless, G-d has decreed their independent existence. And this is the reason for future consolation. For despite this profound spiritual longing, Man shall retain his separate existence.

This is G-d's declaration that He shall be as both "father" and "mother." He will reveal both attributes. The quality of "father" is equivalent to the mystical sphere of *Chachmah* (lit. "wisdom")[11] which is beyond the descending sequence of created being and whose revelation would normally effect total nullification in the lower realms. The quality of "mother" is equal to the mystical level of *Binah* (lit. "understanding"[12]), which prevents the G-dly light derived from *Chachmah* from dissolving worldliness.

On the contrary, it will descend and be comprehend and assimilated within worldly existence, thus accomplishing an

---

11. See *Tanya*, ch. 3 and in many other sources.
12. Ibid.

exalted spiritual union between the spheres of *Chachmah* and *Binah*, which can only occur in the Messianic era.

(Likkutei Sichot vol. 4, pp. 1080-1082)

THE THREE WEEKS

FORTY-TWO JOURNEYS

The following *sicha* discusses the term *Bein Hameitzarim*— "between the straits," which refers to the Three Weeks between the 17th of Tammuz and the 9th of Av. The Rebbe begins with the concept taught by Rabbi Israel Baal Shem Tov that just as the Jewish people took the forty-two journeys described in the Torah reading of Masei, which is always read during the Three Weeks, each individual also takes forty-two journeys. Although these forty-two journeys were included in G-d's master plan for positive reasons, Man's misdeeds can cause them to have the opposite quality. The period of *Bein Hameitzarim* has a similar character; it originally had the potential for great sanctity and was only transformed into a mourning period through Man's misdeeds. Nevertheless, the unfortunate aspects of this period are not irreversible, and through repentance, the Rebbe writes, "they will be transformed into days of joy and happiness."

AN INDIVIDUAL'S FORTY TWO JOURNEYS

Rabbi Israel Baal Shem Tov states[1] that the forty-two journeys made by the Jewish people in the desert after their liberation from Egypt also occur during the course of every individual Jewish life. Thus, in the phrase describing the beginning of these travels: "Who went out of the land of *Mitzrayim*,"[2] the word "*Mitzrayim*" can be understood in two ways: literally Egypt, and limitation and containment (as in *meitzarim*, "boundaries"). Thus, "leaving *Mitzrayim*" (i.e. leaving a place of confinement) refers to birth, followed by the "forty-two journeys" which refer to the journeys of each individual's life. The ultimate goal in biblical times was the Land of Israel,

---

1. Cited in *Sefer Degel Macheneh Efraim, Parshat Masei.*
2. Numbers 33:1.

and this final quest in the life of each individual Jew is the spiritual "land of life."

Considering, however, that some of the journeys were contrary to G-d's will, how, then, can these forty-two travels be a master plan for each Jew, if they include modes of conduct contrary to the will of G-d? The Baal Shem Tov explains that the "journeys" were inherently sanctified; however, as a result of Man's inappropriate deeds caused by his G-d-given free will, the potential "journey" for good was warped and emerged in actuality in a distorted manner. But, when the Jew acts properly in accordance with G-d's command of "And you shall choose life"[3] (indeed this imperative actually endows us with the capability and G-dly aid to accomplish our divine task because it is derived from G-d and stated in the Torah), then all of our journeys without exception progressively ascend and constantly advance in holiness.

The Baal Shem Tov cites as an example the journey related to the site of Kivrot Hata'avah (Graves Of Desire) so named because the Torah tells us "The people of the nation (who had improper desires) were buried there."[4] Spiritually, this refers to the potential of achieving a lofty level of holiness, so exalted that for the Jewish people desire and lust, would not only be absent but "buried"; "desire" would have been so nullified as to make it utterly impossible for this emotion to exist. It was only because of the influence of the realm of evil that "*Kivrot Hata'avah*" was actualized in a manner that was the very reverse of virtue and goodness.

The basic concept of the Baal Shem Tov's teaching has obvious implications for the "travels" journeyed during the course of each Jew's life. Every individual is only too well aware of past journeys intended for the good which regrettably resulted in the very reverse.

---

3. Deuteronomy 30:19.
4. Numbers 12;34.

However, regarding one's future journeys, a Jew has the choice and divine command to use all of his future travel in a manner that will be positive and virtuous. The task of "choosing life" is particularly related to the Torah teachings linked to the Tree of Life[5]—*Chasidut*,[6] the inner teachings of Torah, which cause the inherent good in all things to be revealed; and also transform that which is not good into a "life-curing force."

BETWEEN THE STRAITS

All of the above relates to the period described as *"Bein Hameitzarim"*[7] ("between the straits") the three week period between the fast days of the seventeenth day of *Tammuz* and the ninth day of *Av*, the period during which the Torah portion of *Masei* is always read. The spiritual shortcomings of the Jewish people that led to the condition of being "Between the Straits" could have been actualized in a spiritual manner of exalted holiness.

The same holds true for the sin of the golden calf, which was the root of all subsequent sins.[8] It is known that this transgression occurred because the Jewish nation, at the time of the receiving of the Torah, gazed upon the lofty mystical vision of the *Merkavah*—G-d's throne—and perceived among other things the "face of the ox" upon the *Merkavah*.[9] So that even a matter which, through distorted understanding, resulted in the most fearful sin—the sin of the golden calf—could have been averted had Man utilized his free will in a proper way by means of "And you shall choose life." Moreover, it could have been utilized in a way related to an exalted level of holiness—since the perception of the *Merkavah* at Sinai surpassed to an

---

5. See *Raya Mehemna, Zohar* III 124b; *Tanya, Igeret Hakodesh*, ch. 26.
6. See *Kuntreis Eitz Hachayim*, ch. 13.
7. See Lamentations 1:3.
8. See Exodus 32:34 and Rashi there.
9. *Shemot Rabbah* 42:5.

astonishing degree even the *Merkavah* revelation seen by the prophet Ezekiel.[10]

In the instance of Jeroboam the son of Nebat who is cited in the *Mishnah* in the negative sense "of one who has sinned and caused others to sin,"[11] the Talmud nevertheless, states that he interpreted the book of *Vayikra* in one hundred and three original ways.[12] The Bible states, "And he (Jeroboam) covered himself with a new garment and the two (Jeroboam and the prophet Ahijah the Shilonite) were alone in the field."[13] The Talmud comments: this means that they formulated original concepts in Torah that only the two of them were capable of formulating.[14]

But, due to the influence of evil, Jeroboam was affected so negatively that his ultimate conduct was the exact opposite of virtue. The number 103 is also the numerical value of the word *eigel* (calf) the image he placed to prevent the ascent to Jerusalem.[15] It is self-evident that the same intellect, properly applied, could have been utilized in a profoundly spiritual manner.

The same is true of *Bein Hameitzarim* and its causes: were it not for the distortive effect of corrupting evil, these times could have emerged in a manner of exalted holiness. And though these distressing events have already occurred, *teshuvah* (repentance) is powerful enough to transform intentionally evil acts into acts of virtue.[16]

By means of *teshuvah* the Jewish people can bring about immediate and complete redemption[17] so that these days will be

---

10. See *Yalkut Shimoni, Yitro, remez* 286.

11. *Pirkei Avot* 5:18.

12. *Sanhedrin* 103b.

13. I Kings 11:29.

14. *Sanhedrin* 102a.

15. I Kings 11:29.

16. *Yoma* 86b.

17. Maimonides, *Hilchot Teshuvah* 7:5.

transformed into days of joy and happiness. By means of *Bein Hameitzarim*, the period of limitation and boundaries, we will reach the *"nachalah beli meitzarim"*[18]—the unbounded heritage and spiritual revelations which will be revealed through our righteous *Mashiach*.

(Likkutei Sichot, vol. 4, pp. 1083-1084)

---

18. See *Shabbat* 118a.

THE HOLY TEMPLE

THE GOLDEN HEAD-PLATE
OF THE HIGH PRIEST

Since studying the laws of the Holy Temple is considered the
equivalent of building it, such study receives special emphasis
during the Three Weeks, when we are particularly conscious of the
destruction of the Temple. Indeed, in contemporary times the
Rebbe has generated an intensive world-wide campaign for the
study of the laws of the Temple during this time period. In
addition, this dedicated effort is an expression of the profound faith
and anticipation of redemption through Mashiach when the
Temple laws will again be observed. The current *sicha* concerns a
dispute among the Sages as to the engraving on the *tzitz*, the head-
plate of the high priest. The Talmudic sage Rabbi Eliezer ben Yosi
saw the *tzitz* among the Temple vessels captured by the Romans and
testified as to how it was written. The ensuing discussion leads to
insights into issues that arise when archaeological discoveries seem
at variance with our tradition.

ONE LINE OR TWO LINES

The Torah commands that on the golden head-plate worn
by the high priest "you shall engrave on it, as the engraving on a
signet ring, 'holy to G-d.'"[1] The Talmud relates a dispute
between the Sages and Rabbi Eliezer ben Rabbi Yosi as to the
manner in which the words "holy to G-d" were written. The
Sages maintain that it was written on two lines with the four-
letter name of G-d—the Tetragramaton—on the upper line and
"holy to" on the lower line. Rabbi Eliezer ben Rabbi Yosi,

---

1. Exodus 28:36.

however, states, "I saw it (the head-plate) in the city of Rome, and 'holy to G-d' was written on one line."[2]

Maimonides renders the *halachic* opinion, "It was written on two lines and if it was written on one line; it is permissible, and there were instances when it was written on one line."[3] From this we can understand that notwithstanding the opinion of Rabbi Eliezer ben Rabbi Yosi, the Sages did not retract their opinion, asserting that it was necessary to use two lines. For this reason Maimonides declares the law to be according to the opinion of the Sages, adding that the opinion of Rabbi Eliezer ben Rabbi Yosi only applies to an already engraved head-plate. Maimonides writes, "and at times it was written on one line," referring thus to the testimony of Rabbi Eliezer ben Rabbi Yosi, compelling us to say that *de facto,* once written, it is acceptable, even if written on one line.

The Me'iri commentary declares, "And though one of the great Sages attested to having seen it in Rome written on one line, this did not refute that which was known to the Sages, though his words were actual visual witness."[4]

Even according to Maimonides it seems that the golden head-plate with the one-line inscription worn by the high priest during the Temple service and later seen in Rome was *only* acceptable ex post facto, (although it is preferable that the words should be written on two lines rather than one).

Indeed, the use of a (temporary) one-line head-plate would only be permissible for the brief time necessary to write a two-line head-plate. Are we to say that in such a brief period of time the Temple was captured and the head-plate seized by the Romans, for it appears that this head-plate was actually used in the priestly service proximal to the time of the Temple destruction?![5]

---

2. *Shabbat* 63b.

3. Maimonides, *Hilchot Klei Hamikdash* 9:1.

4. Me'iri, *Shabbat* 63b.

5. The question mark and exclamation points are in the Rebbe's text.

THE MENORAH ON THE ARCH OF TITUS

This can be understood when viewed within the context of a similar matter already discussed at length.[6] On the Arch of Titus, built in Rome by Titus after his conquest of Jerusalem, there is an engraving of a menorah, and there are those who believe this to be an actual replication of the Temple menorah. In that menorah the six branches are depicted as curved.

This is problematic, for Rashi[7] explicitly states that the branches were "diagonal, extending and ascending," that they extended in a direct incline. Indeed, the word *k'nei* for branches is the plural of *kaneh*, a stalk, a straight plant, as can be seen at the banks of every ocean.[8] Maimonides, in his very own handwritten commentary on the *Mishnah*, draws the branches as diagonally straight, and his son Rabbi Avraham attests that his father drew the menorah branches straight and not curved with precise intent.[9] Thus, there is variance between this rendering of the menorah,[10] and the depiction on the Arch of Titus, obviously derived from first-hand observation.

A possible simple resolution of this problem is to say that the menorah on the Arch of Titus is not a true representation of the Temple menorah. This is further corroborated by the number of significant variations from the Temple menorah drawing—the menorah on the arch also contains a dragon image!

It is therefore logical to presume that the menorah on the arch was not derived from the Temple menorah, but from another menorah with certain similarities to the Temple menorah.

It is reasonable to assume that since the menorah in the Temple had great significance, many other menorahs were

---

6. *Likkutei Sichot,* vol. 21, p. 70.

7. On Exodus 25:32.

8. See Exodus 2:3.

9. Rabbi Avraham son of Maimonides, Torah commentary, *Terumah.*

10. See Kapach on Maimonides, *Mishnah* Commentary.

made similar to it and most notably those used for idolatrous practices. This would provide a rationale for the idolatrous dragon image on the arch's menorah.[11] Such a secondary menorah served as a source for the menorah engraved on the arch.

WAS IT THE TRUE HEAD-PLATE?

We may similarly venture a rationale for the opinion of the Me'iri. Though Rabbi Eliezer ben Rabbi Yosi saw a head-plate in Rome, this was not a clear proof that it was indeed the head-plate of the high priest. It may very well have been an ornament, somewhat, but not wholly, similar to the Temple head-plate. Subsequently, this object was placed together with Temple objects to be found in Rome. Indeed, it is possible that the various versions of both the head-plate and the menorah were created as decoys that would be confiscated instead of the authentic head-plate and menorah.

As to the prohibition of duplicating Temple objects of entities, derived from "you shall not make with Me"[12] —it may very well be that a non-Jewish craftsman created this handiwork.

Yet, the Sages had a tradition, in the words of the Me'iri, "known to them," that the inscription "holy to G-d" was written on two lines. Thus, it was clear to them that this was the manner of fulfilling the obligation. The tradition itself forced the conclusion that the head-plate seen by Rabbi Eliezer ben Rabbi Yosi in Rome was not the head-plate of the high priest.

Rabbi Eliezer ben Rabbi Yosi, in contrast did not receive this tradition from his teacher. Upon seeing the head-plate in Rome he was not impelled to presume so remote a possibility that an alien object had been combined with the objects of the Temple. Thus, he viewed this head-plate in Rome as a proof

---

11. See *Avodah Zarah* 42b.

12. Exodus 20:20.

that the head-plate contained the inscription "'holy to G-d' on one line."

The Sages, however, having this tradition, "would not accept as contradictory even visual testimony"; there was no doubt or uncertainty as to their tradition. And as to the Roman head-plate, it is possible to say, as mentioned above, that this was not the authentic one.

THE OPINION OF MAIMONIDES

A difficulty remains: How to resolve Maimonides's position asserting that if it is already an accomplished fact, then even the head-plate of one line is acceptable. Indeed, how is it conceivable that the Romans would be misled or deceived by an object not having an original counterpart in the Temple, and especially in view of the fact that Roman historical literature abounds with specific details about the Temple and the various rituals performed there? It is, perhaps, this question that compels Maimonides to state that if the wearing of the one-line head-plate was already an accomplished fact, then it is permissible and in fact actually occurred, even if only for a brief time. The *Or Hachaim* goes even further to say, "Even according to the Sages (a head-plate with one line) is not invalidated." Therefore, the opinion of Maimonides should not be difficult in your eyes." Thus, we may surmise another rationale for the position of Maimonides to avoid excessive dispute and differences of opinion.

CONTEMPORARY DISCOVERIES

From the above discussion we can also derive[13] an insight which is relevant to our times. In our era, various accumulations of manuscripts, fragments and scrolls have been discovered. They contain variations from our standard texts regarding additional and omitted letters, etc. We must realize that though this appears to be "visual testimony," they are in actuality totally at variance with our tradition. We must also bear in mind our

---

13. *Rishon Letzion*: Sukkah 50.

lack of knowledge as to the actual authors of these "concealed texts"; whether or not they were truly "great Sages." Moreover, it may very well be that the very reason for concealing these works was *specifically because* they did not conform to our established tradition.

Regarding our transmitted heritage and tradition, however, given over from person to person and from generation to generation, extending backwards in unbroken continuity until Moses, we can state with certainty that it is the true and accurate version.

(*Likkutei Sichot*, vol. 26, pp. 200-203)

THE ARK

The Talmud[1] cites different opinions concerning the location where the *aron*—the holy ark—containing the Tablets was concealed. One opinion is that it was hidden in the "chamber of wood." There are also varying views as to its ultimate fate when the Holy Temple was destroyed: one, that it remains hidden on the Temple Mount, another, that it was taken into exile.

Maimonides renders a *halachic* decision that the ark was concealed in its designated hiding place and is still there. Here the Rebbe explores the profound implications of this opinion.

CONCEALING THE HOLY ARK

Maimonides,[2] describing the chamber of the Holy of Holies in the Temple in which the ark containing the tablets engraved with the Ten Commandments rested, states:

There was a stone in the Holy of Holies on the west side, upon which the holy ark rested... At the time that Solomon built the Temple he knew that it would ultimately be destroyed. He therefore built a place in the Temple directly below its resting place, where the ark could be stored in hidden depths reached by winding passages. Later King Josiah commanded that the ark be hidden in the hiding place prepared by Solomon, as it is said, "And say to the Levites, the holy tribe, teachers of all Israel: 'Put the holy ark in the house which Solomon the son of David, King of Israel,

---

1. *Yoma* 53b, 54a.
2. *Hilchot Beit Habechirah* 4:1.

built. It shall no longer be borne on your shoulders;
now serve the L-rd your G-d.'"[3]

Maimonides goes on to explain that the miraculous staff of
Aaron, the first high priest, was also hidden there. These were
not restored in the second Temple. Also the *Urim Vetumim*—
the breastplate of precious stones worn by the high priest—did
not provide prophetic response by the illumination of specific
letters engraved in its gems during the time of the second
Temple, as occurred in the first Temple.

Now, Maimonides explicitly states that the purpose of his
halachic masterwork, *Mishneh Torah*, is solely to provide
knowledge of Jewish Law.[4] We may therefore ask: Why this
inclusion of seemingly extraneous details about the
personalities and procedures related to the hiding of the holy
ark? Moreover, the manner and location of the holy ark is
actually a matter of debate in the Talmud. Maimonides is thus
rendering a *halachic* decision in accordance with one Talmudic
opinion which does not seem to be linked to any practical legal
consequences.

In grappling with this problem, the commentaries on
Mishneh Torah[5] state that it was necessary for Maimonides to
declare this opinion because it is consistent with his position[6]
that the inherent sanctity of the Temple was not nullified when
the first Temple was destroyed. In general, the opinion
concerning the enduring holiness of the Temple is linked to the
ark's being concealed in its original place—and, at the least, the
ark in its place serves as a point of reference concerning the
location of the Holy of Holies within the sacred precincts of the
Temple.

There are a number of problems relating to this opinion.
Firstly, Maimonides' rationale for the principle that the Temple

---

3. II Chronicles 35:3.

4. *Mishneh Torah*, Introduction.

5. See R.Ya'akov Emden's commentary on this text; *Chatam Sofer, Chulin* 7a

6. *Hilchot Beit Habechirah* 6:16.

site was "consecrated for that time and for future times"[7] is that the sanctity of the Temple and of Jerusalem derives from the *Shechinah*, the Divine Presence—and the "Divine Presence never departs or is nullified." This principle does not seen to relate only and specifically to the holy ark.

Moreover, Maimonides should have stated briefly and clearly that the ark was concealed below the site of its designated place. Actually Maimonides states: "(Solomon) built a place to store the holy ark there." The word "there" seems to relate to the "house," i.e. the Temple proper, and not to the Holy of Holies, the chamber in which the ark was placed. Thus, Maimonides does not emphasize the holy ark and its place. Nor does Maimonides quote the text cited in the Talmud, "And it is there to the present day,"[8] which explicitly states that the holy ark is to be found to this very day in its *original location*.

Additionally, why the need for the many details enumerated by Maimonides: the fact that King Solomon built the hiding place, that it was "deeply concealed through winding tunnels," that King Josiah *commanded* that it be hidden, not simply that he hid the holy ark. Why cite a Biblical text which does not seem to prove that "King Josiah commanded the holy ark be buried in the place built by Solomon." Indeed, what laws are to be derived from all these facts?

Puzzling, as well, is that Maimonides' discussion of the concealment of the ark, seems to indicate that King Solomon built the place of concealment based on his own judgment, for "he knew that the Temple would be destroyed." This is problematic, for all the parts and details of the Temple were built in accordance with G-d's command: "It is all in writing, as explained to me from the hand of G-d."[9] How is it conceivable that King Solomon built this hiding place on his own judgment?

---

7. Ibid.

8. I Kings 8:8. The Talmud's discussion is in *Yoma* 53b-54a.

9. I Chronicles 28:19.

As mentioned, Maimonides also informs us in the passage under discussion that the precious stones of the *Urim Vetumim* did not provide prophetic response in the second Temple. Seemingly, this fact is related to the section dealing with the Temple utensils and the garments worn by the priests when serving there. Indeed, Maimonides does mention this in that section, but why is this fact also cited here?

It is therefore necessary to assume that there is some inherent link between the holy ark and the *Urim Vetumim*, aside from the fact that the *Urim Vetumim* did not provide prophetic responses in the second Temple.

Maimonides' inclusion of the description of the concealment of the ark in the section of his work dealing with the Temple structure, rather than in the section describing the vessels and objects used in the Temple, may shed some light on this topic.

The placement of the holy ark in the Holy of Holies is, in Maimonides' opinion, an aspect of the actual structure of the Holy of Holies. That is why Maimonides does not include the holy ark when he enumerates the vessels of the Temple, because he does not consider the ark a vessel, but an actual part of the structure of the Holy of Holies.

This raises a far more challenging question: If indeed there was no ark in its designated place in the second Temple, then the Holy of Holies was lacking in its wholeness. A significant, essential entity, primary to the very structure of the Holy Temple, was missing.

To address this question Maimonides provides lengthy and specific details about the manner of the concealment of the holy ark to show that the second Temple did not lack, indeed, it *had all* the required factors validating it as a Holy Temple.

The holy ark was not hidden as an after-the-fact occurrence because there was no alternative. At the very beginning of the building of the Temple, two places were established: The first an overt location on the foundation stone in the Holy of Holies, and the second, a site "below" the Holy of Holies "in the depths of concealment of winding passages." This second repository was, from the very onset, also considered an intrinsic part of the Holy Temple.

Thus, the later concealment of the holy ark was not determined by the necessity of adverse events; its hiding place was an actual requirement in the building of the Holy Temple. Just as the total construction of the Temple required the building of the chamber of the Holy of Holies, so was it necessary to create a hiding place there for the holy ark. The Holy of Holies was assured of continued existence, and the requirement for the presence of the holy ark was fulfilled in either a revealed or concealed manner.

This is Maimonides' precise intent in declaring "At the time that Solomon built...he knew it would be destroyed in the future and he built a place there..." King Solomon did not act based on his own will. It was G-d's intent, that at the very time of building the Holy Temple, that King Solomon should know of its future destruction, and therefore be commanded to create a place for its safekeeping.

It was necessary for the holy ark to be in the chamber of the Holy of Holies. Had he merely dug below, without knowledge of the purpose of this hiding place, this lack of *kavanah* (intent) would have prevented the sanctification of this specific location for the ark and caused the Holy of Holies to be incomplete.

In light of the above, we gain insight into Maimonides' statement, "And Josiah the King commanded the ark to be hidden in the place built by Solomon." He says this to demonstrate even more pointedly that the place of concealment was created initially as a part of the chamber of the Holy of Holies. Josiah ruled at a time when the Jewish nation was a great power and there was no imminent danger. He did not conceal the holy ark due to fear or immediate threat. Indeed, his act seems similar to King Solomon's placement of the ark in the Holy of Holies. It was done with ceremonial ritual by "the Levites who taught all Israel, and were holy to G-d."

This corresponds to the first ceremony, in the era of Solomon, when "the priests brought the holy ark to its Place." Josiah also specifically commands: "And place the holy ark in the house built by Solomon;" the ark is not being removed or taken away from its designated place. On the contrary, it is being *placed in the Temple itself.*

King Josiah continues, declaring to the Levites that it will not be possible for the "ark to be borne on your shoulders." While it is being borne, there is a period of transition which may affect the sanctity of the ark and their service. However, when the ark is relocated, even in its hiding place, it still retains the essential authority of its initial holiness. In no way is the service of the Levites in the Temple lessened in status or sanctity, as it may be when the ark was dismantled and transported.

"Now serve the L-rd your G-d"—their ritual observance in the Holy Temple has the same validity as in the past, and the authority of the Temple's sanctity is sustained.

We can thus also understand why Maimonides mentions the presence of the *Urim Vetumim* in the second Temple, even though they did not respond miraculously as occurred in the first Temple.

In essence, they are similar to the ark. Even in concealment the ark was part of the total Temple structure, making it permissible to perform the rituals of Temple service. This is also true of the special garments of the priests, including the *Urim Vetumim* the high priest was required to wear as part of his ritual garments when performing his Temple service. Though the *Urim Vetumim* did not shine in the second Temple; nevertheless, they had the very same sanctity they possessed in the first Temple.

Simply stated, the ark contributed to the totality of the Temple structure and the *Urim Vetumim* to the completeness of the high priest's garments.

THREE HOLY TEMPLES – ONE COMPOSITE UNITY

We can now gain new insight, not only about the completeness of the second Temple, but also about a special dimension in the first Temple.

Superficially, the first Temple does not seem to have been an eternal structure; there existed a possibility for its destruction, which was unfortunately fulfilled. However, internally there existed a hidden aspect that was eternal: a hiding place for the holy ark that provides concealment "to our very day."

The first Temple endures for all future times because of its location, the *place* where the Temple is to be found. Maimonides posits that this sanctity endures because of the presence of the ark in its concealment below its original site and the resulting constancy of the *Shechinah*—the Divine Presence. Maimonides provides us here with a new awareness regarding the Temple structure. Although the first Temple was leveled, one part of the structure remained that was "holy for its time and for the future."

We can gain from the above an understanding of the unifying factor of all three Temples, the two of the past and the third to be built speedily by our righteous *Mashiach*. All three Holy Temples form one composite identity; they are not to be seen as three separate structures. The second and third Temples should not be seen as separate edifices, but rather as the rebuilding of the first Temple, for in the first Temple there already pre-existed within its structure a part that was eternal, that would be part of the second and third Temples.

We may speculate that this is analogous to the time of the resurrection of the dead. At that time the body will not be totally recreated,[10] the body will be resurrected from the elemental "*luz* bone" which pre-exists in the human body on earth and is indestructible. The hidden place of the ark is, in essence, equivalent to the *luz* bone; it is the indestructible core

---

10. *Bereishit Rabbah* 28:3.

of the Holy Temple, from which the second and third Temples are derived.

The *halachic* view of Maimonides has many significant implications relating to the destruction of the Temple and the exile of the Jewish people.

The essential core of the Holy Temple was not subject to destruction. It is totally impossible for alien nations to prevail in any way over the House dedicated to the service of G-d. The destruction could occur only because, in the event that the Jewish people did not merit the sustained physical existence of the Temple, recourse was provided for the refuge of the ark. This is similar to the survival of the Jewish people. Alien nations have no authority over the Jewish people. Jews are vulnerable only because of their improper deeds and conduct which cause G-d to relate to them in a punitive and exacting manner.

The very fact that, at the time of joy and exhilaration accompanying the building of the Temple, King Solomon could concern himself with its destruction, and even take practical action anticipating this adverse event, is profoundly significant. The destruction was apart of a divine historical process which will ultimately culminate in the building of the third Temple in its complete and perfect form.

THE HOLY TEMPLE AND REPENTANCE

G-d's destruction of the Temple was not an end in itself; indeed, the goal was the resultant repentance and return of the Jewish people to G-d. The "descent" of the Temple destruction would culminate in an even greater "ascent" of repentance—an example of the well-known Chasidic principle of "descent for the purpose of ascent." This will finally bring about the building of the third Temple, which will endure forever in its most perfect form, for it shall be "the edifice built by G-d—the Temple of G-d established by your hand."[11]

---

11. Exodus 15:17.

By analyzing the three terms used by Maimonides to describe the hiding place of the ark, *Chasidut* sheds light on the spiritual nature of a Jew: 1) The Depths 2) of Concealment and 3) Winding Passages.

Building "a place to hide the ark" seems to anticipate the Temple's destruction, "for in the future it would be destroyed." However, the trauma of this anguished descent results in deep, heartfelt remorse, which leads to atonement and repentance for the deeds of the past and then ascent and elevation to a higher divine service.

Eventually, this level of divine service will merit the revelation of the category of Torah secrets called "depths of concealment"—the loftiest levels of G-dliness, which are alluded to by King Solomon with the phrase "deep, deep—who can comprehend them?"[12]

These high levels of spirituality cannot be revealed by normal, straightforward spiritual effort. Such an intense repentance must occur, not by Man's direct, normal, and natural way of serving G-d, but through the far move profound effort connected with the "winding" and "twisting" ways of the *Baal teshuvah*—the repentant person. Such a repentant evokes and elicits, in a positive way, the lofty mystical levels of the "depths of concealment" which cannot be elicited by *or yashar*— direct, straight light—but only by *or chozeir*—winding, indirect light of great intensity.

This is the lesson we learn from the concealment of the ark in hidden depths reached by winding passages: That every Jew, no matter how low his or her descent, can, though it be through indirect winding passages, reach the highest level of true repentance and knowledge of Torah secrets.

May it be G-d's will that this occur with the building of the third, the final and eternal Temple. May this edifice be built and revealed speedily and actually in our times, at the time of

---

12. Ecclesiastes 7:29.

the true and complete redemption through our righteous *Mashiach*.

(*Chiddusim Ubiurim al Hilchot Beit Habechirah,* ch. 10, p. 55 and ff.)

THE HOLY TEMPLE

THE ARK IN
THE HOLY OF HOLIES

This discourse, focusing the ark and its cover in the Holy of Holies, presents two views as to their function. Obviously, as in all Torah disputes, they are both the word of the "Living G-d."[1] From this discussion, we can gain new insight into the nature of their purpose in the Temple, as well as to the unique manner in which G-d relates and reveals Himself to the Jewish people.

THE STATUS OF THE ARK COVER

One of the Torah's commandments in connection with the construction of the Sanctuary in the desert (and later also for the Holy Temple) was that in the room of the Holy of Holies an ark was to be placed containing the tablets on which the Ten Commandments were engraved. The ark was constructed of an outer chest of pure gold, a closely fitted wooden chest within it, and another pure gold chest within the wooden one. The Torah states that a golden cover—*kaporet*—was to be placed upon the ark. And the two cherubim were to be pounded out from this solid mass of gold.

The Torah states: "And you shall place the ark cover upon the ark from above, and into the ark you shall put the Testaments which I (G-d) will give you."[2]

There is a dispute between the great commentators Rashi and Nachmonides concerning the ark cover. The verse just quoted seems to repeat an earlier command.[3] Rashi explains the

---

1. *Eiruvin* 13b.
2. Exodus 25:21.
3. Exodus 25:16.

351

seemingly unnecessary repetition in the later verse as indicating that first the Tablets should be placed in the newly-built ark, and that only then should the cover be put on the ark.

Rashi believes that the "ark" is considered the "ark" even *without* its cover, which is a separate entity and mitzvah. When the tablets of the Ten Commandments were placed in it, G-d's command for the construction of the ark was fulfilled.

Nachmonides disputes this opinion, and asserts that the ark by definition *must* include its cover, and only when the cover is in place is the commandment for the ark's construction fulfilled.

Rashi's opinion that the ark cover is a separate entity whose place happens to be on top of the ark is also found in the Torah commentary by Rabbi Yosef Rosen, the famed *Ragatchover Gaon*.[4] Since the Talmud[5] describes the cover itself as a "Vessel," and the Torah uses the term *"kaporet"* for the cover instead of the more common term *"kisui"*[6] the *Rogatchover* concludes that the *kaporet* "was not merely a cover, but an entity having a separate identity with the *halachic* requisite that its place be on the ark."

THE ARK AND THE CHERUBIM

The above discussion can be linked to differing views of Rashi and Nachmonides about the holy ark itself.

Nachmonides states[7] that "the primary purpose of the *Mishkan* (Sanctuary) was to serve as an abode for the *Shechinah* (Divine Presence) specifically through the holy ark. As the Torah states, 'And I will meet you (Moses) there and speak to you above the holy ark's cover.'"[8] This encounter can only be accomplished with the placement of the Tablet of the Ten Commandments, G-d's testament, within the ark and then

---

4. *Tzafnat Panei'ach, Terumah* 25:17, *Veyakheil* 37:6.

5. *Sukkah* 5a.

6. See *Torat Kohanim*, Leviticus 16:2.

7. Exodus 25:1.

8. Ibid. 25:22.

covering it with the *kaporet*. This means that both the ark and its cover are considered as a total entity, and that both components are necessary factors making possible G-d's revelation and encounter with the Jewish people: "And I will meet you there."

Rashi, on the other hand, maintains that the ark and its cover have two separate functions. The ark's purpose is to contain the Ten Commandments, G-d's testament to the Jewish people.

Rashi regards the ark cover also as being separate and distinct in its purpose from the holy ark itself. The construction of the ark's cover was stated later, for the second purpose: So that G-d would reveal to Moses His divine will and commands to the Jewish people from above the ark.

Rashi defines the function of the cherubim in terms of the cover's function—as opposed to the separate function of the ark itself—because:

a) The cherubim had to be beaten out from the two extremities of the same solid gold block of the ark cover and not be artificially joined or soldered to it.[9]

b) Their specific relationship to the ark cover is emphatically conveyed by the Biblical command that the wings of the cherubim "should be spread on high above the ark *cover*" with their "faces toward the ark *cover*."[10] Thus, the ark cover serves as the medium through which G-d will "meet" and "speak" from "between the two cherubim."[11]

Nachmonides,[12] however, explains the purpose of the cherubim in a mystical manner, comparing them to the cherubim seen in the prophet Ezekiel's vision of G-d's *merkavah* (chariot). Nachmonides describes the cherubim with the mystical term of *merkavah*: chariot-bearers of G-d's glory. Indeed, the reason for the "spreading out of their wings on

---

9. Ibid. 25:18.

10. Ibid. 25:20.

11. Ibid. 25:22.

12. Exodus 25:20.

high" was to create a supporting "throne on high" while covering the ark which contained the Ten Commandments— G-d's Testament, which was the "Writing of G-d."[13] G-d Himself is described as "He Who sits upon the cherubim."

This is the reason that G-d speaks prophetically to Moses, from "between the two cherubim" on the ark of G-d's testimony. Because, according to Nachmonides, the ark and its cover with the cherubim are all *one organic unit*, all three combining to form "a place for the repose of the Divine Presence." Moreover, as stated before, G-d is described as "He Who sits upon the cherubim," a "throne of G-d's glory."

In contrast, Nachmonides maintains that the cherubim were similar in appearance to those of the prophetic vision of Ezekiel of the mystical heavenly chariot, and therefore G-d is "He Who sits upon the cherubim,"[14] Rashi describes the cherubim as having the "face of a small child."[15] Rashi asserts that the ark cover and the cherubim are not merely component parts of the ark, but as having a separate identity and purpose. It is for this reason that the cherubim had the appearance of the face of "a small child." This was to symbolize the love of G-d for the Jewish people, as reflected by G-d's words in the prophecy of Hosea:[16] "For Israel was a child and I loved him."[17]

According to Rashi, the ark with G-d's Testament of the Ten Commandments expresses the concept of Torah. The ark cover, on the other hand, with its cherubim having "the face of a small child" about which G-d declared "And I will meet you there and speak to you...all that I shall command through you to the Jewish people"[18] underscores the fondness and love of G-d for the Jewish people. This is in harmony with the

---

13. Ibid. 32:16.
14. See *Zohar* III: 73a.
15. See *Tana D'vei Eliyahu,* chap. 14, and *Likkutei Torah, Shir Hashirim* 19a and 19b.
16. Hosea 11:1.
17. *Zohar Chadash* I: 12b.
18. Exodus 25:22.

explanation of Rabbeinu Bechaye[19] who, in analyzing the literal meaning of the text, discusses at length the fact that the two cherubim were masculine and feminine in appearance. This allegorically conveys the love of G-d for the Jewish people. Similarly, the Talmud states: "When the Jewish people ascended on their holiday pilgrimages to Jerusalem, they (the Temple attendants) would pull aside the *parochet* covering (the entrance to the Holy of Holies where the holy ark and its cover with the cherubim was located) and reveal to them the cherubim in affectionate embrace and declare 'Thus is G-d's love for you.'"[20] This all stresses the profound bond of love between G-d and the Jewish people, irrespective of any other factor, as explained at length in Rabbi Bechaye's commentary.

THE ESSENTIAL BOND

We can advance the following Chasidic explanation for the above:

The holy ark containing G-d's Testament of the Ten Commandments conveys the concept of Torah. Nachmonides[21] quotes the *Midrash*[22]: G-d said that all Jews should contribute to the construction of the ark so that "they would *all* merit Torah Knowledge." Since, according to Nachmonides, the ark cover with the cherubim were one entity with the ark itself, then "G-d's meeting" and speaking to the Jewish people is related to Torah, as exemplified by the Ten Commandments in the ark. Jews are bound to the Torah and Torah is bound to G-d.[23] The bond between Jews and G-d is through Torah.

Rashi is concerned with the *peshat*—the simple, elemental meaning of the text. According to Rashi, the ark cover with the cherubim, which is distinct from the ark, expresses the essential bond between G-d and the Jewish people. The *elemental* identity

---

19. Exodus 25:18.

20. *Tanya, Igeret Hateshuvah,* ch. 8.

21. Exodus 25:10.

22. *Shemot Rabbah* 33:3.

23. See *Zohar* III: 73a.

of a Jew as he is united with G-d transcends the link between
G-d and Jew through Torah. *Chasidut* explains the reference in
the *Zohar* to "three bonds"[24] linking G-d, Torah, and the Jews
(for there actually seem to be only two: Jews with Torah and
Torah with G-d) as including a third bond: a direct one
between G-d and Israel.[25] This bond transcends Torah. We are
told that G-d's plan for creation of the Jewish people preceded
even His intention to create the Torah.

This is the inner meaning of the fact that the cherubim
were required to have the face of a small child. The elemental
love of a father for a son is not related to the surpassing
qualities of the child, but to their essential mutual identity.
Similarly the primary love of Jews for G-d is expressed through
the cherubim, which have the face of a small child.

We can now understand a basic difference between Rashi
and Nachmonides about the placement of the cover "Upon the
ark from above." According to Nachmonides, the ark cover
with the cherubim is also related to the Ten Commandments—
"the testament"—within the ark. Nachmonides cites the verse
"from amidst the two cherubim upon the ark of testament" to
corroborate his position. Rashi views the placement of the
cover "upon the ark from above" as indicating that the ark cover
is *higher* than the ark, actually protecting the ark, i.e. shielding
and protecting Torah. The essential bond between the Jewish
people and G-d draws down spiritual influence from "Above
into Torah" "to increase therein"—to enable the study of Torah
in ever-increasing measure and to effect a greater degree of
holiness in that study.[26]

The ark cover is called *kaporet*, which is related to the word
kaparah, forgiveness and cleansing (from sin).[27] The power for
forgiveness from sin is derived from the source of all Jewish

---

24. Ibid.
25. See *Likkutei Sichot*, vol. 18, p. 408.
26. See *Zohar* I 12b.
27. See *Shemot Rabbah* 50:4; *Tanchuma, Vayakheil* 10.

souls, a spiritual level so lofty that it transcends Torah. If a Jew is lacking in his observance of Torah, i.e. if there is a defect in his bond with G-d through Torah, then he has the ability to set it aright and correct the lack and defect by the *kaporet*— repentance. Through his deep efforts for atonement, he can achieve a superior level of "a higher repentance," similar to that of those true repentant souls who surpass even *tzaddikim* who are "perfect in their righteousness." They can achieve the most surpassing kind of *kaparah* (atonement) gaining closeness to and gratifying Man's Maker." [28]

(*Likkutei Sichot*, vol. 26, p. 175-182)

---

28. *Tanya, Igeret Hateshuvah*, ch. 2.

THE FIFTEENTH DAY OF AV

FROM THE DEPTHS TO THE HEIGHTS

> The Fifteenth of Av does not receive much attention in discussions of the Jewish holidays, yet the *Mishnah*[1] speaks of it in the same breath with Yom Kippur. What is the unique spiritual quality of this day? The answer relates to the day's quality of being an "ascent", following the profound "descent" of Tisha B'Av, and ultimately to the Messianic Redemption.

ONE OF THE GREATEST HOLIDAYS?

The *Mishnah* states that the Jewish people had no festivals that could compare with the Fifteenth of *Av* and Yom Kippur.[2] This astonishing statement implies that the Fifteenth of *Av* possesses a surpassing quality compared to all other holidays, including Pesach and Shavuot.[3] That it is in some ways superior to Shavuot can perhaps be explained[4] by the fact that on the fifteenth day the "new moon is in its fullness."[5] The Jewish people are compared to the moon,[6] thus, the moon's "fullness" indicates a greater level of spirituality. However, how can the Fifteenth day of *Av* surpass Pesach, which occurs on the fifteenth day of *Nissan* and Sukkot which is on the fifteenth day of *Tishrei*? On both Pesach and Sukkot "the moon is in its fullness."[7]

---

1. *Ta'anit* 26b.
2. Ibid.
3. See *Sefer Hama'amarim 5670*, p. 218 and ff., 221 and ff.
4. See *Pri Eitz Chaim*, end *Sha'ar Chag HaShavuot, Drush al sod Tu b'Av*
5. *Zohar* I 150a; 225b.
6. See *Sukkah* 29a; *Bereishit Rabbah* 6:3.
7. See *Sefer Hama'amarim*, ibid.

One rationale for the significance of the holiday of the Fifteenth of *Av*[8] is that it occurs after the awesome descent at the beginning of the month. Indeed, great sin and intensive punishment was followed by a corresponding great ascent "ascent after descent." Through the spiritual endeavor of repentance of "*Bacho tivkeh*" ("She weeps bitterly")[9] repeated and intense weeping—the resultant ascent was with great consolation, far surpassing the ascent of the fifteenth day of *Nissan*—Pesach, and the fifteenth day of *Tishrei*—Sukkot.

FROM THE DEPTHS TO THE HEIGHTS

A further explanation is that the ascent of *Av* is not measured and sequential, but, an intensive elevation from one extreme to another in a very brief measure of time and in one instant. The ascent of the month of *Av* begins immediately after the tragedy of *Tisha b'Av*, which proceeds from great depths to lofty heights. On *Tisha b'Av* also, the *Midrash* relates, *Mashiach* was born. *Mashiach* exemplifies the essence of repentance, as in the statement "*Mashiach* will make *tzadikim* repent."[10] Consequently, the potentiality for redemption occurred immediately. Thus, the consolation commences on *Tisha b'Av* and is revealed in its fullness on the Fifteenth of *Av*. Significantly, the death decree for the generation of Jews wandering forty years in the desert, after their departure from Egypt, ceased on this day. Actually, this decree ended on the ninth day of *Av*, a day on which many perished in previous years. However, the Jewish people were in a state of uncertainty as to which specific day was the ninth day of *Av* because they had no precise calendar and relied on the phases of the moon to determine time. When the fifteenth day of *Av* came, with the characteristic "moon in its fullness," and no one had perished,

---

8. See *Sefer Hama'amarim 5670*, ibid.

9. Lamentations 1:2.

10. *Likkutei Torah, Derushim Le*Shemini Atzeret 92; *Shir Hashirim* 50b; and see *Zohar* III 153b.

they knew with certainty that the death decree for the desert generation no longer applied.

SURPASSING YOM KIPPUR

However, the aforementioned ascent on the ninth day of *Av* is not the total fulfillment of a Jew's spiritual endeavor. As the time advances from the ninth day of *Av* the spiritual ascent and elevation subsequent to the spiritual decline of *Av* becomes progressively revealed. Finally on the fifteenth day of *Av* the ascent is complete. This is why it is a surpassingly great holiday, as the Talmud states: "the Jewish people did not have holidays comparable in their joyousness to the Fifteenth day of *Av* and Yom Kippur." The Fifteenth day of *Av* is compared to, and cited even before Yom Kippur. The joy of Yom Kippur is that it is a day "wherein there is forgiveness and pardon," consequently, the dimension of repentance must also pertain to the Fifteenth of *Av*. Yet, it possesses an aspect surpassing Yom Kippur (being enumerated before Yom Kippur) because the repentance is of a "short interval of time and in a brief instant." Yom Kippur, however, (ideally) entails lengthy preparation, commencing from the first day of *Elul*.

Moreover, in contrast to the Fifteenth of Av, it also includes many elaborate and complex details. Similarly, the fulfillment of Pesach also requires the structured progression of counting *Sefirah* until the time of Shavuot, when the Jews were deemed worthy of receiving the Torah.

Perfection of this subsequent ascent from the profound and painful descent of the ninth day of *Av*, occurs on the Fifteenth of *Av*. When the Holy Temple stood, the distinctiveness of this day was perceived in a revealed manner through the unusual degree of festivity, etc. Even during the period of exile there are various customs commemorating this particular day due to the numerous reasons cited in the Talmud as to its importance in Temple times.

May G-d similarly grant us, that our spiritual endeavor of repentance during the time of exile shall cause G-d to "Gather you in from captivity and have mercy upon you...G-d will return and gather you in from all the nations."[11]

The Divine Presence is also in exile in a manner that the children of Israel will be gathered "one by one,"[12] and G-d will also gather each Jew individually due to the soul's quality of "one." He will then lead the entire Jewish nation "with our youths and our elders, with our sons and our daughters,"[13] to greet our righteous *Mashiach*, "and all their silver and gold with them."[14] And, thus, may all the "sparks of G-dliness" be uplifted from exile, a refining so total that the exile is voided of these "sparks of G-dliness" and "I [G-d] will cause the spirit of impurity to be removed from the land."[15] Then it will be openly seen that the Jewish people "did not have any holidays comparable to the Fifteenth day of *Av*, and this will once again occur in the material world, in Jerusalem the Holy City and in the Holy Land in general, speedily at the time of the coming of our righteous *Mashiach*.

(Sefer Hama'amarim 5748)

---

11. Deuteronomy 30:3.
12. Isaiah 27:12.
13. Exodus 10:9.
14. Isaiah 60:9.
15. Zechariah 13:2.

TWENTIETH OF AV

ALTRUISM—
A SPIRITUAL HERITAGE

This *sicha* discusses the twentieth day of *Av*. In addition to the traditional Torah-*Chasidut* contents, it is also a Torah eulogy for a towering spiritual personality, Rabbi Levi Yitzchak Schneerson, the Rebbe's father, who passed away in exile, as a result of his altruistic and heroic efforts for the promulgation of Judaism, on the 20th of *Av*, 5704.

The basic premise, that the quality of one's altruism can be transmitted to one's physical and spiritual descendants, is awe-inspiring and inexpressibly moving. It makes us conscious of our links to the past and of our obligation to the future of our people. Through this awareness, we gain a glimmer of insight into the authentic relationship between *Rebbe* and *Chasid*. We are also movingly reminded of the *Chasid's* role in relationship to his immediate Jewish environment and the world community at large. Hewn upon our minds, this awareness can ultimately elicit those spiritual qualities that are dormant and concealed at present; and it is the actualization of these traits that will hasten the advent of *Mashiach* with great mercies.

A FAMILY HOLIDAY

The *Mishnah*[1] relates that the twentieth day of *Av* was observed as a holiday by a specific family, for on this day their offering of wood was used upon the altar in the Holy Temple.

For a period of time, wood had been unavailable, and several families had volunteered to supply the wood for the altar. When the supply brought by one family was exhausted, another family would provide it in their stead. Thus, a

---

1. *Ta'anit* 26a.

particular group of families provided for the needs of the Temple. Later, a custom was established that the families who had offered the wood, when it was difficult to obtain, would now (when wood was available) retain their privilege; each family's wood was still used on the very same day of their earlier offerings to mark their kindness and generosity, and this day was commemorated as a holiday by that family.

A TALMUDIC DISPUTE

Two opinions are cited in the Talmud[2] concerning the identity of the family who had given the wood for the twentieth day of *Av*. Rabbi Meir is of the opinion that "these were the descendants of David who descended from Judah." Rabbi Yosi states that "they were descended from Joab, the son of Zeruiah."[3] Two questions arise from this. First, how is it possible for a Talmudic controversy to focus upon a matter of fact? Second, how can the all-pervasive Talmudic principle "that all positions in a controversy are the words of the Living G-d"[4] apply in this instance?

These questions can be resolved by establishing that the aforementioned dispute is *not* about a factual matter, i.e., the family of origin. In fact, both Rabbi Meir and Rabbi Yosi were descendants of David and Joab as a result of subsequent marriage. The primary dispute between Rabbi Meir and Rabbi Yosi is about the unique familial trait which impelled them to generously provide the necessary wood for the altar on the twentieth day of *Av*. Rabbi Meir is of the opinion that the merit of King David evoked this act, while Rabbi Yosi contends that the merit of Joab son of Zeruiah was the primary cause.

What was, in fact, the unique significance of providing wood for the twentieth day of *Av*? Why did this evoke Talmudic speculation about the special spiritual heritage and ancestral merit which enabled them to perform this deed?

---

2. *Ta'anit* 28a.

3. See II Samuel 2:13.

4. *Eiruvin* 13b.

The Talmud states: "From the fifteenth of *Av* onward, the power of the sun begins to wane, and wood is no longer cut to be arranged upon the Temple altar, for the wood is no longer dry."[5] The law states that wormy wood is unacceptable for the altar.[6] Therefore, from the time the intense mid-summer power of the sun begins to decline, which is the fifteenth day of *Av*, wood is no longer cut lest it be defective for Temple service.

The first sacrifices brought after the fifteenth day of *Av* were on the twentieth day of *Av*. However, the wood had to be cut earlier to avoid the aforementioned defect. In addition, it was necessary to prepare the wood days in advance with elaborate caution, so that it would be acceptable for Temple service. Consequently, the family bringing the wood for the twentieth of *Av* (and also the family whose offering was on the twentieth day of *Elul*) displayed unique merit, exceeding the significance of the earlier wood-offerings made when the wood was immediately available and did not require excessive preparation. Since the offerings after the fifteenth day of Av expressed greater motivation, the Talmud proceeds to speculate on the spiritual source of the notable deed.

JOY IN HELPING A FELLOW JEW

Another important point: the wood itself was not itself considered a *sacrifice*. It was obviously required for the altar upon which sacrifices were offered, but the sacrifice itself, which was consumed in flames upon the wood, was not necessarily the family's own, or even a communal sacrifice in which they had a share. Sacrifices from all Jews were offered upon the altar. Even sin-offerings and guilt offerings brought by persons who had transgressed and now sought atonement were placed upon the wood of the altar. Nevertheless, the family expended elaborate efforts in preparation of the wood, not motivated by self-gratification, but moved by the desire to

---

5. *Ta'anit* 31a.
6. *Middot* 1:5; Maimoides, *Hilchot Isurei Mizbei'ach* 6:2.

aid even a Jew who had sinned. They strove to enable him to bring a sacrifice through which he could achieve atonement.

Of even greater significance is the fact that they made available something that was in limited supply in order to aid a sinful fellow Jew. They did this with such joy that the day of the wood offering became established as a family *Yom Tov*.

This then, is the controversy between Rabbi Meir and Rabbi Yosi. Was the power for such exemplary conduct derived from King David or from Joab son of Zeruiah?

SCHOLAR AND WARRIOR

The Talmud states: "Were it not for David then Joab would not have been capable of waging war, and if not for Joab, then David would have been unable to preoccupy himself with Torah."[7] Joab's military triumphs were due to the merit of David's Torah studies, and David's ability to study Torah undisturbed by worldly distraction was due to Joab's military efforts on King David's behalf.[8]

(The fact that the Talmud derives the significance of their efforts from the very same verse also indicates that their deeds were integrated.[9] Joab's success in battle was not merely thanks to the *merit* of David's Torah, but Joab actually *shared* in the substance of David's Torah, because "if not for Joab them David would have been unable to preoccupy himself with Torah." Therefore the Torah of David aided Joab to victory.)

Both David and Joab strove to serve G-d with self-nullification and self-sacrifice. David's self-nullification, however, expressed itself in the spiritual labor of Torah study. Because of this self-nullification, which was the unique aspect of David's Torah study, he merited that: "G-d is with him,"[10] i.e., "that the law was in accordance with his opinion."[11] The

---

7. *Sanhedrin* 49a.

8. See *Chiddushei Agadot, Maharasha, Sanhedrin*, ibid.

9. See *Likkutei Sichot*, vol. 3, p. 782 and sources cited there.

10. Samuel 18:14.

11. *Sanhedrin* 93b.

self-nullification and self-sacrifice of Joab, on the other hand, expressed itself in the labor of coping with the world, even battling victoriously against those nations that opposed Israel, and thus causing an "abode for the Almighty"[12] in the realm of the mundane.

Since matters of holiness and sanctified service is interrelated. Thus, David and Joab assisted each other. Joab's military efforts aided David's study, and David's Torah labors helped Joab achieve victory in war. There was, however, a significant difference in their efforts: David's primary concern (at that time) was Torah, and he was secluded and isolated from worldly matters; the focus of Joab's endeavor was waging war, and he had to grapple and cope with the world.

Rabbi Meir and Rabbi Yosi differed as to which deeds were of greater significance. The name "Meir" is derived from the word *or*,[13] meaning light or manifest spirituality, beyond the finitude of the world. The Hebrew word for "the world" is *ha'olam*, which is interpreted in Chasidic thought as derived from the word *helem*, meaning "concealment"[14]—that is, the concealing veil of natural laws. Therefore, Rabbi Meir zealously preoccupied himself with the concept of self-nullification intrinsic to Torah study as embodied in King David.

Rabbi Yosi's name is numerically equivalent to the word *Elokim*,[15] which is in turn numerically equal to the word *hateva*[16]—nature, i.e. the fixed laws of worldliness. Thus, he was actively concerned with the significance of conflict and the spiritual service involved in reigning over the world—as expressed by the deeds of Joab.

Another rationale for the discussion between Rabbi Meir and Rabbi Yosi may be alluded in a dispute between the

---

12. See *Tanya*, ch. 36.
13. See *Eiruvin* 13b.
14. *Likkutei Torah*, Numbers 37d.
15. Zohar III 223a; and see *Hemshech "Vekacha" 5637*, ch. 80.
16. *Pardeis, Sha'ar* 12, ch. 2.

Babylonian[17] and Jerusalem Talmud[18] concerning the holiday celebration of the fifteenth of *Av* . The dispute, as explained elsewhere,[19] ultimately concerns whether an individual is obligated to exert himself in a small way if this effort will ultimately result in an outcome of great importance.

The Jerusalem Talmud maintains that since the present effort is wholly incomparable to the ensuing benefit, the individual is obligated to perform the minor act, though much time may pass till the major benefit occurs.

The Babylonian Talmud, on the other hand, asserts that we must concern ourselves with the present situation. If the effort is exerted at present, then the greatness of the resulting benefit that will not occur until some time in the future does not outweigh the effort, even though the resulting benefit will far surpass the present minor effort in significance. Consequently, the individual is not obliged to perform the act of lesser significance.

The beneficial result of King David's undistracted Torah study surpassed by far the difficulties endured by Joab at the time of battle, yet this great benefit occurred subsequent to Joab's military achievements. According to the position of the Jerusalem Talmud, Joab was thus *obligated* to wage war. The Babylonian Talmud, however, would assert that Joab's actions were altruistic and of his own free will, not subject to external obligation or necessity.

Therefore, Rabbi Meir's position conforms with that of the Jerusalem Talmud: it was the present lesser effort which later achieved the result of David's deeds attaining their greatest significance.

Rabbi Yosi, however, is in agreement with the Babylonian Talmud: Joab's deeds were in themselves of major significance,

---

17. *Ta'anit* 31a

18. End *Ta'anit*

19. See *Likkutei Sichot*, vol. 4, pp. 1336-1338.

since they were not required by law, and he acted of his own free choice in an altruistic and idealistic manner.

INSTILLING SELF-SACRIFICE IN OUR CHILDREN

A lesson: When an individual possesses something so rare that it is unobtainable in the entire world, then he should be prepared to give it away in order to help a fellow Jew—even if that fellow Jew has stumbled and transgressed, and even if the offering and gift do not bear the name of the donor. Moreover, he should regard as a privilege the opportunity to aid another Jew. He should experience joy to the extent that he commemorates this action by the fixing of a special *Yom Tov* for his entire family.

In order to instill this trait in one's children, either children in the physical sense, or as defined by the Torah, "Your children"[20]—"These are your students"[21] —one's own conduct must be permeated with the vitalizing quality of *mesirat nefesh*— altruistic self-sacrifice. The service of both the individual who is wholly involved in the study of Torah and the individual in the labor of commerce, in battle and conflict with the mundane, must be characterized by *bitul* (self-nullification) and *mesirat nefesh* (self-sacrifice).

In this manner we will raise a generation prepared to bestow their own possessions upon others, and to do so joyously in order to aid a fellow Jew.

The trait of altruistic love for a fellow Jew is of such great significance[22]—indeed it is the very opposite of *sinat chinam*, baseless hatred which caused the destruction of the second Temple[23]—that it will bring about the true, complete, redemption very soon.

(*Likkutei Sichot*, vol. 4, pp. 1103-1104)

---

20. Deuteronomy 6:7.
21. *Sifrei Devarim* 6:7.
22. See *Likkutei Sichot*, vol. 2, p. 598.
23. See *Yoma* 9 b.

ELUL
THE DIVINE KNOT

THE ETERNAL BOND
BETWEEN G-D
AND THE JEWISH PEOPLE

The Thirteen Attributes of Mercy are a significant component of
the *selichot* and High Holy Day prayers. Moreover, it is stated in
Jewish mystical sources[1] that in the month of *Elul* there is a spiritual
revelation of the Thirteen Attributes. In this *sicha*, the Rebbe
explains the concepts linking the recitation of The Thirteen
attributes of Mercy with the *talit* and *tefillin* knot.

"YOU SHALL SEE ME FROM THE BACK"

After the traumatic incidents of the sin of the golden calf
and the breaking of the Ten Commandments by Moses, the
Torah describes how Moses turned to G-d with profound
prayers for divine forgiveness. The Torah also relates that
Moses then asks, "Reveal to me Your glory."[2]

G-d's response is that while wrapped in the *talit*, He will
reveal His Thirteen Attributes of Mercy, which the Jewish
people can evoke in all future generations when they pray for
divine forgiveness.[3] Answering Moses' request, G-d declares,
"You will see Me from the back, but My face will not be seen."[4]
Rashi comments on this verse that G-d showed Moshe the knot
of the *tefillin* that are worn on the head.

---

1. See beg. *Pri Eitz Chaim, Sha'ar Rosh Hashanah; Mishnat Chasidim, Masechet Elul*. 1:3;
    Likkutei Torah, Deuteronomy 32a.
2. Exodus 33:18.
3. Rashi, Exodus ibid.
4. Ibid.

It thus seems that there is an inherent link between G-d's recitation of the Thirteen Attributes of Mercy, His being wrapped in the *talit,* and the head-knot of *tefillin.* What is this relationship?

We are told that "forgetfulness is derived from evil."[5] It does not exist in the realm of holiness, for "there is no forgetfulness before the throne of Your [G-d's] glory."[6] Indeed, Jews are the "faithful sons of the faithful."[7] A cornerstone of our faithfulness is our firm and sincere belief that "In the beginning G-d created Heaven and earth"[8]—all of creation and all that exists therein. Inherent in this belief is the ongoing nature of creation, "for He renews with His goodness every day, constantly, the deeds of creation."[9] G-d constantly renews all creation *ex nihilo,* from the nothingness that existed prior to the six days of creation.

This raises a significant problem: How can a person, even the most sensual and self-indulgent, lapse into sin, while profoundly aware that at this very moment his existence is dependent upon G-d's constant re-creation? How can he neglect G-d's Will, as expressed in Torah and *mitzvot,* while knowing that his entire existence, and even the potentiality of the impulse for evil, are all deriving, this very moment, from G-d the Creator.

This problem is compounded when we realize that those things that seem to be hindrances, in our path of living a life of Torah and *mitzvot,* are *themselves* part of G-d's constant creation. How is it then possible for someone to act so illogically, in flagrant contradiction to something that is absolutely true to him? It is because, although fully cognizant of the truth—at the time of sinning there is a lapse, and *forgetfulness,* of this spiritual awareness.

---

5. See *Hilchot Talmud Torah* of Rabbi Schneur Zalman, 2:10 and sources cited there.
6. *Berachot* 32b; *Hilchot Talmud Torah* , ibid.
7. *Shabbat* 97a.
8. Genesis 1:1.
9. *Siddur,* p. 44.

When spiritual memory functions normally, it inevitably results in dispelling all matters of evil in thought, speech, and deed. A Jew at such times can even ascend to the lofty level of "All your deeds should be for the sake of Heaven"[10] and "Know Him in all your ways";[11] he does not experience alien or improper thoughts.

TEFILLIN, TALIT AND REMEMBRANCE

The inner spiritual quality of the commandments of wearing *talit* and *tefillin* are connected with remembrance: "And you shall seen them and remember" (the *tzitzit*—fringes of the *talit*);[12] "And they *(tefillin)* shall be for a remembrance between your eyes."[13] Since these *mitzvot* serve as a reminder of G-dliness, they cause a correction and uprooting of sin. This resultant awareness of our relationship to Heaven can therefore be followed by G-d's declaration: "I shall bestow grace" and "I shall have Mercy."[14]

The *Zohar*[15] states that Rabbi Chiya and Rabbi Yosi would tie knots to use as signs not to forget the Torah they had learned. Indeed, later commentaries state that this is the source for the Jewish adage that tying a *knip*—a knot—is auspicious for remembering something important.

How are knots related to repentance? Our Sages tell us that "if a person transgressed...what shall he do and live? If he was accustomed to learning one page, he should learn two pages; if one chapter, then he should learn two chapters."[16] Rabbi Schneur Zalman, the Alter Rebbe, in *Igeret Hateshuvah*[17] explains: "This is comparable to a rope that was torn asunder;

---

10. *Pirkei Avot* 2:12.
11. Proverbs 3:6.
12. Numbers 15:39.
13. Exodus 13:9.
14. Exodus 33:19.
15. *Zohar*, Exodus 190a; see also *Likkutei Levi Yitzchak* on this passage.
16. *Vayikra Rabbah*.
17. Ch. 9.

when retying it, the place where it was severed is usually knotted several times over."

In the realm of the physical, a knot can help prevent forgetfulness and encourage remembrance. Moreover, we repair something torn or damaged by tying a double or triple knot for strength. Similarly, a spiritual knot can "repair," nullify and atone for evil and sin.

To create a powerful bond to holiness one should tie a strong, reinforced "knot" by learning Torah and doing *mitzvot* with an extra measure of involvement. This will prevent forgetfulness, the cause of sin, and encourage remembrance of our Creator, and of our obligations to serve Him. *Tefillin* express the dedication and service of a Jew to Hashem with his total being. The head *tefillin* convey the subjugation of mind and intellect to G-d's Will, while the arm and hand *tefillin*, which face the heart, emphasize the need to master and control one's wishes and desires.[18]

This is the link between G-d's revelation to Moses ("You shall see Me from behind"), the back knot of the head *tefillin*, and the recitation of the Thirteen Attributes beseeching G-d's Mercy: G-d revealed to Moses, and to us, the spiritual quality which cleanses from sin deriving from the *tefillin* knot, and how it evokes the quality of remembrance, with emphasis upon conscience awareness, and constant dependence upon G-d as Creator.

The Jewish people are collectively responsible for the observance of all *mitzvot* of the Torah. Rabbi Yitzchak Luria, the Arizal, states that although women are exempt from many *mitzvot* that are observed at specific times, they share in the merit of time-bound *mitzvot*, such as *tefillin*, when men observe them. Moreover, women inspire and guide their children in their Torah education; thus they also share in their sons' *mitzvot* of *tefillin* and other obligations.[19] By taking precautionary

---

18. See *Shulchan Aruch, Orach Chaim*, ch. 25; *Shulchan Aruch Harav*, ibid., sec. 11; and see letter dated 11 *Nissan* 5728, *Haggadah shel* Pesach (Kehot), p. 620.

19. *Berachot* 17a.

measures to prevent "forgetting," by intensified "remembrance" of all matters of holiness and Judaism, we will speedily merit the fulfillment of the prophetic assurance "And G-d's glory shall be revealed and all humanity together shall see that the mouth of G-d has spoken."[20]

We will not have to rely upon memory, for we shall actually *see* with our own eyes how all creation, including humanity, is re-created anew, from utter non-being, by G-d's utterance. This will occur at the time of the coming of *Mashiach,* may he come and redeem us and lead us upright to our land, speedily and in our times.

(Likkutei Sichot, vol. 21, pp. 232-37)

---

20. Isaiah 40:5.

CHAI ELUL
BIRTHDAY OF RABBI ISRAEL BAAL SHEM TOV AND RABBI SCHNEUR ZALMAN OF LIADI

THE MIRACLE OF BIRTH

Chai Elul, the eighteenth day of Elul, is the birthday of both Rabbi Israel Baal Shem Tov, the founder of general *Chasidut*, and Rabbi Schneur Zalman of Liadi, the founder of Chabad Chasidism, known as the Alter Rebbe. Now celebrated by Jews the world over, this day invites us to ponder not only the phenomenon of birth and the significance of birthdays but, most importantly, the purpose of our own existence and service to G-d.

THE SIGNIFICANCE OF BIRTHDAYS

A birthday has significance for all Jews,[1] not only for spiritually distinguished Jews but even for individuals on the humblest level, from the "heads of your tribes" to those who "chop wood and draw water."[2] Torah—the all-encompassing blueprint[3] for human and Jewish conduct—even mentions[4] the birthday of Pharaoh, a non-Jew, thereby indicating the profound significance linked to the day of birth.

For this reason, Rabbi Yosef Yitzchak Schneersohn of Lubavitch, revealed[5] a special regimen of conduct, previously concealed and observed only by unique spiritual personalities, to be observed on one's birthday.

---

1. See *Sefer Hasichot 5748*, vol 2, p. 399.
2. Deuteronomy 29:10.
3. *Zohar* vol 2, p. 161b.
4. Genesis 40:20.
5. See *Hayom Yom*, 11 *Nissan* and *Likkutei Sichot* vol. 5, p.86.

This regimen calls for introspection, additional time for Torah study, giving more charity than usual, and other actions. The elaboration and fuss relating to the day of birth indicates its relevance for every single Jew, regardless of stature.

But all this raises a perturbing question, for while the term "birthday" refers to the moment of emergence into the outside world, most fetuses are already normal and healthy beings. Even before birth they exist as a full-fledged, physiologically developed human beings, their hearts beat, their limbs move, they actually "eat" and "drink" (even if only through the umbilical cord[6]), and they even have such minor features as hair and nails.[7] What unique event takes place in the brief instant of transition from the pre-natal state to new existence? What meaningful changes occur as a result of birth?

Certainly, there is a singular advantage to the fetus's remaining in the pre-natal state. Following birth, effort must be expended even for the child to breathe; the doctor must pound upon the child's back to facilitate his breathing. Indeed, in most instances a child emerges not with a smile, but an abrasive wail evoked by the jarring changes. It is therefore puzzling why the transitional moment of birth should be regarded as an event worthy of celebration in subsequent years.

Viewed within the context of Torah, this question becomes more pointed. The Talmud tells us that, while the child is still within his mother, a "flame gives light above his head and he is taught the Torah in its entirety." This light resembles the light of the Divine Presence resting upon the head of the scholar, a "radiance shining upon his head." Thus, the mystical light upon the child illuminates not his potential for learning but the knowledge he has already obtained in the womb. Furthermore, since the unborn child is "*taught* the Torah in its entirety," we must assume that the child is successful in both learning and knowing the complete Torah.

---

6. See *Torah Or*, p. 55a and p. 124b.
7. *Tanya*, ch. 2.

However, the Talmud relates that "upon his emergence into the atmosphere of the world, an angel comes to strike him and cause him to forget the entire Torah." It seems, then, that at the moment he enters the world, there is no spiritual growth but, to the contrary, retrogression and descent. Having learned and known the complete Torah as a fetus, the child must now laboriously learn anew, and even this is postponed according to his development: "At the age of five the child studies the written Torah; at the age of ten *Mishnah*..."[8]

Why, then, the great "to-do" and celebration over the physical birthday? Physiologically, the child is already fully developed, his spiritual growth, however, seems actually to have suffered a reversal. In his pre-natal environment he is privileged to have the mystical spiritual light "shining upon his head" and "to be taught the Torah in its entirety." Why, therefore, the yearly joyous observance of one's birthday, the time when spiritual knowledge was lost?

THE MOMENT OF BIRTH

In order to fully understand all aspects of worldly existence, we must look in the "Torah of light"[9] which provides illumination and clarification for all matters, for "G-d (Himself) looked into the Torah and created the world."[10] Thus, any complex and puzzling matter can be clarified by the all-inclusive wisdom of the Torah.

Indeed, the Torah is multi-faceted, ranging from esoteric profundity to tangible ritual. The concept of birthday being of concerns to all Jews without exception, must, therefore, be explained with clarity within the *halacha*, the unalterable code of law applicable to all Jews everywhere, and it must not require sophisticated analysis to be understood.

---

8. *Pirkei Avot*, ch. 5.

9. Proverbs 6:23.

10. *Bereishit Rabbah*, beg.

The *halacha* includes a clear, definitive law that defines the uniqueness of birth. The Talmud[11] states that "A fetus is part of its mother," which Rashi explains to mean that the fetus is "as one of her limbs." According to the *halacha,* then, a fetus is not legally a separate entity, but, part of the mother.

The uniqueness of birth is that it is precisely at this time that the child becomes a completely *independent* living organism. Before birth, even though fully developed, its existence is subordinate to its mother's identity; at birth it achieves selfhood.

True, even after birth the child requires the aid of others since, at first, it is helpless and incapable of tending to even its most basic needs. Even after reaching maturity humans still require the sustaining aid of the human community. Maimonides explains at length,[12] that Man is, by nature, a social creature. Life's needs are so complex and varied that only as a participant in a structured society can he receive the support and aid to obtain them; alone he could not adequately perform the many tasks necessary for survival. Further, Man alone would be incapable of fulfilling the purpose of Creation, that is, to "achieve intellectual awareness of his Creator." Yet despite all of the above, the newborn child still has a separate unique identity acquired at the moment of birth.

As for the spiritual aspects of the newborn child, it is true that up to this point the child possessed the "light upon its head" and was taught the Torah in its entirety. However, this was not accomplished through its own effort and striving as a separate being, but received as a magnanimous gift, a bestowal from Above. From the time of birth onward, all of his spiritual accomplishments result entirely from his own efforts. It is for this very reason that upon "emerging into the atmosphere of the world, the angel comes and strikes him upon his mouth and causes him to forget the entire Torah." He is thus enabled to

11. *Chulin* 58a.

12. *Moreh Nevuchim* and *Mishnah Torah,* introduction.

acquire independence as a separate being, to strive and be self-reliant. Once born, Man must depend only on his capability, his "own measure" of creativity, and not on the "bread of shame,"[13] earned without the pride and satisfaction of sweat and toil.

It is therefore to his advantage that the angel expunges his Torah learning. Only in this way can he function as a separate being and utilize his own efforts. Our Sages state, "A person prefers 'one measure' of his own (harvest) to 'ten measures' (given to him as a gift) from his friend."[14] The "one measure" for which he struggles is far more rewarding and meaningful than the "ten measures" received from a benefactor. This is especially true in learning "Torah in its entirety" by one's own efforts.

Hence, the "commotion" created concerning the festive observance of one's birthday. On each birthday Man is obligated to remember that on this day he not only achieved a new dimension of existence—independence and selfhood—but that he inherited the profound obligation to study Torah with maximum effort. On this day in particular he should involve himself in intensive self-evaluation, reflecting on whether he has utilized his spiritual potential to fulfill the divine purpose of Man's creation and existence that "I (Man) was created to serve G-d my Maker."[15]

CONTINUAL REBIRTH

Although this concept is highlighted on one's birthday, it should obviously motivate a person's actions throughout the year. How much greater is its meaning when viewed from the religious perspective: Each day, each person becomes a new being. This is eloquently expressed in the *Modeh Ani* prayer, which is recited daily upon awakening: "I offer thanks to You...for You have mercifully restored my soul within me."

---

13. See Jerusalem Talmud, *Orlah* 1:3. *Likkutei Torah*, Leviticus 7d.

14. *Bava Metzia* 38a.

15. *Kiddushin* 82b.

Thus, everyday, Man is reborn and recreated. The concept of ongoing re-creation from non-existence is elaborated on in the teachings of Rabbi Israel Baal Shem Tov, and explained at great length by the Alter Rebbe in *Sha'ar Hayichud Vehaemunah*.[16] It is also mentioned in our daily prayers: "(G-d) Who renews in His goodness, every day, constantly, the deeds of Creation."

One cannot be content with past achievement in Torah study and the fulfillment of its commandments, when aware of the fact that a person's very existence is continuously renewed. Though these achievements are certainly part of his identity and being, they are nonetheless a gift given to him with G-d's daily restoration of his soul. And to merely rely upon past capabilities is not to serve G-d with his own initiative and effort. Since he has awakened reborn—a new person—he must exert new effort and add to his striving to serve his Creator. He must bring his deepest, latent soul-powers to the fore in order to fulfill G-d's Divine command that "Man is born to labor"[17]—to strive constantly to serve G-d through his own initiative.

This, then, is the central concept of the celebration of a birthday: each person must know that on that very day he has been born anew and therefore cannot be satisfied with past deeds. He must progress from "valor to valor."[18] Every day he stands confronted by a new challenge, and he must respond with previously concealed creative power.

Rabbi Schneur Zalman, the first Rebbe of Chabad-Lubavitch,[19] and subsequent leaders of Chabad, compare exile and Messianic redemption of the Jewish people to the phases of pregnancy and birth. May it be G-d's will that our reflection and action on the true meaning of the "day of birth" bring

---

16. *Tanya*, p. 152 ff.

17. Job 5:7.

18. Psalms 84:8, and see *Berachot* 64a.

19. *Torah Or*, Genesis 55a.

about the transition of the Jewish people from pre-natal exile to the illuminating moment of Messianic "birth" and redemption speedily and in our days.

(Based on *Hitvadiot 5742*, vol. 4, pp. 2179-2185)

ELUL

THE UNITY OF ISRAEL—
HUMILITY IN
THE PRESENCE OF G-D

In a sicha *analyzing Parshat Nitzavim, read on the last Shabbat of the month of* Elul, *the Rebbe discusses the service of achieving unity with other Jews as a preparation for Rosh Hashanah. By realizing the essential equality of Jews in the face of G-d's transcendent greatness, the Jew, is able to evoke humility within himself and create a bond with the rest of the Jewish people which goes beyond intellect. This is a precondition for the renewal of the essential bond between G-d and the Jews which occurs on Rosh Hashanah. The theme of honest self-appraisal is illustrated by a story involving Rabbi Hillel Paritcher.*

ACHIEVING UNITY

Parshat Nitzavim, as stated in *Likkutei Torah*[1] and cited by Rabbi Yosef Yitzchak Schneersohn, the sixth Lubavitcher Rebbe,[2] is always read on the Shabbat before Rosh Hashanah, whether it is read together with *Parshat Vayelech,* or by itself.

Every Shabbat is related to and encompasses the days of the subsequent week. [3] Thus, before Rosh Hashanah we read[4] *Atem nitzavim hayom* ("All of you stand this day"). "This day," interpreted in the light of *Chasidut,* refers to Rosh Hashanah, the "day" of great judgment.

---

1. Deuteronomy 44a.

2. *Reshimah, Parshat Nitzavim, Sefer Hasichot 5707*, p. 150.

3. *Zohar* II 63b, 88a.

4. Deuteronomy 29:9.

When this "Day" of Rosh Hashanah arrives, it is necessary that "All of you stand." All souls must join before "G-d your L-rd." The emphasis here is on *all* Jewish souls equally, from "the heads of your tribes to the hewers of wood and drawers of water."

Rashi[5] explains that the "hewers of wood" were the Canaanites who came to convert in the manner of the Gibeonites at the time of Joshua. They had concealed their true Canaanite identity and were accepted in Israel only because an oath of friendship had been made before the revelation of their true identity.[6] On Rosh Hashanah even these "hewers of wood" ascend before G-d together with all other Jews, "All of you," united collectively into one identity.

The concept of all Jews united into one great corpus, one identity, goes beyond mutual tolerance and acceptance. One who holds the rank of a "head" or leader may tolerate and endure another Jew of humble degree, but the relationship described here is far more significant, not mere tolerance, but integration and interdependence. This is comparable to parts of a human body such as the head and the feet, which are interdependent, neither of which possessing perfection without the other.

This is the spiritual labor required on Rosh Hashanah— "this day." In order to fulfill the spiritual task of that solemn day, we read in the Torah on the Shabbat before Rosh Hashanah, "You stand this day all of you...the heads of your tribes...the hewers of your wood and the drawers of your water." Through reading this in the Torah, the spiritual power to actually achieve this unity is evoked within us.

This is similar to the Chasidic[7] explanation of the addition to the liturgy on the High Holy Days of the verses of *Malchiot*— G-d's Majesty; *Zichronot*—G-d's remembrance of significant

---

5. Deuteronomy 29:10.

6. Joshua 9:15.

7. *See Ma'amarei Admor Hazakein 5564*, p. 217 and ff.

events; and *Shofrot*—Biblical incidents involving the blast of the *shofar*. Through reciting these passages of *Malchiot, Zichronot* and *Shofrot* we assert and maintain that G-d *should* rule, *should* remember, and that this is evoked through sounding the *shofar*. Our recitation of these verses actually brings these lofty ideals into the realm of worldly existence.

AN ESSENTIAL BOND

After the verses, "you stand this day... from your hewers of wood to the drawers of water," the Torah declares[8] "that you should enter into the covenant of G-d your L-rd." The sequence of verses implies that "you stand...all of you" serves as a necessary prelude to "entering into the covenant"—the creation of a covenant and bond between G-d and the Jewish people on the day of Rosh Hashanah.

In normal human relationships, it may occur that two individuals are connected by bonds of strong love based on a specific factor or rationale, such as admiration of a superior trait, or anticipation of an act of generosity or kindness. If a person involved in such a relationship is aware of a personal defect or shortcoming, he may be anxious, lest it be discovered and weaken the bond of love. This anxiety is magnified if the inadequacy involves something greatly significant, since it can cause complete loss of love, possibly even evoking the opposite emotion.

Hence, while the love is still intense, the two people enter into a *brit* (a covenant) that their love should endure eternally. The bonds of a *brit* are beyond reason and understanding; one puts one's selfhood aside, transcends intellect, and enters into a covenant linking oneself to another person. This bond of united selfhood is so intense that it enables the love to endure eternally.

This describes the love between G-d and Israel. During Rosh Hashanah Israel's love of G-d is heightened, their

---

8. Deuteronomy 29:11.

spiritual labor during the previous month of *Elul* having removed all the sins which could obstruct this inner love. Consequently, G-d and Israel enter into a covenant. Jews unite with G-d in an essential bond beyond reason and understanding. Nothing in the world can weaken it.

In order to evoke G-d's acquiescence in joining with the souls of Israel in a bond transcending reason and intellect, the labor of "All of you united as one" is necessary. This joining requires humility and self-submission, transcending reason and intellect. For in conduct-based on logic and rationale—one person is in the category of "head," and the other person is a "drawer of water." Viewed through the limiting prism of social status, how is it at all possible for the two to be seen as equal?

The transcendent union of G-d and Israel can only be achieved by the devotion inherent in the phrase "You shall love G-d... *bechol me'odecha*[9]" ("with your allness"), recited in the *Shema*. Man, by submitting his finite "allness"[10] to the will of G-d, causes the revelation of the absolute "Allness" of the divine.

The union of "All of you as one" must be real. The individual must be aware that he is truly equal to his fellow Jew. This awareness must transcend any sense he has of himself as a "head," and his perception of another as only a simple person. Perhaps, a definitive identification of the leader— "head"—and one who is a—"leg"—cannot be made. Human tendency is to exaggerate one's own self-worth and to underestimate the value and dignity of another. Even if the self-evaluation as "head," and the perception of another as a "leg" is accurate, the "leg" nevertheless possesses a superiority. Since the body functions as a composite entity, the "head's" fulfillment and perfection depend on the leg.

We can thus understand why the Gibeonites were made the hewers of wood for the Sanctuary and the Temple. All of the

---

9. Deuteronomy 6:5.

10. See *Torah Or*, Genesis 39c.

Israelites were not present in the Temple, nor did all Jews live in Jerusalem. There was only a specially designated group of Israelites known as *Anshei Ma'amad*[11] who represented all Jews during the daily Temple offerings. The Gibeonites were assigned to serve the Temple because true perfection and fulfillment is found specifically in the "leg," the humblest, nethermost degree.

This is the significance of the oath taken by the Gibeonites upon their acceptance to the ranks of Israel—a commitment which is beyond reason and understanding, affecting the very essence of the soul;[12] and this essence is manifested specifically by those on the level of "leg."

On Rosh Hashanah before the blowing of the *shofar*, we beseech G-d to "choose us, our heritage, the grandeur of Jacob, whom He loves, *selah*."[13] This means He "shall choose us," Israel, His fixed choice to the exclusion of any other possibility. G-d's choice is derived from His very essence, which is beyond all limitations and boundaries, and is thus truly capable of free choice and free from external influence.[14] Contemplating this, one realizes how utterly impossible it is to compare G-d to any created being. In mystical terms, far greater than the incomparability between the loftiest level of created existence (the world of *Atzilut*) to the lowest level of existence, the realm of the mundane (the world of *Asiyah*)—is the utter incomparability of the Almighty to the world of *Atzilut*.[15] The most incredible disproportions that Man can possibly envision cannot illustrate the utter impossibility of describing the transcendence and exaltedness of G-d in relation to created beings. How then is it possible for him to pray and plead to G-d in His Essence that "He shall choose us?" If a person meditates

---

11. *Ta'anit* 26a.

12. See *Kitzurim Veha'arot Letanya*, p. 48 and ff.

13. Psalms 47:5.

14. See *Torat Shalom*, p. 120 and ff. *Likkutei Sichot*, vol. 4, p. 1309, p. 1340 and ff. , vol. 23, p. 219.

15. R. Moshe Cordovero in *Sefer Alimah*, quoted in *Pelach Harimon*, *Sha'ar* 3, ch. 1.

on this and tries to honestly evaluate his own worth in relation to his Creator, then he will no longer be concerned with measuring the value of a fellow Jew.

RABBI HILLEL'S QUESTION

The well-known chasid, Rabbi Hillel Paritcher[16] yearned intensely to meet Rabbi Schneur Zalman, the Alter Rebbe,[17] but every time he would arrive at a city where the Rebbe was scheduled to appear, he would find that the Rebbe had already left. He decided to anticipate the Rebbe by arriving in a certain town beforehand. But, having been so frequently frustrated in the past, and still fearing that he would again be denied access, Rabbi Hillel secreted himself in the room designated for the Alter Rebbe's use, and hid under the bed.

Rabbi Hillel had also prepared a question about a point in the Talmud tractate *Arachin*, which deals with vows of charity based on the evaluated worth of a person, either oneself or of another. Immediately upon entering the room, even before Rabbi Hillel could emerge from his hiding place, the Alter Rebbe said, in his famed Chasidic melody, "When a young man has a question in the Tractate of "Evaluations"—*Arachin*, he must first evaluate himself." Upon hearing this, Rabbi Hillel fainted. By the time he was discovered and revived, the Rebbe had already departed.

Rabbi Hillel never had a subsequent opportunity to see the Alter Rebbe. He ultimately journeyed to the Alter Rebbe's successors, the Mitteler Rebbe, Rabbi DovBer, and Rabbi Menachem Mendel, the Tzemach Tzedek, but this was the only time that he was in the presence of the Alter Rebbe, and even then he was unable to see him.

REALISTIC SELF-APPRAISAL

The explanation and implication of this narrative is this: *Arachin*—vows of charity offerings based on a person's worth—

---

16. R. Hillel son of R. Meir *Halevi* Malisov.

17. See also *Likkutei Dibburim* 524a.

are not based upon conventional logic. For in the matter of *Arachin*, a person's value is based on his age rather than on attributes and capabilities. All people in the same age range have identical worth.

At first glance, a devoted Jew can ask, "I have dedicated all my days to Torah and prayer, which are a source of gratification to G-d. The host of heaven is also content with these efforts. Even according to human reckoning, my accomplishments are of great value. The years of the other person, on the other hand, have been wholly wasted and is one of those of whom it is said,[18] 'Better that they had not been created.'"[19] How, then, is it possible to equate the worth of two individuals who are the same only in numbers of years? The answer is that when a person "has a question in Tractate *Arachin*, he must first realistically evaluate himself."

Inevitably the awareness of one's own insignificance in relation to the Infinite grandeur and majesty of G-d, and the knowledge of the great unbridgeable abyss between Man and his Creator, will evoke humility within Man. Authentic self-appraisal and introspection will banish all arrogance and vanity in relation to a fellow Jew. This, in turn, will unite all Israel in essential unity and make them worthy of divine compassion and mercy.

(*Likkutei Sichot*, vol. 2, pp. 398-401)

---

18. *Eiruvin* 13b.
19. See *Likkutei Torah*, Deuteronomy 29a.

SUPPLEMENT

TEFILLIN—
MITZVAH OF UNITY AND VICTORY

> We conclude with a particularly rousing and inspiring talk by the Rebbe, in which he addresses a list of questions posed by detractors concerning the Rebbe's campaign, launched in 1967 (before the Six-Day War), to promote the observance of the mitzvah of *tefillin*, a campaign which has become one of the signature activities of the Lubavitch movement worldwide. Many of the points addressed in the *sicha* involve issues which are the hallmark of the Rebbe's leadership, *Ahavat Yisrael*, the power of a single mitzvah to "tip the balance" and make the whole world meritorious, and the obligation of every Jew towards his fellow. As the Rebbe states, "In every instance that another Jew performs the mitzvah of *tefillin*, the world is further inclined toward the side of virtue, bringing closer the end of the exile and hastening our redemption."

To prevent any slackening of the significant efforts of those vigorously involved in promoting the *Tefillin* Campaign, I am replying to the many questions and "reservations" submitted to me about the Campaign, although it is not my custom to engage in polemics.

QUESTION ONE:

Why, of all the six-hundred thirteen *mitzvot*, was *tefillin* specifically chosen?

ANSWER:

a) At the very beginning of the intensive emphasis upon this mitzvah, it was explicitly underscored that the concern with this mitzvah was based on our Sages' explanation of the Biblical verse: "And all the nations shall see that the name of G-d is called upon you, and they will fear you;"[1] "'the name of

---

1. Deuteronomy 28:10.

G-d' refers to the *tefillin* upon the head."[2] Since the particular need of that hour was that the enemy fear the Jewish people and be prevented from fulfilling their intention to inflict harm, the exertion of great effort to arouse others in the fulfillment of this mitzvah of *tefillin* was therefore encouraged.

In further explanation of the above:

Every mitzvah is a command of G-d. Every mitzvah must be fulfilled because of our submission to the yoke of the Heavenly Kingdom, as indicated in the blessing recited when performing a mitzvah, "Blessed are You...*King* of the universe, Who has *commanded us*." Moreover, when a person is in distress or need, he tries intensely to fulfill the mitzvah most appropriate to his particular situation and need, for each mitzvah possesses a special, unique quality of its own.

This concept has been described by our Sages: "He who states, 'This money is being given to charity, so that my son should live,' etc. is wholly righteous."[3] Why was the mitzvah of charity specifically mentioned? Any one of the many *mitzvot* could have been cited. But since this person desires that "his son shall live," he strives to perform a mitzvah that specifically corresponds to the unique quality appropriate to his plea. Elsewhere our Sages say about the mitzvah of charity: "G-d has said, the soul of the poor man was quivering and on the verge of expiring due to hunger, and you provided sustenance and enabled him to live.... Tomorrow your son or daughter may be taken ill or be at the verge of death...and I shall save them from death."[4] It is for this reason that a father begging for the life of his son chooses to do an act of charity.

As stated, since it was necessary to cast the fear of the Jewish nation over its adversaries, the benefit to fellow Jews of the mitzvah of *tefillin* was highlighted and repeatedly emphasized

---

2. *Berachot* 6a.

3. Pesachim 8a.

4. *Tanchuma, Mishpatim* 15.

because we have been divinely assured that by means of this mitzvah, "they will fear you."

All Jews are responsible for each other,[5] and most assuredly in matters of reward, for a "good attribute always surpasses a bad one"[6] (see question 2). Therefore, the efforts to encourage the performance of this mitzvah should be exerted, not only among our brethren in *Eretz Yisrael*, who are in particular need of "And they shall fear you," but also among our fellow Jews throughout the world. The performance of the mitzvah of *tefillin* by every individual Jew, wherever he may be, has the power to effect "And they shall fear you" in relation to the entire Jewish people.

This matter is self-evident, most particularly in this instance, when the fear of enemies threatening Israel was also related to their fear of Jews living in all other lands.

b) The Six-Day War, when great efforts were exerted for the *Tefillin* Campaign, occurred a few days before the holiday of Shavuot, the time of the giving of the Torah. *Chasidut* repeatedly emphasizes that Jewish holidays do not merely commemorate past happenings, but that there is an actual reoccurrence, on the spiritual level, of the historical event.[7] As a result, on the days immediately preceding the time of the receiving of the Torah, there must be a reawakening concerning Torah study. Our Sages have declared regarding *tefillin*: "Fulfill this mitzvah and I will regard it as though you assiduously pursue the study of Torah day and night."[8]

At that time of the giving of the Torah, the Jewish people were similarly instructed concerning the observance of the entire Torah, and they expressed their acceptance by stating "We shall do" even before "We shall learn."[9] Our Sages tell us regarding *tefillin*: "The Torah in its entirety is equated to the

---

5. *Shevuot* 39a.

6. *Sotah* 11a.

7. See *Sefer Leiv David* of the *Chidah*, ch. 29.

8. *Midrash Tehillim*, beginning.

9. Exodus 24;7; *Shabbat* 88a.

mitzvah of *tefillin*."[10] Many laws are derived from this statement. Thus, *tefillin* are very much related to the receiving of the entire Torah.

Question Two:

What is the great significance of influencing *one* individual Jew to put on *tefillin* for a *single* time? Is it really worth such great effort to sway another Jew to perform the mitzvah once?

Answer:

a) Indeed! Let them attempt it repeatedly and with many Jews.

b) Maimonides[11] explicitly states as a *principle of Jewish law* that *every* Jew is obliged to see himself as in a state of ethical balance, possessing in equal measure deeds of virtue and deeds of transgression, and to view the entire world as also in such a condition of equal balance. If he performs but *one* mitzvah, he tips the Heavenly scale to the side of virtue, bringing to himself and the entire world rescue and deliverance. The individual who *accepts* the *halachic* rulings of Maimonides will most assuredly endeavor in an appropriate manner to perform the decisive act which will cause the scale of judgment to incline toward virtue, and thus cause rescue and deliverance.

c) There is a particular law regarding the "head which has not worn *tefillin*."[12] Maimonides[13] states that this phrase applies only to one who has never worn *tefillin* during the course of *his entire life*. This means that having performed the mitzvah once, he is no longer in the above category. There are differing opinions from other Talmudic commentators concerning this phrase. Maimonides, however, states this as a *definite legal ruling*, and the interpretations of the great *halachic* authorities, Rabbi Yitzchak Alfasi (the *Rif*), Rabbeinu Chananel, and Rabbi Yitzchak Abba Mari, (the *Baal Ha'itur*), based upon a responsum of the *Geonim*, all agree to his decision.

---

10. *Kiddushin* 35a.

11. *Hilchot Teshuvah* 3:4.

12. *Rosh Hashanah* 17a.

13. *Hilchot Teshuvah* 3:5.

d) It is explicitly stated in the *Mishnah*[14] that "One mitzvah brings about the performance of another mitzvah." Influencing someone to perform the mitzvah of *tefillin* will inevitably cause the performance of another mitzvah. Indeed, concerning a matter explicitly stated in the *Mishnah*, an opinion not in agreement with the *Mishnah* is totally invalid. The law of the *Mishnah* is always final.[15]

QUESTION THREE:

Superficially, it would appear that it is forbidden to influence irreligious persons to observe the ritual of *tefillin*, since the law requires a clean body and great care for a "clean mind" free from evil thoughts.[16] Our Sages state that "A person is not spared from three kinds of sin, one of them being 'evil thoughts.'"[17]

ANSWER:

a) Firstly, there is no basis for presuming that even those who are at present far from the fulfillment of Torah and *mitzvot* will succumb to improper thoughts precisely at the time of performing the mitzvah of *tefillin*.

b) Even if there should be some grounds for this fear, the *Magen Avraham* commentary on the *Shulchan Aruch* comments, and Rabbi Schneur Zalman, the Alter Rebbe, cites[18] as law: "This [prohibition] applies only if he is *certain* that he will succumb to these thoughts. But in the case of *uncertainty* he should not desist from the mitzvah of *tefillin*."

c) Our Sages have stated: "All persons have an avid interest in something new;"[19] this is self-evident. It follows then, that when someone sees something to which he is unaccustomed, he will be particularly engrossed and undistracted then by other thoughts. And it is quite apparent that those unaccustomed to

---

14. *Pirkei Avot* 4:2.

15. See *Tur* and *Shulchan Aruch, Choshen Mishpat,* beg. ch. 25.

16. *Shulchan Aruch, Orach Chaim,* ch. 38.

17. *Bava Batra* 164b.

18. *Shulchan Aruch,* ibid., sec. 4.

19. See *Sifri,* Deuteronmy 6, 6.

the mitzvah of *tefillin* will be wholly preoccupied with it when actually performing the mitzvah.

d) Rabbi Moshe of Coucy, author of *Semag,* states:[20] "There is no evil person not worthy of the mitzvah of *tefillin*; we can learn this from the Torah scroll which has greater sanctity [than *tefillin*] since everyone without exception may hold the Torah during the course of prayer. This is because everyone can conform to the law of purity at the time of prayer." *Semag's* reference to an "evil person" cannot be interpreted to mean one considered evil because of some particular kind of misconduct, for he cites as proof that "*All* take hold of the Torah scroll." Is there, then, anyone who will deny to a fellow Jew the privilege of holding a *Sefer Torah*?!

The words of the *Semag* are particularly relevant to our discussion, in accordance with the *halachic* principle that "common Jewish practice" serves as a guide for law and religious conduct.

It was the practice of the *Semag himself* to promulgate the observance of the mitzvah. He expounded, exhorted, and declaimed on the mitzvah of *tefillin* among the "Exiles of Israel", in Spain and other lands, and to people who accepted the mitzvah of *tefillin, mezuzah* and *tzitzit* only due to his inspirational religious guidance.

When the *tefillin* Campaign was first announced, I did not want to cite the *Semag,* nor his statement in that text: "G-d desires that an evil person perform the mitzvah of *tefillin* even more than one who is righteous; and the primary reason for the command of *tefillin* was that it serves as a reminder to those who are evil, to level out before them a path of virtue." I did not do so because the above is not that relevant to the matter under discussion. In our times, virtually all those who are presently remote from Torah and its *mitzvot* are in the *halachic* category of a "small child taken captive,"[21] one who is consequently ignorant about proper religious conduct. Contemporary religious

---

20. *Mitzvat Aseh* 3.
21. See *Shabbat* 68b.

non-observance is primarily caused by ignorance and the tragic inadequacy of contemporary Jewish education.

There are many statements in works of Jewish law indicating the need for profound devotional thoughts at the time of performing various *mitzvot*. For example, the words[22] of Rabbi DovBer, the Mitteler Rebbe, that the *kavanah* for immersion in the *mikveh* is the "intention of self-nullification and the giving over of one's soul to G-d." Regarding prayer we find: "He should think as though the Divine Presence was directly before him...and before prayer he should think of G-d's exaltedness and of the lowness of Man, and remove all thoughts of physical pleasure from his heart."[23] These thoughts *enhance* the significance of the mitzvah, simply since it is the will of G-d.

THE POTENTIAL OF TORAH ACTIVISM

The above is a response to the complaints I received. The crucial issue of this discussion is that all the reservations are based upon speculation and vague misgivings; in no way do they justify neglecting the *explicit Biblical* injunction to improve the conduct of a fellow Jew: "Repeatedly admonish your neighbor."[24] Every Jew is obliged to observe this mitzvah, even if it entails remonstrating with one individual "a hundred times,"[25] endeavoring that he too learn Torah and observe *mitzvot*. Our Sages of blessed memory have declared "All Jews are responsible for each other."[26]

As for those who justify inactivity because they doubt the effectiveness of their actions—we can give several replies.

a) The primary emphasis in the obligation of attempting to correct the conduct of a fellow Jew is based upon the *effort and attempt* to have him observe Torah and its commands. Even if

---

22. *Siddur im Dach* 159d.

23. *Orach Chaim* 98:1.

24. Leviticus 19:17.

25. *Bava Metzia* 31b.

26. *Shevuot* 39a, *Sanhedrin* 27b

the efforts are of no avail, the mitzvah of remonstrating has been *fulfilled*. This can be compared to the mitzvah of searching for *chometz*; even if no *chometz* is found, the mitzvah has been performed.[27] However, if one does not strive to correct the behavior of others, he has violated an obligatory mitzvah as a result of his passive behavior. This endeavor is required even if he is unequivocally certain that the other individual will be unresponsive.[28]

b) If the obligation to reprimand a fellow Jew would be based on the effectiveness of such an attempt, it would still be necessary to make an effort when we are uncertain about the outcome of our actions. Since the obligation to reprimand is Biblical in origin, we are required to apply the principle of *sefeika de'oraita lechumra*: when uncertain, in the case of a Biblical law, we conform to the stricter alternative. Namely, we cannot be passive or non-involved, but must attempt to correct the conduct of others, even when doubtful about the consequences of our efforts.

c) The above contentions had some basis only before the beginning of the *Tefillin* Campaign. After the very first day, when experience revealed that *hundreds of individuals* responded positively, and only a small minority demurred, then the matter was no longer in the category of doubt or speculation.

The Talmud explicitly states: Even those who are *perfectly righteous* are obligated to reprove individuals who are *utterly evil*, and they will be held responsible for the deeds of the evildoers if they do not attempt to influence them to correct their ways.[29]

We have already enumerated the following concepts: the obligation to criticize one who has departed from the proper path; the responsibility which each Jew bears towards a fellow Jew; the obligation of "loving one's neighbor as one's self;"[30]

---

27. Rema, *Orach Chaim*, 432: 2; *Shulchan Aruch Harav*, ibid., sec. 11.

28. *Orach Chaim*, Chapter 608. See also *Shulchan Aruch Harav*, ibid.

29. *Shabbat* 54b-55a.

30. Leviticus 19:18.

viewing the world as equally balanced between virtue and evil and that one mitzvah can tip the scales of the world to virtue, which is cited as a principle of Jewish law by Maimonides.

In addition, there is the factor expressed in the adage of our Sages: "More than what the benefactor does for the poor man, the poor man does for his benefactor."[31] Experience has shown that the effort of benefiting fellow Jews with the mitzvah of *tefillin* has added intensity and spiritual radiance to the lives of those actively involved in the promulgation of *mitzvot* in general and the mitzvah of *tefillin* in particular.

May it be the will of G-d that their deeds encourage many others, including those highly pious in their conduct, to actively participate in the *Tefillin* Campaign. In every instance that another Jew performs the mitzvah of *tefillin*, the world is further inclined toward the side of virtue, bringing closer the end of our exile and hastening our redemption.

The *Midrash Tehillim* states that the verse "Let us tear their ropes asunder, and cast away their cords from us,"[32] refers specifically to the *tefillin* worn upon the head and arm of Jews; for (as the verse continues) when "the nations all clamor and the peoples [of the world] speak in vain," then the Jewish nation must strengthen itself with the mitzvah of *tefillin*.

May the merit of this mitzvah bring about the true and complete redemption through our righteous *Mashiach* very soon.

(*Likkutei Sichot*, vol. 6, pp. 271-275)

---

31. *Vayikra Rabbah* 34:8.

32. Psalms 2:3.

INDEX

OF SOURCES CITED

INDEX OF TOPICS

In Honor of
YITZCHAK BARBER
On the occasion of his Bar-Mitzvah
22 Shevat 5762

❧ • ❧

DEDICATED BY HIS PARENTS
MR. & MRS. SHIMON AND LEAH BARBER

❧ • ❧

לזכות
התת' **יצחק שיחי'**
לרגל הבר מצוה שלו

ולזכות
אחיותיו **חנה מיכלא** וחי' ואחיו **הלל דוד**
שיחיו

נדפס ע"י הוריהם
הרה"ת **אליעזר שמעון** וזוגתו מרת **הינדא לאה** שיחיו
בארבער

זקניהם
הרה"ת הר' **יצחק** ע"ה וזוגתו תבלחט"ט מרת **רבקה מאטל** שתחי'
בארבער
הרה"ת הר' **משה אהרן** וזוגתו **שרה** שיחיו
קזיניץ